ESSENTIALS

of Risk Ma

in Finance

ESSENTIALS SERIES

The Essentials Series was created for busy business advisory and corporate professionals. The books in this series were designed so that these busy professionals can quickly acquire knowledge and skills in core business areas.

Each book provides need-to-have fundamentals for professionals who must:

- Get up to speed quickly, because they have been promoted to a new position or have broadened their responsibility scope.
- Manage a new functional area.
- Brush up on new developments in their area of responsibility.
- Add more value to their company or clients.

Other books in this series include:

For more information on any of the above titles, please visit www.wiley.com.

ESSENTIALS
of Risk Management
in Finance

Anthony Tarantino

with Deborah Cernauskas

WILEY

John Wiley & Sons, Inc.

Published by John Wiley & Sons, Inc., Hoboken, New Jersey.

Published simultaneously in Canada.

For general information on our other products and services or for technical
support, please contact our Customer Care Department within the United States
at (800) 762–2974, outside the United States at (317) 572–3993 or
fax (317) 572–4002.

Wiley also publishes its books in a variety of electronic formats. Some content that
appears in print may not be available in electronic books. For more information
about Wiley products, visit our web site at www.wiley.com.

Library of Congress Cataloging-in-Publication Data:

Tarantino, Anthony.
  Essentials of risk management in finance/Anthony Tarantino with Deborah
Cernauskas.
      p. cm. — (Essentials series)
   Includes bibliographical references and index.
   ISBN 978-0-470-63528-5 (pbk.); ISBN 978-0-470-94633-6 (ebk);
   ISBN 978-0-470-94634-3 (ebk); ISBN 978-0-470-94635-0 (ebk)
   1.   Financial risk management.   I. Cernauskas, Deborah, 1956–   II. Title.
   HG173.T3457 2011
   658.15'5—dc22

                                                              2010032745

Printed in the United States of America
10 9 8 7 6 5 4 3 2 1

Do not store up for yourselves treasures on earth, where moth and rust destroy, and where thieves break in and steal. But store up for yourselves treasures in heaven, where moth and rust do not destroy, and where thieves do not break in and steal. For where your treasure is, there your heart will be also.

Matthew 6:19–21

Business is with deed and not with the result.

Hindu poem of Bhagavad-Gita

Contents

Preface

Beginning in 2007, the world suffered through the worst economic crisis since the Great Depression of the 1930s. The most sophisticated risk management strategies and techniques in the hands of global financial industry leaders failed in a spectacular and catastrophic manner. Quantitative and qualitative modeling, the core foundation of computational finance, also failed, even though it was in the hands of the most respected scientists and mathematicians utilizing massive computing assets and resources. However, organizations that applied prudential risk management approaches have fared far better. This included taking a holistic and enterprise-wide approach, plus an ethical tone-at-the-top, thus avoiding the seductive and nearly irresistible appeal of mortgage-backed securities and related investments.

The catastrophic failure in risk management and computational finance among the world's leading financial institutions demonstrates the need for a more holistic, interdisciplinary, and enterprise-wide approach to risk management, which combines accounting, economics, mathematics, operations, and technology. It also demonstrates the need for the correct tone-at-the-top, in which ethical considerations are weighed as heavily as shortsighted business considerations in risk or opportunity decisions.

To avoid repeating painful failures in risk management and ethics, it is essential for today's accounting, business, finance, audit, IT, and not-for-profit managers to accept that risk management is everyone's job. It is also important to understand that the complexity of markets, financial products, and risk management techniques is a risk. The global financial crisis (also known as the Great Recession of 2008–2009) contains elements of every type of risk, which combined to overwhelm regulators, investors, and corporate governance.

This basic survey book is designed to provide a short and easy-to-follow introduction to financial risk management, covered in its major components: credit, market, operational, legal, and reputational, along with the relationship between corporate governance and risk management, and the techniques to control risk. We will also use the new ISO 31000 and 31010 risk standards to provide readers with the means to conduct their own risk assessments and risk alignments.

There are some mathematical concepts included, but they are kept at levels that general readers will find easy to grasp.

Readers will acquire a good basic understanding of the major areas of risk exposure that all organizations, both public and private, face in operating in today's complex global marketplace. Risk management is an essential element in all business activities. As a consequence, notions of risk management have quickly changed from a cost of doing business and distraction to acceptance as an essential part of any viable organization.

This Essentials book involves an analysis of contemporary theories and techniques in risk management used in a variety of industries. It also provides insights into best practices and next generation techniques.

Readers entering new careers will find that the book prepares them for government, not-for-profit, business, and IT positions in which risk management will play an ever-expanding role. Experienced professionals will find it a handy reference guide. Although limited as an overview, this book provides extensive references and links so readers can easily dive deeper into the coverage areas.

Organization of this Book

The book provides an overview of financial risk management in the introduction. The second chapter surveys the major risk management standards, frameworks, and associations in widespread use today.

Chapter   1 Introduction to Risk Management

Chapter   2 Risk Frameworks and Standards

The new ISO 31000/31010 risk management framework and Six Sigma for its approach to risk assessments and risk alignments are discussed in the following chapters.

Chapter   3 Conducting Your Own Risk Assessment and Alignment

Chapter   4 Six Sigma in Risk Assessments

Essentials of Risk Management in Finance uses the Basel II categories of risk management, which identify operational, credit, market, and liquidity risk. We treat legal risk, financial crimes, and internal controls as subsets of operational risk. We treat portfolio risk as a subset of market risk. We also include other important areas of risk—reputational, information/data, and product. The Basel committee also identified reputational risk as important, but beyond the scope of the current framework. We treat it as a consequence of other operational risk failures. The categories and subcategories of risk are:

Chapter   5 Operational Risk

Chapter   6 Legal Risk

Chapter   7 Financial Crimes (Fraud and Corruption)

Chapter   8 Internal Controls (U.S. and International SOX)

Chapter   9 Environmental and Product Risks—Sustainability

Chapter 10 Data Governance and Risk

We next discuss risks associated with the marketplace and invest-ment portfolios.

Chapter 11 Market Risk—From Value at Risk to Black Swans

Chapter 12 Volatility, Risk Aversion, and Portfolio Management

We then provide an overview of the risks associated with credit, which is a universal issue for all those not doing business on a cash basis.

Chapter 13 Credit Risk

We continue with a discussion of corporate governance, including the compensation issues around the principal/agent problem, and alter-natives to Western approaches (i.e., Islam).

Chapter 14 Corporate Governance and Compensation

Chapter 15 Faith-Based Risk Management—Shariah

We end with a brief overview of the most dangerous types of risk enterprises face: reputational, liquidity, and solvency.

Chapter 16 Reputational Risk

Chapter 17 Liquidity and Solvency: Enterprise-Ending Risks

Basel III Update

While this book was going to press, the oversight body of the Basel Committee on Banking Supervision announced revisions to the Basel II capital accords resulting in more stringent capital requirements. Basel III outlines a stepped process whereby banks will move from a 2 percent core capital ratio to a 7 percent core capital ratio over the next several years. An additional round of regulations for systemically important global banks is under development by the Basel Committee.

Basel III will profoundly impact us all and requires a survival guide. While we discuss Basel III in general terms in this book, we are preparing an *Essentials of Basel III* to fully prepare you for the tightening of credit markets, the impact on commodity prices, and what to expect from the central banks of major economies like the United States, China, Japan, and the European Union. Bankers fear that tougher capital requirements will stifle lending and economic growth.

Acknowledgments

This text would not have been possible without the support and encouragement of the faculty and students of Santa Clara University's Leavey School of Business. Thanks to George Chacko, Sanjiv Das, and Carrie Pan, faculty in the finance department at SCU, for guidance and mentoring. The text is based on the MBA and undergraduate risk management classes taught in 2009 and 2010.

We also wish to acknowledge the support and encouragement of our Wiley colleagues and friends: Tim Burgard, our senior editor; Helen Cho, our senior editorial assistant; and Laura Cherkas, our production editor.

Special thanks go to Alexandra Tarantino for final editing of production proofs.

CHAPTER 1

Introduction to Risk Management

To avoid repeating the painful failures in risk management that occurred during the global financial crisis of 2007 to 2009 (also known as the Great Recession), it is essential for today's business, IT, risk, compliance, and audit managers to understand the big picture of risk management and to accept that risk management goes along with every position in business, technology, accounting, and finance. This is also true for many managers in the not-for-profit and government sectors.

This book is designed to provide an introduction to financial risk management, including operational, credit, market, reputational, liquidity, solvency, legal, and portfolio risk. These categories are based on the Basel II Capital Accords used by the global banking industry, but are applicable to all enterprises and organizations.

You will acquire an understanding of the major areas of risk exposure that all organizations, both public and private, face in operating in today's complex global marketplace. Risk management is an essential element in all business activities.

You will also be provided with actionable methods, techniques, and tools to improve risk management in your organization. This includes the basics of conducting risk assessments and risk alignments.

Definition of Risk and Financial Risk Management

Definitions of *risk* typically refer to the possibility of a loss or an injury created by an activity or a person. Risk management seeks to identify, assess, and measure risk and then develop countermeasures to handle it—not to eliminate risk.

Financial risk management applies a systematic and logical approach to uncertainties in operations, reputation, credit, liquidity/solvency, portfolios, and markets. Without risk management, an organization would simply rely on luck to avoid disasters. Risk management typically means seeking to mitigate and minimize the impact of risk, which is fundamentally different from avoiding it entirely. An organization that is completely risk averse is not likely to be attractive to investors and may be doomed to ultimately fail.

Risk should not be viewed as inherently bad. All opportunities come with some degree of risk—two sides of the same coin.

Gambling, Investment Risk, Chance, and Probability

Gambling can be defined as playing a game of chance for money or stakes. It requires one to risk money, or other things of value, on the outcome of something involving chance. *Investing* is to put money or other things of value to use by an expenditure or purchase in an investment vehicle that offers profitable returns. An investment vehicle may be a security or derivative, and can range from an asset-backed security to a stock or bond. An investment vehicle is used to make a profit on capital invested in it.

There is not a clear distinction between gambling and investment risk, but one can argue that risk taking in investments is good and adds capital to markets and thus contributes to society. One can also argue that gambling is inherently bad and adds limited value to society, although it does support some economies—Native American tribes, Las Vegas, and so on. Ironically, gambling risks are more identifiable, measurable, and quantifiable than investment risks. Investment risks can be mitigated, whereas gambling risks typically cannot.

Risk can also be viewed as *probability* or the *chance* of making an incorrect decision. The risks of making a wrong decision are unique to the decision being made and may be realized only if a wrong decision is made. Unlike gambling, chance, and probability, risk management offers mitigation techniques.

Enterprise and Systemic Risk

Enterprise risk can be viewed as all processes that present risk to an organization. *Enterprise risk management (ERM)* comprises the methods and processes used by organizations to manage risks and seize opportunities related to the achievement of their objectives. The goal of ERM is to provide a framework for risk management that:

- Identifies specific events, situations, and environments relevant to the organization's objectives and their applicable risks and opportunities.
- Assesses those risks in terms of their likelihood and consequences.
- Develops a risk mitigation strategy appropriate to the exposure (balancing the mitigation costs and benefits).
- Monitors and reports on the risk mitigation progress.

ERM mitigation strategies include:

- Avoidance: Ending the activities and processes that created the risk.

- Reduction: Reducing the likelihood and/or the consequences the risk through mitigation.

- Transference: Transferring or sharing a portion of the risk via insurance or other vehicles.

- Monitoring: Ongoing tracking and auditing of mitigation counter measures.

- Acceptance: Accepting the risk and taking no action.

Systemic risk is a term now in common use because of the global financial crisis and is typically used to explain the risk to an entire national economy and society caused by enterprise risk failures of large institutions deemed too big to fail. It is probably more accurate to describe these organizations as too interconnected to fail. Their size does present risk to the overall economy, but it is their ability to create a domino effect in which their failures cascade down into the failure of several other organizations that compels national treasuries to intervene. Lehman Brothers and AIG are the poster children for systemic risk failures in the last few years.

EXECUTIVE INSIGHT

Systemic Risks Increase after the Global Financial Crisis

Systemic and enterprise risks are distinct but very much interrelated. The catastrophic enterprise risk failures of Lehman Brothers, AIG, and several global banks presented a systemic risk to the United States and several Euro Zone economies. Interestingly, the large majority of my Santa Clara University MBA students expressed concerns that the global financial crisis has increased our systemic risk for two reasons. First, national governments have set a bad precedent of bailing out large corporations rather than letting them fail, and thus have rewarded their reckless risk taking. Second, the major consolidation of banks reduces the distribution of risk so that the surviving banks present an even larger systemic risk. Their concerns are well founded, especially because there has been little government action to address the huge unregulated credit default swap (CDS) and derivatives markets or to reform rating agencies.

Relationships among Governance, Risk, and Compliance

Just as risk and opportunity go hand in hand, risk goes hand in hand with governance and compliance. *Governance* is the relationship between those who govern and those whom they govern over. *Compliance* is the system of laws, regulations, and standards that control the governance and risk management process. It may be best to understand the compliance side of this triangle as a hierarchy with laws at the top and enterprise-level tasks at the bottom.

- Laws are created by national, state, and local legislatures.
- Regulations are created by agencies and typically make the rules that public and private companies must adhere to.
- Standards are created by regulatory agencies and international organizations that establish the audit standards by which compliance to regulations are validated.
- Enterprises create policies (higher level) and procedures (detailed level) to comply with standards by which they will be audited.
- Procedures lead to a large number of specific and auditable tasks to enforce policies, standards, regulations, and laws.

The Hierarchy of Laws, Regulations, and Standards

A common misconception is that enterprises only comply with national and state laws. Although this is true on the surface, enterprises are measured by how they pass statutory (legally required) audits against compliance and risk standards and frameworks (addressed in Chapter 2). These audits are conducted by government regulators and external auditors. Standards are the detailed and actionable face of laws and regulations. In the case of the Sarbanes-Oxley Act (less than 30,000 words), public companies in the United States must follow the audit standards from the Public Company Accounting Oversight Board (PCAOB). The PCAOB's Audit Standards 1, 3, 4, 5, and 6 total more than 50,000 words. Auditors create audit questionnaires, process charts, risk/control metrics, audit test scripts, findings, and remediations that typically run into thousands of pages. Enterprises create general policies and detailed procedures to pass PCAOB and other statutory audits. Each procedure comprises a multitude of required tasks and supporting documentation.

The pyramid graphic in Exhibit 1.1 is a good way to view this hierarchy.

Risk Management and Internal Controls

The process that an organization, its internal auditors, its external auditors, and its regulators would typically follow to validate the effectiveness of internal controls that impact financial reports would typically include these steps:

- Identify business processes, especially those impacting financial reporting.
- Identify the risks associated with each process.

EXHIBIT 1.1

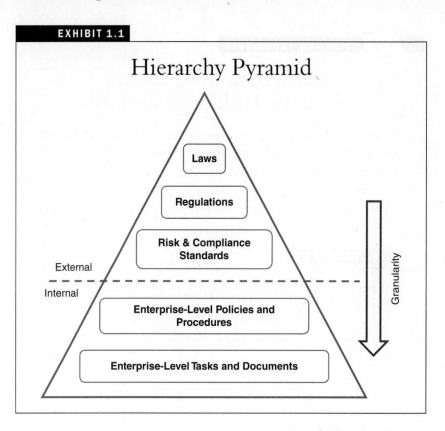

- Identify the internal controls used to mitigate the risks for each process.
- Create a hierarchy of business processes, risks, and controls.
- Identify the tests to be used in determining the effectiveness of the internal controls.
- Test the internal controls and publish findings.
- Provide an opinion (findings) as to the effectiveness of the controls.
- If the controls are found to be ineffective, recommend changes (remediation) and retest the controls—alternatively, change the process to reduce the risk and retest.
- Create and maintain a documentation library of the processes, risks and controls, tests, findings, remediations, process narratives, and process flow charts.

The Relationship among Processes, Risks, and Controls

Exhibit 1.2 is a simple means to visualize the relationship among processes, risks, and controls. These exist in a many-to-many relationship, which means one control can cover multiple risks and one risk can be covered by multiple controls. One process may come with multiple risks as well.

EXHIBIT 1.2

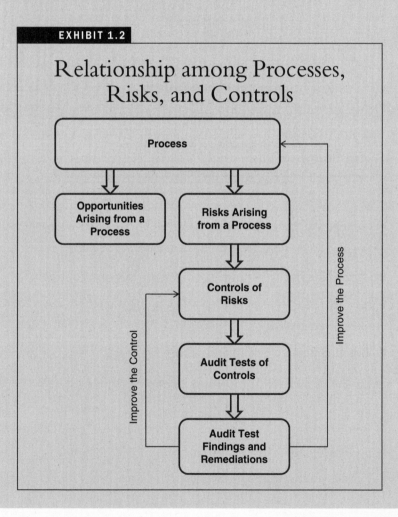

Relationship among Processes, Risks, and Controls

Risk Management in Corporations

Under Western legal models, there are three actors in corporations: directors, employees, and shareholders. Each has a role in risk management.

- *Directors* provide the oversight and stewardship over all corporate assets, both human and otherwise. This includes aligning the corporations risk appetite with its risk exposure, yet it is common for Western boards to put the burden of risk management on executives. Evidence of this is that risk committees at the board level exist in few corporations.[1]

- *Employees* do the day-to-day work of managing the corporation's resources and assets. They execute the risk strategy and practices of the corporation. Notice that corporate executives are not treated under the law as separate actors but as employees.

- *Shareholders* provide the money in the form of risk capital and share risk equal to their investments. Under the Anglo-American model, shareholders have little say in risk management and can only vote with their feet—selling their shares. Their involvement in corporate operations is typically limited to interaction with the board, and not with corporate employees. Large institutional investors have exerted greater demands over boards, but typically not in the areas of risk management.

A corporate executive's approach to risk management is heavily influenced by the corporate governance model in place. In the United States and United Kingdom, agency theory is preferred; in Germany, Japan, and Islamic nations, stewardship theory is preferred. Under the Western agency theory, executives are driven to achieve short-term objectives that tend to translate into greater risk taking. In good times, the agency approach can achieve greater growth and profitability than the more conservative stewardship approach. In bad times, the conservatism of the stewardship approach can help to insulate a corporation from major losses. The major elements of each approach can be summarized as follows:

Executives	Agency Theory (e.g., U.S., U.K.)	Stewardship Theory (e.g., Islam, Germany, Japan)
Act as	Agents	Stewards
Behavior model is	Self-serving, individualistic	Pro-organizational, collectivistic
Motivated by	Their own interests	Their principals' interests
Alignment with principals' interest	Limited or divergent	Closely aligned

The agency approach comes with a chronic and significant issue known as the principal/agent problem. This is a classic dilemma for any organization that is not family-owned and run. Employees are agents with self-serving interests. Principals (owners and corporate board members) attempt to align the interest of their employees (agents) and the organization (principals) with a wide variety of compensation models. The problem can never be solved, only mitigated. When the interests of principals and agents are poorly aligned, corporations can be exposed to material risk through shortsighted and reckless employee behavior or outright fraud. The global crisis exposed multiple examples of highly compensated executives who drove their corporations over a cliff, in part because their compensation models contained few incentives to act as stewards protecting the long-term interests of their employers.

Evolution of Risk Management

Financial risk management as a discipline has progressed since the pivotal year of 1921, when Frank Knight published his *Risk, Uncertainty, and Profit,* and John Maynard Keynes published his *A Treatise on*

Probability. Knight pioneered the notion that uncertainty, which cannot be measured, is different from risk, which is measurable. Keynes pioneered the mathematical and philosophical foundations of risk management. Keynes argues for a greater reliance on perception and judgment when considering probabilities and warns against an over-reliance on numbers.

In 1956, Russell Gallagher published his *Risk Management: A New Phase of Cost Control* in the *Harvard Business Review,* arguing that a professional insurance manager should also be a risk manager. Because of the nature of its business, the insurance industry was the first to embrace professional risk management with its concern for avoiding unaffordable potential losses—actuarial risk.

In the 1980s, new risk societies were created to promote risk management—the Society for Risk Analysis in Washington and the Institute for Risk Management in London. Their efforts have made the concepts of risk assessment and risk management well understood in business and government circles.

In the 1990s, the U.K.'s Cadbury and Turnbull committees issued reports advocating that corporate boards take responsibility for setting risk management policies, for assuring that the organization understands all its risks, and for accepting oversight for the entire process.

It was also in the 1990s that the title chief risk officer (CRO) was first used by GE Capital to describe a manager who is responsible for the totality of risk exposure to an organization. Chief risk officers and risk managers are now commonplace in the financial services industry and they are spreading into other industries.

Risk management as a distinct discipline may be fairly new, but risk management is as old as man. Noah is an early example of risk mitigation techniques in practice—building a giant ark of no commercial or recreational value in the belief that he was not crazy and really had talked to God. Good managers have always understood that risk management must be addressed in every opportunity pursuit.

Ethical and Moral Foundations to Risk Management

Historically, investors in most companies were individuals ranging from the very rich to the working class. Over recent decades, however, institutional investors representing insurance companies; banks; investor groups; and mutual, hedge, and pension funds have become dominant players in the market. Institutional investors have been able to advocate for stronger corporate governance and oversight. Although oversight has improved, it has not necessarily improved the voice of small investors, or improved risk management. The growth of mutual funds and pension plans has given small investors at least an indirect voice.

The need for institutional investors to access equity capital on a global level has increased the demand for improved governance, typically manifested through improved financial transparency, accountability, and representation of minority shareholder interests. The process has increased demand for what is commonly referred to as *tone-at-the-top*—corporate boards and executives providing the stewardship, culture, and organization committed to corporate governance.

Tone-at-the-top, as the jurist said about pornography, is hard to define, but you know it when you see it. The fundamental issue around tone-at-the-top may come down to the basic ethics and morality of those in positions of corporate power. If there is no moral and ethical foundation to the tone-at-the-top, then rules, regulations, and sanctions will ultimately fail. Morally bankrupt wrongdoers are often too clever and powerful to be caught, at least initially.

These are some suggestions to help establish an ethical tone-at-the-top approach to risk management:

- The organization's board and executive management have embraced ethical risk management as a continuous process that is critical to meeting the organization's objectives.

- The board of directors has demonstrated its full support for risk management as an integral part of the organization—there is a management consensus as to the main drivers around risk.

- The board and senior management have designed an over-arching risk management policy that includes objectives and responsibilities.

- The board has created a risk committee at the board level.

- The board has ensured the alignment among the firm's business objectives, revenue drivers, and its risk exposure and appetite. Risk environment and risk appetite are aligned.

- There is a chief compliance and risk officer (one person) at a minimum and ideally both a risk officer and a compliance officer (two people).

- The organization has an ongoing process to assess and track the benefits of improved risk management.

- The organization understands its main risk weaknesses and has compared them to their peer organizations and the best-in-class organizations.

- The organization has invested in high-caliber management with the skills, training, compensation rewards, and resources to improve risk management.

- The board has endorsed financial rewards for whistleblowers as a means to expose unethical and illegal behavior.

- The board draws from the management talent pool of the country and region so that it is sufficiently diverse as to age, sex, and ethnicity. (There is positive correlation between increased female board representation and improved governance.)[2]

Tone-at-the-Top at Lehman Brothers

Richard Fuld, chairman of the board (CoB) and chief executive officer (CEO) of now-defunct Lehman Brothers, testified to Congress in October 2008 after the collapse of his firm a month earlier. When asked if he thought his $354 million salary over the past five years was justified in light of Lehman's shareholders being wiped out and the loss of 20,000 jobs, Fuld responded that his compensation was determined by the compensation committee. The Congressman snapped back asking who the compensation committee reported to. Fuld calmly responded that they reported to him as chairman of the board.

Fuld's holding both the CEO and CoB positions is known as *duality*, which is common in the United States, but much less common and discouraged in much of the world. CEO/CoB duality creates obvious conflicts of interests in which Fuld could orchestrate his own compensation package with few checks and balances. CEO/CoB duality also challenges risk management checks and balances with one person responsible for short-term execution (CEO) and long-term stewardship (CoB).

Lessons from Miyamoto Musashi, Japan's Greatest Samurai

The problems with risk management can be summarized in the teachings of the legendary Samurai master swordsman, Miyamoto Musashi, in his *Book of the Five Rings*.

Musashi, who lived in fifteenth-century Tokugawa, Japan, won more than 30 duels and is considered by many as the greatest Samurai swordsman of all time. He retired to a life of solitude and wrote a short book about sword-fighting techniques that many of us believe applies to business in general and specifically to risk management. In Musashi's business, risk failure meant death or disgrace.

There are at least two great risk lessons from Miyamoto Musashi.

1. Never take a hard focus on the point of your opponent's sword. The attack will never come from the point of the sword, directly in front of you, but from some other direction. (This is true in Western fencing as well.) He advises to take a soft focus in order to prepare for an attack in any direction. The reactionary and myopic nature of regulatory reforms did little to prevent the largest financial crisis since the 1930s because reforms were focused on the point of the sword.

2. Never favor one weapon—master all of them. If you do have a favorite, you will be defeated when forced to use your least favorite weapon. Risk managers must master all the tools at their disposal as well.

Risk is like this. The biggest threats never come from the most visible point of attack. Risk managers in most organizations are experts in specific areas of risk, for example, credit risk in banking, but the global financial crisis involved a failure of every major type of risk. Few organizations were masters of each area of risk management and fewer still were able to take a holistic approach to their enterprise risk.

Effective risk management must take a more holistic approach because the next risk problem will not look like the last one and may come from a completely different direction. What does this mean to you in business, assuming you are not assigned to address one specific area of risk? A few thoughts:

- Do not assume government regulations, rating agencies, or financial audits will protect you.

- Do not assume risk experts understand multiple areas of risk and how they impact one another, sometimes referred to as risk complexity. (The global crisis involved failures in each type of risk we address in this text.)

- You are more expert in complex risk management than you may think. Remember the lessons of Miyamoto Musashi to keep a soft focus and follow the guidance from the 9/11 Commission that concluded the attacks were caused by a lack of imagination on the part of those responsible for our protection. Keeping a soft focus and your imagination will help to identify and address the next Black Swan coming your way.

Summary

Although we use the Basel II framework to categorize the various types of risk, there is no universally accepted framework for risk management. Just as medicine has become highly specialized, risk management requires specialization for each type of risk. The skills required of a loan officer in credit risk are quite different than those required by an IT security manager in such areas of operational risk as external and internal fraud. This book does not attempt to dive deep into each area of risk, but does provide an introduction and points you in the right direction for additional information. Like medicine, the disciplines in risk management are progressing rapidly, indicating that continuing education is essential. Common techniques in use today did not exist 10 to 20 years ago.

The global financial crisis has taught us that even the most sophisticated risk management techniques and tools in the hands of well-funded professionals can be seriously flawed, especially when obsessive greed trumps common sense. The fundamental problem with risk management comes from what are often called Black Swans, outlier events, rare but disastrous risk management failures that are extremely difficult to predict using statistical forecasting and other historical observations.

Failures in risk management typically result in a reactionary regulatory and mitigation process that addresses the problem in a myopic fashion. This typically does little to prevent or curtail the next crisis. An example is the enactment of the Sarbanes-Oxley Act (SOX), which was designed in response to the financial reporting abuses and scandals of the late 1990s.[3] A related example is the Basel II capital accords that were in force for many European Union (EU) banks at the onset of the crisis.[4] Unfortunately SOX did nothing to prevent major U.S. banks from failing after they reported strong quarterly and annual results. Basel II failed in a similar fashion for the EU banks.

Notes

1. See Chapter 24 in Anthony Tarantino and Deborah Cernauskas, *Financial Risk Management, Six Sigma and Other Next Generation Techniques* (Hoboken, NJ: John Wiley & Sons, 2006).
2. Ibid.
3. See Chapter 9 in Sanjay Anand and Anthony Tarantino, *Sarbanes Oxley in Leading Economies* (Upper Saddle River, NJ: Prentice-Hall, 2010).
4. See Chapter 41 in Anthony Tarantino, *Governance, Risk, and Compliance Handbook* (Hoboken, NJ: John Wiley & Sons, 2008).

CHAPTER 2

Risk Frameworks and Standards

After reading this chapter, you will be able to:

- Understand at a high level the major risk frameworks in use today.
- Grasp how Basel II and Basel III will shape global banking.
- Comprehend the major IT risk standards used by risk managers.
- Recognize the limitations in the COSO framework and U.S. SOX.

There exists a large variety of risk frameworks and risk standards that guide risk managers in various regions, industries, and disciplines. The terms *frameworks* and *standards* are used interchangeably throughout the text because both are referenced by regulators as an acceptable approach to risk management. Accounting standards such as Generally Accepted Accounting Principles (GAAP) have been in widespread use for many decades, but risk standards are relatively new. Relative to accounting standards, there is much less consensus around risk frameworks. In a similar vein, certification programs for risk managers are relatively new and not widely accepted—there is no risk equivalent to a certified/chartered public accountant (CPA).

We provide an overview of the major financial risk standards in use: COSO for internal controls that impact financial reporting; COSO II and ISO 31000/31010 for enterprise risk management; COBIT, ITIL, and NIST for IT risk; XBRL to automate financial reporting; Basel II and the upcoming Basel III for the banking industry; and Solvency II for the insurance industry. We also list the major risk associations operating today.

Coso

COSO is the most globally accepted risk and compliance framework. It addresses internal controls that impact financial reporting, and dates back to a 1987 recommendation by the Treadway Commission, which created the Committee of Sponsoring Organizations (COSO).[1] While COSO is often described as a financial reporting standard, it is also a risk management framework over internal controls. With the exception of France, COSO is in almost universal use and mentioned as an acceptable framework for the U.S. Sarbanes-Oxley Act (SOX) and related corporate laws for public companies throughout the world.

COSO defines internal controls as a process, affected by an entity's board of directors, management, and other personnel, designed to provide reasonable assurance regarding the achievement of objectives in the following categories: effectiveness and efficiency of operations, reliability of financial reporting, and compliance with applicable laws and regulations. The COSO framework identified five interrelated components:

1. Control environment
2. Risk assessment
3. Control activities
4. Information and communication
5. Monitoring

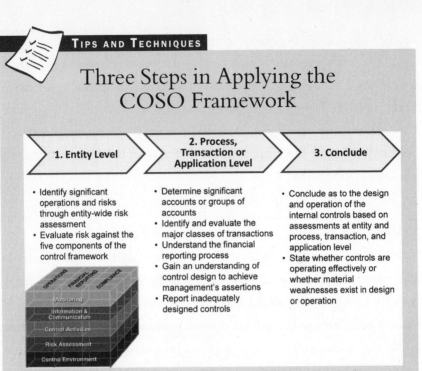

TIPS AND TECHNIQUES

Three Steps in Applying the COSO Framework

1. Entity Level

2. Process, Transaction or Application Level

3. Conclude

- Identify significant operations and risks through entity-wide risk assessment
- Evaluate risk against the five components of the control framework

- Determine significant accounts or groups of accounts
- Identify and evaluate the major classes of transactions
- Understand the financial reporting process
- Gain an understanding of control design to achieve management's assertions
- Report inadequately designed controls

- Conclude as to the design and operation of the internal controls based on assessments at entity and process, transaction, and application level
- State whether controls are operating effectively or whether material weaknesses exist in design or operation

COSO has been criticized as a volunteer organization with limited resources, no legal existence, no corporate governance structure, no funding mechanisms, and no physical address, that is not overseen by any regulatory body. COSO was not well accepted prior to the scandals that brought on the Sarbanes-Oxley Act of 2002. SOX gave COSO much greater acceptance, and not just in the United States.[2] As a risk framework, COSO can be criticized for not permitting reasonably consistent quantitative/qualitative measurements of internal control.

COSO for Small Public Companies

Most compliance frameworks and standards do little to address the challenges that smaller enterprises face in complying with regulatory and risk management requirements. The COSO committee attempted to

Three COSO and SOX Failures in the Global Financial Crisis

1 It is widely acknowledged that reckless risk taking and the self-interest of banking executives contributed to the global financial crisis. Although the 1992 COSO framework does include some discussion about the importance of an ethical tone-at-the-top, it provides little in the way of specifics on how to measure whether controls to ensure sound ethics are effective.

2 COSO and SOX address controls over internal controls, but few of the marquee accounting scandals and transparency failures were caused by a lack of internal controls. Ironically, Enron, the most notorious scandal of its time, was caused by the abuse of off-balance-sheet accounting practices, not a failure of internal controls. SOX Section 401 was designed to prevent off-balance accounting fraud and abuse, but has done little to prevent major banking firms from hiding debt in off-balance-sheet arrangements with firms closely related to them. It is alleged that Hudson Castle, a small investment firm run by former Lehman personnel, was created by Lehman as an alter ego to hide major Lehman debt from regulators and rating agencies.[3]

3 COSO and SOX provide five interrelated components over internal controls, but lack a means to quantify and prioritize risk. COSO and SOX apply a pass/fail system that struggles with prioritizing risks. Internal and external audits typically look at everything that impacts financial reporting. The new U.S. audit standard under the PCAOB is supposed to be risk-based, but auditors face regulatory and investor criticism and litigation if they ignore hundreds of insignificant internal controls. So it appears that the check-box approach to risk management, in which the significant few will not receive the attention they deserve, is destined to continue.

address this with its release of *Internal Control over Financial Reporting—Guidance for Smaller Public Companies* in 2006.[4] The goal of this guidance is to help small corporations adapt COSO's framework to their unique requirements, and thus improve their ability to meet compliance requirements and lower their compliance costs.

The small company guidance provides procedures on how to comply with compliance requirements without adding a large new staff or investing in major new technologies. For example, in smaller companies it is not unusual for one person to wear many hats, which can violate proper segregation of duties (SOD). The COSO framework suggests alternatives, such as detective (after-the-fact) controls in which managers periodically review reports to identify improper behavior and violations of company policies. It also scales down documentation requirements from the massive volumes required by larger enterprise.

Enterprise Risk Management (COSO II)

The COSO committee updated its COSO framework in September 2004 with its enterprise risk management (ERM) process.[5] Using a graphical cube, the four objectives categories—strategic, operations, reporting, and compliance—are represented by vertical columns, the eight components by horizontal rows, and an entity's units by the third dimension. The goal is to provide the flexibility to attack an organization's ERM from a global or entity level down through its divisions or locations, and down to its subsidiaries. ERM's graphic looks like a Rubik's Cube, implying that risk is not strictly a serial process in which one component impacts only the next, but is a multidirectional, iterative process in which almost any component can and does influence another. ERM also adds the concept of event management to COSO I. This is an important change in that COSO I's internal controls work best for repetitive tasks and processes.

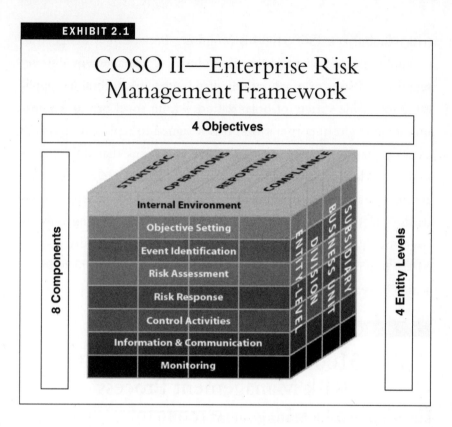

COSO II—Enterprise Risk Management Framework

One-off special events can cause grief to controls designed for day-to-day and repetitive processes.[6] See Exhibit 2.1.

ERM appeared to provide a much improved risk framework, but it has enjoyed only limited acceptance and suffers from the same limitations as the original COSO framework—the lack of risk quantification and prioritization. ERM makes a compelling case for the multidirectional and iterative process, but it is difficult to convert this notion into a viable and auditable risk framework.

ISO 31000 and ISO 31010

ISO 31000, codified by the International Organization for Standardization, was published in November 2009, and provides a promising standard on the implementation of risk management. ISO 31000 is an ISO family and includes ISO 31010 (risk techniques) and ISO 73 (risk vocabulary). ISO 31000 is promising because it is designed to be applicable and adaptable across industries, management systems, regions, and sizes of organizations. It provides risk techniques applicable to a wide variety of organizations—from small private companies to large global corporations. It is designed to replace a myriad of existing methodologies, standards, and paradigms that differ across regions, industries, and subject matters. ISO 31000 can be viewed as a replacement to Australian/New Zealand risk management standards AS/NZS 4360:2004 and has the attraction of being only 22 pages or 7,900 words in the basic standard. The appendix to ISO 31010 provides a comprehensive list of risk management techniques, which are easy-to-follow guidelines. See Exhibit 2.2.

EXHIBIT 2.2

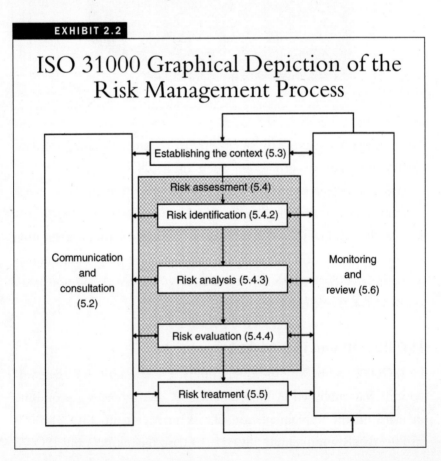

ISO 31000 Graphical Depiction of the Risk Management Process

- Establishing the context (5.3)
- Risk assessment (5.4)
  - Risk identification (5.4.2)
  - Risk analysis (5.4.3)
  - Risk evaluation (5.4.4)
- Risk treatment (5.5)

Communication and consultation (5.2)

Monitoring and review (5.6)

ISO 31000 and 31010 help develop an understanding of risks and provide inputs to conducting risk assessments. The two standards (actually a family of standards) also help in deciding whether and how risks need to be treated. They describe risk analysis as determining the probabilities and consequences for risk events and then considering the existence and effectiveness of controls. The probabilities and consequences are then combined to determine a level of risk. Risk analysis involves consideration of the causes and sources of risk, their probability, and consequences that those consequences can occur. An event can have multiple consequences and can impact multiple objectives. Existing risk controls and their effectiveness should be taken into account.

In Chapter 3, we provide a more complete discussion on the use of probabilities and consequences in conducting both a risk assessment and risk alignment. Alignment is the process of bringing together the risk appetite of an organization as expressed by its board of directors with the actual risk exposure as expressed by the organization's risk and business managers.

ISO 31000 differentiates among qualitative, semi-quantitative, and quantitative approaches to risk management. *Qualitative assessment* defines consequence, probability, and level of risk by significance levels, such as "high," "medium," and "low," which may combine consequence and probability, and evaluates the resultant level of risk against qualitative criteria.

Semi-quantitative methods use numerical rating scales for consequence and probability and combine them to produce a level of risk using a formula. Scales may be linear or logarithmic, or have some other relationship; formulae used can also vary.

Quantitative analysis estimates practical values for consequences and their probabilities and produces values of the level of risk in specific units defined when developing the context. Full quantitative analysis may not always be possible or desirable due to insufficient information about the system or activity being analyzed, lack of data, influence of human factors, and so on, or because the effort of quantitative analysis is not warranted or required. In such circumstances, a comparative semi-quantitative or qualitative ranking of risks by specialists, knowledgeable in their respective field, may still be effective. Even where full quantification has been carried out, it needs to be recognized that the levels of risk calculated are estimates. Care should be taken to ensure that they are not attributed to a level of accuracy and precision inconsistent with the accuracy of the data and methods employed.

COBIT, ITIL, and NIST

The IT Governance Institute established the Control Objectives for Information and related Technology (COBIT) guidelines in 1996.[7] COBIT defines 34 significant processes, links 318 detailed controls activities to them, and defines an internal control framework for all of them. These guidelines, which continue to be updated and expanded, are the most commonly used framework in the United States for the creation and evaluation of IT controls. Though COBIT is widely accepted in the United States and other countries, many companies outside of the United States have embraced an IT best practice framework that is fairly similar to COBIT. The Information Technology Infrastructure Library (ITIL) is controlled by the U.K.'s Office of Government Commerce and shares many of COBIT's characteristics.[8] For multinational public companies listed in the United States and Europe, the need to follow both COBIT and ITIL complicates IT audit and compliance requirements. The good news here is that they are compatible and do not conflict with each other to any major extent.

After the enactment of SOX, the COBIT standards have been updated to better suit the act's requirements. COBIT enforces the key

Financial Problems Roll Downhill into IT

Information and data accuracy, accessibility, security, con-sistency, and completeness are critical to any and all risk and compliance frameworks. It is no exaggeration to say that financial problems typically roll downhill into the office of the chief information officer (CIO). SOX and SOX-like statutory audits will always include an IT component. It was typical for our SOX audit teams to divide into two groups—one focused on finance and other focused on IT. The IT group benefited from a well-accepted and defined framework known as COBIT (Control Objectives for Information and Related Technology). Outside of the United States, IT risk managers often rely on a similar framework known as the ITIL (Information Technology Infrastructure Library).

Today's IT managers will typically need to closely coordinate their efforts with accounting and internal audit managers and proactively stay abreast of changes in regulatory requirements.

areas that corporations must address in establishing and monitoring their IT controls. Among others, these areas include communication, control objectives, security access, and audit guidelines. Since the signing officers must assume responsibility for the design and monitoring of these controls, it is understandable that COBIT instructs corporations to begin their processes by opening the channels of communication between the executive and the IT division. ITIL plays a similar role for organizations outside the United States.

Once these objectives have been clearly defined under COBIT or ITIL, the corporation can begin designing its controls. This can involve internal modifications to existing systems or, in some cases, the acquisi-tion of new applications. IT controls should be tested at the design stage as well as following implementation.

Although U.S. SOX and related international versions of SOX do not provide specific guidance in terms of how companies need to go about achieving compliance and IT risk management, there is information available through the ITIL and the National Institute of Standards and Technology (NIST).

The ITIL is a system of international documents designed to facilitate the creation and maintenance of IT controls. Developed by the Office of Government Commerce (OGC), ITIL is meant to assist companies in the creation of IT controls, thereby reducing costs, improving IT services, and increasing productivity. One feature that makes this resource useful to corporations seeking SOX-related compliance is that it provides a framework for the creation of IT controls rather than a rigid platform.

Similar to ITIL, NIST also seeks to aid in the improvement of IT services and productivity. As a federal agency, however, NIST's specific goals are directed toward the promotion of U.S. innovation and industrial competitiveness. NIST further differs from ITIL in that it provides platforms for IT control design rather than simply offering a framework. For example, NIST's Role-Based Access Control (RBAC) serves to restrict system access from unauthorized users. This system enables companies to track user information and activity, including login times, durations, and file modifications.

TIPS AND TECHNIQUES

Navigating between COBIT and ITIL

Global organizations often have to navigate between the COBIT and ITIL—the two major IT frameworks in the world today. The following matrix developed by Brian Barnier and Richard Marti helps by showing their many overlaps and their differences.*

	COBIT® 4.1	ITIL® 3
Owner	IT Governance Institute	UK Office of Government Commerce
Purpose	Provides a comprehensive framework for the management and delivery of high-quality information technology-based services. It sets best practices for the means of contributing to the process of value creation.	Is an approach to IT service management. ITIL is a cohesive best practice framework, drawn from the public and private sectors internationally. It describes the organization of IT resources to deliver business value, and documents processes, functions, and roles in IT service management.
Audience	IT planning and governance leaders, IT operations, IT–business liaison, IT risk managers, IT auditors.	IT service planners, IT service managers, IT operations, IT auditors.
Key components	Plan and Organize, Acquire and Implement, Deliver and Support, Monitor and Evaluate	Service Strategy, Service Design, Service Transition, Service Operation, Continual Service Improvement
In short	How to manage IT operations	How to operate IT

TIPS AND TECHNIQUES (CONTINUED)

	COBIT® 4.1	ITIL® 3
How it helps you	If you are seeking a control framework to measure IT outcomes as a means to improve return, reduce risk or improve quality, then this is the leading approach for you.	If you are seeking consistency, efficiency, reduced process errors, and improved quality of IT service delivery, then this is the leading approach for you.
Related disciplines	Should link upward to Val IT and downward to ITIL. Horizontally, can link with business risk management and control techniques (e.g., COSO).	Should link upward to COBIT. For more detailed information, users can turn to domain-specific standards for disaster recovery, information security, and such. The most detailed guidance comes from best practices for using systems management software and configuring specific IT resources.

*See Brian Barnier and Richard Marti, *Information Technology Risk*, in Chapter 5 in Anthony Tarantino and Deborah Cernauskas, *Risk Management in Finance: Six Sigma and Other Next Generation Techniques* (Hoboken, NJ: John Wiley & Sons, 2009).

Extensible Business Reporting Language

Extensible Business Reporting Language (XBRL) provides organizations with a viable method for complying with requirements for the timely reporting of financial information, such as U.S. SOX Section 409. As an XML-based standard for defining and exchanging financial information, XBRL also provides many security benefits to meet an organization's IT control objectives, such as those found in U.S. SOX Sections 302 and 404.

Prior to XBRL, financial information was communicated in flat text formats requiring regulators, analysts, and investors to key in information manually. The XML-based tags of XBRL automate the process. This makes it possible to easily compare financial data from peer organizations and over different reporting periods. This will also help organizations internally by increasing the speed of financial reporting and analysis. The SEC and the European Central Bank have been strong advocates of XBRL adoption; and it is reasonable to expect its use to become mandatory in the coming years.

Basel II for Banks and Solvency II for Insurers

The Basel II Capital Accords were developed by the Bank for International Settlements (BIS) to improve market discipline, reporting, transparency, and capital reserve management in banking. The BIS web site (http://bis.org) contains many comprehensive guidelines to address operational, credit, market, and liquidity risks. Basel is the town in Switzerland where the BIS resides (basil is the herb). BIS is the world's oldest international organization and is widely accepted as the standard setter for financial services.

The Basel Committee on Banking Supervision (BCBS) was established in 1974 by the central bank governors of the Group of Ten (G10) countries[9] in the aftermath of serious disturbances in international currency and banking markets and deterioration in capital ratios. The committee does not possess any formal supranational supervisory authority. Rather, it formulates broad supervisory standards and guidelines and recommends statements of best practice. The BCBS has been devoted in recent years to capital adequacy by implementing a weighted approach to the measurement of risk, both on and off the balance sheet.

The global financial crisis has greatly increased demands by national governments, investors, and taxpayers to increase regulatory oversight. Basel III is still in development, but early indications are that financial reserves and reporting requirements will increase. Although the Dodd/ Frank Financial Reform Act of 2010 is independent of Basel III, it is a good indication of the increased scrutiny that bankers can expect in the next two years.

TIPS AND TECHNIQUES

Why Basel II and Basel III are Important Far Beyond Banking

Capital ratio is the percentage of a bank's capital to its risk-weighted assets and determines its legal lending limits. Basel II established capital ratios for the largest banks, which are bound to increase under Basel III with the catastrophic failures in the global financial (banking) crisis. Basel II was in full force for many large European banks that suffered massive losses due to poor investment and loan decisions—mostly tied to subprime mortgages, and financial products such as mortgage-backed securities, credit default swaps, and related derivatives.

A natural reaction to the crisis is for regulators to increase reserve levels. Unfortunately, this translates into less money to lend—credit is scarcer. Therefore, Basel II and III impact anyone who needs credit by making money more expensive. Money is also scarcer as banks increase their lending requirements— very ironic after their embrace of subprime "liar loans," in which sound banking practices were ignored.

Basel II, Basel III, and the BIS are important to all risk managers because they establish comprehensive guidelines for credit, market, operational, and liquidity risk that are applicable outside of banking. Basel II's basic definitions and classifications of risk are used throughout this book.

Economic versus Regulatory Capital

Banks are in the business of taking risk and they hold capital as a buffer against potential losses, to provide them with financial flexibility, and as a sign of strength to their customers. *Economic capital* is the amount of risk capital that is required by a firm to cover credit, market, and operational risk. Economic capital is also the money to cover worst-case scenarios, assuring the survival of the organization by demonstrating that it has a solvent balance sheet. *Regulatory capital* is the mandatory capital that regulators require to be maintained. Regulatory capital is used externally while economic capital is used internally. Ideally, risk capital should equal economic capital.

Solvency II

In banking, think capital adequacy; in insurance, think solvency. The concepts are closely related, and both are behind global initiatives that will transform the financial services industry. *Solvency* is used in the insurance industry to measure an insurer's ability to pay its debts with available cash. Solvency has not traditionally referred to a calculation but rather has been treated as a statement of fact—you are either solvent or you are not. Financial ratios are now being applied to predict solvency problems. Solvency is different from profitability, which is the ability of a company to earn a profit. A company can make a profit without being solvent or be solvent and lose money. The game is over (bankrupt) when a company is both unprofitable and insolvent. The European Commission (EC)'s Financial Services Action Plan (FSAP) developed a new solvency regime known as Solvency II.

International Association of Insurance Supervisors

The EC has relied on the International Association of Insurance Supervisors (IAIS) to provide the guidance around Solvency II, which is designed to replace the 30-year-old Solvency I guidance by 2010 to 2011. It is intended to provide a more quantitative and qualitative risk-based focus to minimum capital requirements and supervision. The IAIS was established in 1994 and represents insurance regulators and supervisors of more than 180 jurisdictions in more than 130 countries, constituting 97 percent of insurance premiums in the world. The IAIS objectives:

- Contribute to improved supervision of the insurance industry on a domestic and international level in order to maintain efficient, fair, safe, and stable insurance markets for the benefit and protection of policyholders.
- Promote the development of well-regarded insurance markets.
- Contribute to global financial stability.

Solvency Foundations

In 2005, the IAIS published a series of guidance white papers that lay the foundation for an improved insurance solvency framework and infrastructure. The IAIS objectives are to improve industry supervision by:

- Enhancing risk and solvency management for insurers, reinsurers, and related financial groups.
- Enhancing financial transparency and cross-border comparative analytics.

- Promoting a level playing field across the insurance industry.

- Promoting international collaboration and cooperation.

- Reducing unwarranted regulatory arbitrage.

- Increasing government, investor, and consumer confidence in the insurance industry.

- Enhancing improved industry efficiency and productivity.

Solvency II is closely aligned with Basel II as the two committees work hand in hand. The risk in universal banks has blurred the traditional distinctions between insurance and banking, making a coordinated effort imperative. Exhibit 2.3 demonstrates their close alignment.

EXHIBIT 2.3

Solvency II versus Basel II		
Pillar	**Solvency II**	**Basel II**
One	**Minimum Capital Requirements:**	**Minimum Capital Requirements:**
	• Target and minimum solvency capital requirement.	• Minimum acceptable capital levels.
	• Minimum solvency capital depends on the dollar value of policies written.	• Internal ratings-based (IRB) approach to determining credit risk charge.
	• Calculation takes a risk-based approach around assets, liabilities, and underwriting information.	• Explicit treatment of operational ("event") risk in capital calculations—3 approaches with increasing complexity.
	• Target solvency capital typically the same as economic risk capital to cover disaster scenarios.	• Computation of capital charge.
		• Credit risk—3 approaches with increasing complexity.
		• Operational Risk—3 approaches with increasing complexity.
Two	**Supervisory Review Process:**	**Supervisory Review Process:**
	• Insurer supervisors monitoring the amount of their existing capital.	• Banks assess their own solvency relative to risk profile.
		(*continued*)

EXHIBIT 2.3		
Solvency II versus Basel II		
Pillar	Solvency II	Basel II
	• Improving cooperation and standardization among regulators across national borders. • Assessment of internal controls, risk management, and segregation of duties, stress testing of IT infrastructure and systems, senior management capabilities, and the balance between assets and liabilities.	• Supervisors review the bank's assessments and capital strategies. • Banks hold capital in excess of minimum requirements. • Regulators intervene at an early stage if capital levels deteriorate. • Perspective of the supervisor.
Three	**Disclosure and Market Discipline:** • Improved public access to the insurer's financial and risk management information. • Efforts to comply with accepted best practice frameworks.	**Disclosure and Market Discipline:** • Increased disclosure of capital structure. • Increased disclosure of risk measurement and management. • Increased disclosure of risk profile. • Increased disclosure of capital adequacy. • Qualitative and quantitative information in three general areas: corporate structure, capital structure and adequacy, and risk management.

Risk Management Certifications and Associations

With the growing interest in risk management, it was to be expected that programs would emerge to train and certify risk professionals. These groups include:

• Global Association of Risk Professionals (GARP)

• Professional Risk Managers International Association (PRMIA)

• Risk Management Association (RMA)

Both GARP and PRIMA offer training and certifications, but acceptance is spotty as the exams do not approach the rigor required to become a certified public accountant.

TIPS AND TECHNIQUES

Other Risk Frameworks You May Encounter

Besides the major risk and compliance standards we overview here, you may encounter or wish to consider these:

A Risk Management Standard (ARMS) 2002. ARMS is a brief and process model driven with no charge for public download. It was created in the U.K. by three organizations: Association of Insurance and Risk Managers (AIRMIC), Association of Local Authority Risk Manager (ALARM), and Institute of Risk Management (IRM). It is supported by Federation of European Risk Management Associations and has been translated into several languages. There is much additional good information at the individual association web sites.

Open Compliance and Ethics Group (OCEG) Foundation "Red Book." It is a business-level open standard and there is no charge for public downloads of the base document. It provides guidance about the core processes and capabilities to enhance culture and address governance, risk management, and compliance requirements. Beyond the open standard, extensive implementation guidance is also available.

Lean and Six Sigma. A data-driven method of problem solving and waste reduction with the goal of making processes more efficient and effective, therefore reducing their risk. Lean Six Sigma Black Belts are gaining acceptance beyond the traditional role of reducing process variability in manufacturing. Most large banks have major Six Sigma and Lean programs.

The Conflicting Mind–Sets and Skill Sets of Accounting and Risk Professionals

In most organizations, the role of chief risk officer falls on the shoulders of the chief financial officer (CFO). Risk officers and board-level risk committees typically do not exist in most organizations outside of finance. This creates a dilemma because the skills required of a good accounting and finance executive diverge from those of a good risk manager.

There are conflicting mind-sets between accounting and risk managers. Accounting is a well-established discipline, with an accepted certification process, that requires great attention to detail. By nature, it is backward-looking and myopic. Risk management is much newer and evolving. By nature, it is forward-looking and requires a soft focus (like our great Samurai hero in Chapter 1) and imagination. Why is imagination important? On a U.S. national security level, the 9/11 attacks on the World Trade Center and the Pentagon were the greatest risk management failures since the 1941 attack on Pearl Harbor. The 9/11 Commission weighed a great deal of evidence and testimony and concluded that the risk management failure was caused by a simple lack of imagination on the part of those charged with protecting the national security of the United States.

Organizations hurt themselves by putting the burdens of complex risk management on the shoulders of one accounting professional, no matter how talented that person may be. Risk management is a demanding discipline that requires unique skills—skills quite different from accounting.

Accounting enjoys a widely accepted certification and training process that has been in place for decades. As noted, risk certifications are emerging, but they are not well accepted or comprehensive. Reading this book is evidence of the challenges facing any risk certification protocol. Most financial institutions have focused only on credit risk. Operational risk is relatively new as a discipline and outside of financial services, risk managers are the exception. It is hard to imagine a certified risk manager who is truly knowledgeable in all the areas we cover here—credit, market, operational, legal, reputation, liquidity, and portfolio risk.

Summary

The good news is that there are several risk frameworks in widespread use. The bad news is that there is little consensus to standardize around one of them. The most recent crisis calls into question both the COSO and Basel frameworks, under which many banks suffered major losses. These organizations have complied with COBIT and ITIL as well, although IT is not considered a major contributor to the financial losses in banking.

The new ISO 31000 and 31010 standards do hold promise and look to be flexible for small and large organizations alike. The appendix of ISO 31010 contains comprehensive lists and introductions to a great variety of risk and compliance tools. Some of these are used outside of risk management and many have been in widespread use for many years.

Risk management is as much an art as a science, making the acceptance and apportionment of one universal standard unlikely—the one that has come the closest is COSO. Its major weaknesses should now be apparent with the continued revelations of major accounting scandals by organizations under the full force of the COSO-based U.S. Sarbanes-Oxley Act.

Notes

1. Committee of Sponsoring Organizations of the Treadway Commission, COSO Enterprise Risk Management—Integrated Framework (AICPA, 2004).

2. See Tim Leach, "COSO—Is It Fit for Purpose?" Chapter 2 in Anthony Tarantino, *Governance, Risk, and Compliance Handbook* (Hoboken, NJ: John Wiley & Sons, 2006).

3. Louise Story and Eric Dash, "Lehman Channeled Risks through 'Alter Ego' Firm," *New York Times,* April 12, 2010. www.nytimes .com/2010/04/13/business/13lehman.html.

4. COSO, *Internal Control over Financial Reporting—Guidance for Smaller Public Companies* (2006). Available at www.coso.org.

5. Committee of Sponsoring Organizations of the Treadway Commission, COSO Enterprise Risk Management—Integrated Framework (AICPA, 2004).

6. See Chapter 21 in Anthony Tarantino, *Manager's Guide to Compliance* (Hoboken, NJ: John Wiley & Sons, 2006).

7. See the official IT Governance Institute web site for more information on COBIT. www.isaca.org/Template.cfm?Section=COBIT6 &Template=/TaggedPage/TaggedPageDisplay.cfm&TPLID=55& ContentID=31519.

8. See the official ITIL web site for more information: www.itil-officialsite.com/home/home.asp.

9. The Committee's members come from Belgium, Canada, France, Germany, Italy, Japan, Luxembourg, the Netherlands, Spain, Sweden, Switzerland, United Kingdom, and the United States. Countries are represented by their central banks (e.g., U.S. Federal Reserve Bank of New York, Bank of England, etc.) and generally meet quarterly.

CHAPTER 3

Conducting Your Own Risk Assessment and Alignment

After reading this chapter, you will be able to:

- Comprehend your risk appetite and capacity.
- Conduct your own risk assessments.
- Be familiar with the types of risk analysis.
- Create a formal risk statement.

For the past decade, there has been an extensive and organized effort by organizations to assess their risks, especially in financial services. The new ISO 31000 and ISO 31010 frameworks provide guidelines in this process that make good sense and build on years of work by risk professionals.[1] But before an organization embarks on a risk assessment, it is imperative that it come to a consensus at the board and executive level as to its risk appetite. Once the risk appetite is agreed on, an organization can conduct ongoing risk assessments to determine the alignment between its appetite and risk exposure. Although this may seem basic and fundamental to the well-being of any organization, the enterprise-threatening risk failures by major financial institutions during the recent financial crisis demonstrate the reality of poor alignment.

By following a structured approach to establishing a risk appetite statement, an organization can gain a better understanding of its strategic goals, culture, marketplace, regulatory requirements, and financial sensitivity to risk. There are four basic steps.

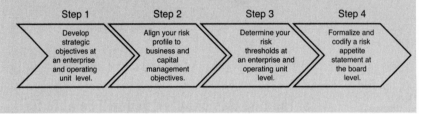

Step 1	Step 2	Step 3	Step 4
Develop strategic objectives at an enterprise and operating unit level.	Align your risk profile to business and capital management objectives.	Determine your risk thresholds at an enterprise and operating unit level.	Formalize and codify a risk appetite statement at the board level.

It has become clear that boards of financial firms and organizations (corporations and municipalities, retirement funds, etc.) that invested in mortgage-based financial products were clueless to the risk exposure. In some cases, this was the result of a misalignment in which risk managers knew of the dangers, but their warnings never reached the board. This appears to have been the case with Washington Mutual (WaMu), the largest U.S. savings and loan provider, prior to its collapse and fire sale to JPMorgan Chase. Ronald Cathcart was WaMu's chief risk officer from 2006 to 2008. He was banned from attending board meetings because of his constant warnings to WaMu senior management as to the dangers in subprime.[2] In other cases, neither the board nor risk managers recognized the dangers—they were aligned, but wrong in their assessment.

Determining Risk Appetite

Prior to conducting a risk assessment it is essential to establish the risk appetite of your organization—its capacity to take on risk in the pursuit of its organizational objectives.

Organizational Objectives

The risk appetite of an organization must consider its strategic objectives, which may include:

- Market share
- Competitors' strategic directions
- Reputation in the marketplace
- Earning stability/growth
- Investor returns and expected returns
- Regulatory requirements and standing among regulators
- Capital adequacy/external credit ratings

Understanding the objectives is not as straightforward as one may think, as there is a wide range of stakeholders in any organization that may have divergent and conflicting attitudes toward its risks. Expectations of these groups may differ significantly, or even be in conflict, but often include maintaining business growth, profitability, and earnings stability, ensuring regulatory compliance, being an employer of choice and a good corporate citizen. Depending on the nature of the organization, key stakeholders may include:

- Shareholders
- Board of directors
- Management
- Employees
- Regulators
- Customers and suppliers
- Taxpayers and voters

As the strategy of the organization changes, its appetite for risk must be revisited to confirm that it will support the achievement of its objectives.

Growth Changes Require Realignment

Should an organization's growth targets double? The organization's risk appetite would need to be reconsidered to reflect the increased risk taking and capital requirements needed for such a target to be achieved.

An extension to an organization's strategic objectives is its business plan, which outlines how the business intends to meet its objectives and stakeholder expectations. Regulators compel an ongoing realignment in the financial service sector. Many companies within the financial services sector will also have comprehensive capital management plans outlining capital requirements for achieving strategic objectives. These requirements need to reflect and inform the risk appetite statement.

Risk Capacity

Risk capacity involves determining how much risk is currently being taken in the context of the organization's capacity to take on risk. To align the risk profile to the capital management or business plan an organization should undertake the following steps:

Step 1. Identify potential risks the organization is exposed to that may prevent it from achieving its strategic objectives.

Step 2. Measure the aggregate risk profile and the level of expected losses (ELs) and unexpected losses (ULs) from Black Swans (very rare events that create catastrophic losses) that the organization is willing to accept in the event the risk occurs.

Step 3. Understand the current risk taking capacity (e.g., the capital management plan and business plan as well as the degree to which these allow a buffer for future risks).

Step 4. Consider the amount of available capital, insurance, and other mitigants (the buffer) between the risk-taking capacity and the aggregate risk profile, including provision for ELs and ULs.

Step 5. Determine the size of the buffer based on the risk appetite of the organization. The organization has to strike a balance between its competing strategic objectives (e.g., availability of capital versus cost of capital). The strategic objectives, if clearly articulated, should provide a strong guideline for the level of anticipated risk appetite.

Step 6. Identify zero tolerance risk exposures (e.g., compliance or safety breaches) for reputational purposes.

Specific Risk Tolerances

Next is the identification of tolerance ranges for specific risks (to ensure the appetite remains within the bounds of the capital management and/or business plan).

These are the typical measures of risk used to monitor exposure compared with the stated risk appetite. They break down high-level risk appetite into actionable measures at a business unit level and help to ensure that appropriate reporting and monitoring processes can be put in place for the effective management of these risks. As such, these thresholds should be clearly articulated and measurable.

Formalize and Codify a Risk Appetite Statement at the Board Level

Finally the organization will need to formalize the results of the above process through the documentation of the organization's risk appetite in a formal risk appetite statement. The risk appetite statement should then be approved by the board prior to communicating the document to the wider organization.

Link Risk Appetite to Performance Monitoring and Reporting

As business strategy is linked to performance management, risk monitoring and reporting should be linked to risk appetite—as both contribute to the quality of business performance. It is important that performance is assessed in terms of its compliance with the organization's risk appetite.

Strong financial performance can often mask the risks that are actually being taken to achieve that performance, as was shown by the collapses of Lehman Brothers and Bear Stearns.

It is one thing to make risk or reward trade-offs; it is another to understand exactly what they are.

Standard risk and incident reporting methodologies should be used to monitor breaches of risk appetite and tolerance levels. This monitoring and reporting is fundamental.

TIPS AND TECHNIQUES

The Value of a Clearly Articulated Risk Appetite

There are significant advantages to including a well-defined risk appetite statement within an organization's formal governance documentation. The definition and articulation of risk appetite has a positive influence on organizational behavior, which includes creating the needed tone-at-the-top. It gives managers an improved understanding of what risk management means to their roles and helps them to apply effective risk management practices. The benefits include:

- **Increasing the capacity to take on risk.** The ability to take on risk is determined by more than just a capacity to absorb losses. The ability to manage risks based on skill sets and experience, systems, controls, and infrastructure is also crucial.

- **Improving allocation of risk resources and assets.** Understanding risk appetite helps an organization in the efficient allocation of risk management resources across a risk portfolio, and may enable the pursuit of business opportunities that, without an understanding of the appetite, would otherwise be rejected.

- **Defining the limits on new business ventures.** A clearly defined risk appetite takes much of the guesswork out of putting limits on new business, such as mergers and acquisitions (M&A), and product introductions.
- **Developing sharper, more intelligent risk reporting.** Reporting frameworks are more sensitive to risk tolerance levels, allowing more meaningful early warning indicators and risk limits.

Conducting Risk Assessments

While there is an active debate as to the most effective approaches to risk management, there is a near universal consensus as to the value of a self-assessment as an essential first step.

Why Conduct a Risk Assessment?

ISO 31010 (31010–4.1) makes the case for conducting risk assessments, arguing that it provides evidence-based analysis and information to make informed decisions on how to treat specific risks. The benefits of a risk assessment include:

- Providing risk information for key stakeholders in the organization.
- Understanding the impact of risk on objectives.
- Understanding the nature of risks to select the optimal counter measures.
- Comparing the pros and cons of various risk mitigation techniques and technologies.
- Establishing a prioritization in risks based on occurrence and severity.
- Meeting regulatory, rating agency, and investor requirements and demands.

How to Conduct a Risk Assessment Exercise

- Obtain the support of the chief executive officer (CEO) and chairman of the board (CoB) to conduct the survey.

- Request the CEO and CoB to impress on all participants the criticality of conducting the risk appetite survey.

- Ask the CEO and CoB to excuse themselves from the process— their presence may be too intimidating for participants fearing to take exception to stated policies and objectives.

- Construct a method of surveying board members and executive managers to determine the firm's risk appetite.

- Optionally, assure the participants of their anonymity, at least initially. Otherwise participants may be intimidated or simply follow the lead of the more powerful and outspoken participants.

- Ideally, create an online method to conduct the survey and create a tight time frame for the survey to prevent participants from sharing their responses.

- Use facilitated survey participant workshops to normalize the results; that is, what may initially appear to be different risk responses may actually be the same once articulated and compared with other responses.

- Use a simple probability and severity matrix (described later in this chapter) to rank and prioritize the identified risks.

Risk Assessment Core to Risk Management Process

Risk assessments are the core activity in an organization's risk management process. Risk assessment is not a stand-alone activity and should be fully integrated into the other components in the risk management process. The risk management process contains the following elements:

EXECUTIVE INSIGHT

How Not to Conduct
a Risk Assessment

On the surface, it would make sense to base a risk assessment on an organization's general ledger—its financial statement. The logic is obvious—focus the greatest risk management efforts on those areas with the greatest impact on the bottom line. Adding to the argument is that this is the risk-based approach advocated by the COSO framework and most audit standards.

The problem is that risks can arise from areas that may not be significant to the bottom line or appear on the bottom line. The giant French bank Société Générale did not have a general ledger entry for Jérôme Kerviel, who nearly destroyed the firm with his rough trading activities. The quality and safety crisis that gripped and severely wounded Toyota in 2009 and 2010 cannot be easily tied to its general ledger.

- Communication and collaboration with all relevant stakeholders.
- Establishing the context or scope of the process.
- Conducting risk assessments.
- Deploying risk treatments and mitigations.
- Monitoring and reviewing the risk management process.

How and When to Assess Risk

Organizations should have a policy and methodology for deciding when and how risks should be assessed. Risk managers need to clearly understand:

- The context and objectives of the organization.
- The extent and type of risks that are tolerable, and how unacceptable risks are to be treated.

- How risk assessment integrates into organizational processes.

- Methods and techniques to be used for risk assessment, and their contributions to the risk management process.

- Accountability, responsibility, and authority for performing risk assessment.

- Resources available to carry out risk assessment.

- How the risk assessment will be reported and reviewed.

Risk assessment is the overall process of risk identification, risk analysis, and risk evaluation. Risks can be assessed at an organizational level, at a departmental level, for projects, individual activities, or specific risks. Different tools and techniques may be appropriate in different contexts.

Risk assessment provides an understanding of risks, their causes, consequences, and their probabilities. This provides input to decisions about:

- Whether an activity should be undertaken.

- How to maximize opportunities.

- Whether risks need to be treated.

- Choosing between options with different risks.

- Prioritizing risk treatment options.

- The most appropriate selection of risk treatment strategies that will bring adverse risks to a tolerable level.

Defining Risk Criteria

Defining risk criteria in a risk assessment involves deciding:

- The nature and types of consequences to be included and how they will be measured.

- The way in which probabilities are to be expressed.

- How a level of risk will be determined.

TIPS AND TECHNIQUES

Many-to-Many Relationship among Business Objectives, Risks, and Risk Mitigation Processes

It would be nice to operate in a one-to-one relationship world in which a single business objective came with one risk and one risk mitigation process. Unfortunately, this is rarely the case. Typically there exist many-to-many relationships in which many risks may stem from one business process and require multiple risk mitigation processes. However, one risk mitigation process may address multiple risks across multiple business objectives.

- The criteria by which it will be decided when a risk needs treatment.

- The criteria for deciding when a risk is acceptable and/or tolerable.

- Whether and how combinations of risks will be taken into account.

- General data sources.

- Organizational risk appetite.

Having completed a risk assessment, *risk treatment* involves selecting and agreeing to one or more relevant options for changing the probability of occurrence, the effect of risks, or both, and implementing these options. This is followed by a cyclical process of reassessing the new level of risk, with a view to determine its tolerability against the criteria previously set, in order to decide whether further treatment is required.

Risk Identification

Risk identification is the process of finding, recognizing, and recording risks. Its goal is to identify what might happen or what situations might exist that might affect the achievement of the objectives of the system or organization. Once a risk is identified, an organization needs to identify existing controls, such as design features, people, processes, and systems. (This is a core process in financial audits which evaluate the effectiveness of internal controls.)

Risk Analysis

Risk analysis develops an understanding of risks providing an input to risk assessments and to decisions about whether risks need to be treated and about the most appropriate treatment strategies and methods. It consists of determining the consequences and their probabilities for identified risk events, taking into account the presence (or not) and the effectiveness of any existing controls. The consequences and their probabilities are then combined to determine a level of risk.

TIPS AND TECHNIQUES

Creating a Probability/ Consequence Matrix

To rank risks, the first step is to find the consequence descriptor that best fits the situation then defines the probability with which those consequences will occur. The level of risk is then read off from the matrix. Many risk events may have a range of outcomes with different associated probabilities. Usually, minor problems are more common than catastrophes. Therefore, there is a choice as to whether to rank the most common outcome or the most serious or some other combination.

In many cases, it is appropriate to focus on the most serious credible outcomes as these pose the largest threat and are often of most concern. In some cases, it may be appropriate to rank both common problems and unlikely catastrophes as separate risks. It is important that the probability relevant to the selected consequence is used, not the probability of the event as a whole.

The level of risk defined by the matrix may be associated with a decision rule, such as to treat or not to treat the risk.

There are limitations in using a probability/consequence matrix:

- It may be difficult to define rating scales unambiguously.
- Its use can be subjective with wide variations between raters.
- It can be difficult to compare or combine risk levels for various consequence categories.

Risk analysis involves consideration of the causes and sources of risk, their consequences, and the probability that those consequences can occur. Factors that affect consequences and probability should be identified. An event can have multiple consequences and can affect multiple objectives. Existing risk controls and their effectiveness should be taken into account. More than one technique may be required for complex applications.

EXECUTIVE INSIGHT

Red Light/Green Light Heat Maps Work

It seems silly and simplistic, but simple red light/green light heat maps can provide a compelling message. Busy executives have little time and less patience to dive deeply into a complex and lengthy analysis. A probability/consequence lends itself to this graphical tool, which clearly shows the critical few areas of risk that require the most attention.

There is one reservation in their use. About 7 percent of men are red/green color-blind. A workaround is to write the names of the colors in the matrix boxes and to group colors together logically. I am red/green color-blind and could discern the differences in a chart such as Exhibit 3.1 if it were in color.

EXHIBIT 3.1

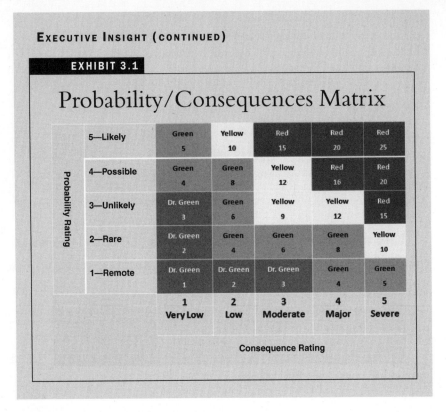

Probability/Consequences Matrix

Probability Rating		1 Very Low	2 Low	3 Moderate	4 Major	5 Severe
5—Likely		Green 5	Yellow 10	Red 15	Red 20	Red 25
4—Possible		Green 4	Green 8	Yellow 12	Red 16	Red 20
3—Unlikely		Dr. Green 3	Green 6	Yellow 9	Yellow 12	Red 15
2—Rare		Dr. Green 2	Green 4	Green 6	Green 8	Yellow 10
1—Remote		Dr. Green 1	Dr. Green 2	Dr. Green 3	Green 4	Green 5

Consequence Rating

Qualitative, Semi-quantitative, and Quantitative Risk Analysis

Approaches to risk analysis can be grouped into three categories: qualitative, semi-quantitative, and quantitative. There are pros and cons to each approach, and ideally they should be deployed together and not exclusively. Banking regulators realize the value of combining risk categories by mandating their combined use in the most advanced risk management approaches.

Qualitative Assessments

Qualitative assessments define consequence, probability, and level of risk by significance levels such as high, medium, and low; may combine consequence and probability; and evaluate the resultant level of risk against

EXHIBIT 3.2	

Definitions of Probability Criteria

Rating	Criteria
Likely	Balance of probability will occur, or could occur within weeks or months
Possible	May occur shortly, but there is a distinct possibility that it could occur within months or a year
Unlikely	May occur but most probably will not occur within months or a year
Rare	Occurrence is very unlikely within the next three years
Remote	Theoretically possible that it will occur, but highly unlikely

qualitative criteria. In cases where the analysis is qualitative, there should be a clear explanation of all the terms employed, and the basis for all criteria should be recorded. Exhibit 3.2 is an example of probability definitions.

Semi-quantitative Assessments

Semi-quantitative assessments are methods that use numerical rating scales for consequence and probability and combine them to produce a level of risk using a formula. Scales may be linear or logarithmic, or have some other relationship; formulae used can also vary.

Quantitative Analysis

Quantitative analysis estimates practical values for consequences and their probabilities, and produces values of the level of risk in specific units defined when developing the context. Full quantitative analysis may not always be possible or desirable due to insufficient information about the system or activity being analyzed, lack of data, influence of human factors, or because the effort of quantitative analysis is not warranted or required. In such circumstances, a comparative semi–quantitative or qualitative ranking of risks by specialists, knowledgeable in their respective field, may still be effective. Even where full quantification has been carried out, it needs to be recognized that the levels of risk calculated are estimates. Care should be taken to ensure that they are not attributed a level of accuracy and precision inconsistent with the accuracy of the data and methods employed.

Chapter 5, "Operational Risk," provides a more detailed discussion of the types and examples of qualitative and quantitative analysis.

Controls Assessment

Integral in any risk assessment is an evaluation of the effectiveness of controls in place over those risks. The level of risk depends on the adequacy and effectiveness of existing controls. Controls assessments should also address the costs versus benefits of various control options. Where existing controls are found to be significantly deficient, not standardized, and/or labor intensive, it may be necessary to develop a business case for a technology and process optimization investment to standardize and automate controls.

Questions to consider in a controls assessment include:

- What are the existing controls for specific risks?
- Are existing controls effective?
- Are existing controls auditable by internal and external auditors?
- Do existing controls meet regulatory and investor requirements?
- Do existing controls help meet the highest rating agency scores?

This last question can be important. In banking and insurance, capital and solvency reserve ratios are based on the effectiveness of credit and operational risk. Unlike Sarbanes-Oxley and the COSO frameworks, it is not a pass/fail system and rewards those who meet the highest standards. It can also be important outside of finance to those seeking the lowest borrowing and insurance rates.

Consequences and Probability Analysis

Risk can be quantified in a variety of ways. The most basic and most essential of these is the probability or likelihood that a risk event will occur and what the consequences or severity will be if it does occur. Even the smallest of organizations can and should assess these two elements of risk.

Consequence Analysis

Consequence analysis determines the nature and type of impact that could occur assuming that a particular event situation or circumstance has occurred. An event may have a range of impacts of different magnitudes, and affect a range of different objectives and different stakeholders. Consequence analysis should:

- Take into consideration existing controls that treat consequences.
- Consider relevant contributory factors that impact consequences.
- Relate consequences of risks to the original objectives.
- Consider both immediate and longer-term consequences.
- Consider secondary consequences, such as those impacting associated systems, activities, equipment, or organizations.

Probability Analysis

Typically there are three approaches used to estimate probability. They may be used individually or in combination.

1. **Historical data.** This is the use of historical data to identify situations or events that occurred in the past and use such data to predict the probability of their reoccurrence in the future. The data must be relevant to the type of system, facility, organization, or activity being considered, and also to the operational standards of the organization involved. If there is a low historical frequency of occurrence, then any estimate of probability will be uncertain.

2. **Probability forecasts.** These are predictive techniques such as fault tree analysis and event tree analysis. They are used when

historical data are unavailable or inadequate. Simulation and modeling techniques may be used to generate probability estimates.

3. **Expert opinion.** This can be used in a structured and systematic process to estimate probability. Optimally, expert judgments should rely on all relevant available information, including historical, system-specific, organizational-specific, experimental, design, and so forth. The methods available include the Delphi approach, paired comparisons, category rating, and absolute probability judgments.

TIPS AND TECHNIQUES

The Delphi Technique in Risk Assessments

The Delphi technique is a procedure to obtain a reliable consensus of opinion from a group of experts. Although the term is often now broadly used to mean any form of brainstorming, an essential feature of the Delphi technique, as originally formulated, was that experts expressed their opinions individually and anonymously while having access to the other experts' views as the process progresses.

The Delphi technique can be applied at any stage of the risk management process or at any phase of a system life cycle, wherever a consensus of views of experts is needed.

A group of experts are questioned using a semi-structured questionnaire. The experts do not meet, so their opinions are independent. This helps to reduce intellectual or boss-employee bullying.

A simplified Delphi procedure would look something like this:

❶ A team is formed to undertake and monitor the Delphi process.

❷ A group of experts is selected.

❸ A round-one questionnaire is developed and tested.

❹ The questionnaire is issued to the panel of experts individually.

❺ The first-round responses are analyzed, combined, and distributed to panelists.

❻ Panelists respond and the process is repeated until consensus is reached.

Delphi strengths include anonymous views, so unpopular opinions are more likely to be expressed; all views being equally weighted, avoiding the problem of dominating personalities; ownership of outcomes; and not needing people to be brought together in one place at one time.

Limitations include the labor-intensive and time-consuming nature of the process and that participants need to be able to express themselves clearly in writing.

Post-Assessment Activities

Once an organization has conducted an assessment, it would be expected to develop a series of projects and sustaining activities to address the major risk areas identified. It may be helpful to develop Six Sigma teams to attack the risk projects. Six Sigma can be a good fit for risk improvement projects as its goal is to improve the efficiency and effectiveness of processes using data–driven problem-solving tools.

The original team that conducted the assessments should not be dissolved, as it is needed to monitor the action items identified in the risk assessments and to reconduct the assessments on an annual or semiannual basis.

Summary

This may be the most important chapter in the book because it offers the reader general guidelines, techniques, and sample forms for conducting risk assessments. Leading organizations have been conducting such alignments for many years, but few firms take the next step that we suggest—to align the risk appetite as defined by the board of directors and executive leadership with risk exposure as defined by business and

Lack of Risk Alignment in Many Organizations

A 2009 survey by KPMG provides evidence that many organizations are poorly aligned between their actual risk exposure and what their board and executives express as their risk appetite.[3]

Many financial institutions and institutional investors did not understand the risk in the complex financial products they purchased. They foolishly relied on rating agency assessments, which are typically backward-looking and reactive—only downgrading organizations after bad news becomes public.

risk managers. This is a critical process for all well-run organizations. The good news is that the methods we describe are adaptable to fit small and large organizations alike.

For those who need encouragement to proceed, the new ISO standards, ISO 31000 and 31010, will help to codify risk assessments as an accepted best practice.

Notes

1. This chapter makes extensive use of the ISO 31000 family of standards—ISO 31000: 2009, www.iso.org/iso/catalogue_detail .htm?csnumber=43170 and ISO/IEC 31010: 2009. www.iso.org/ iso/catalogue_detail.htm?csnumber=51073. Both are available for downloading from the ISO web site, www.iso.org, for a fee.

2. Michael Corkery, "Now Meet Two WaMu Whistleblowers," *Wall Street Journal*, April 13, 2010, http://blogs.wsj.com/deals/2010/ 04/13/now-meet-two-wamu-whistleblowers.

3. KPMG, "Understanding and Articulating Risk Appetite" (white paper, 2009), www.kpmg.com.au/Portals/0/ias_erm-riskappetite 200806.pdf.

CHAPTER 4

Six Sigma in Risk Assessments

After reading this chapter, you will be able to:

- Appreciate the value of Six Sigma in risk management.
- Comprehend the DMAIC methodology.
- Calculate a project prioritization index.
- Follow the logic of a SIPOC analysis.
- Listen to the voice of your internal and external customers.

Six Sigma is a well-established and accepted practice in problem solving, process improvement, and waste reduction. There is growing acceptance of Six Sigma as a best practice in operational risk management in general and in conducting risk assessments in particular. Process variations outside of tolerances, excess inventories, and excess lead times typically translate into greater costs and greater risks. Six Sigma excels at attacking these problems—and not just in manufacturing environments. Most major banks have deployed both Six Sigma and Lean teams in a number of areas.

Six Sigma

Sigma is the Greek alphabet letter used to represent the standard deviation of any process. A Six Sigma quality level is said to

EXECUTIVE INSIGHT

You Do Not Have to Be a Six Sigma Master Black Belt to Use Six Sigma

Six Sigma includes training and certification programs that mimic martial arts belt ranks—lower levels are typically green, middle levels are typically brown, and the highest levels are always black. It is preferable to use black belts and master black belts (the highest rank) to utilize the tools and techniques we describe in this chapter, but it is not essential.

Experienced project managers will typically be familiar with and have used the more popular techniques and tools found in Six Sigma. Six Sigma applies data-driven analysis to problem solving with the goal of making a process more efficient and effective. This approach was not invented by Six Sigma and has been in widespread use since Frederick Winslow Taylor, Frank Gilbreth, and Lillian Gilbreth (who is considered the mother of industrial engineering) developed management theory and industrial engineering in the early twentieth century. (Two of the twelve Gilbreth children wrote the book *Cheaper by the Dozen* about the Gilbreth family. Little wonder that the Gilbreths became efficiency experts.)

represent 3.4 defects per million opportunities. Six Sigma began as the use of statistical methods to improve quality, business process efficiencies, and profitability. Today it is a methodology for continuous improvement in customer satisfaction and profitability that goes far beyond reducing defects to focus on general business process improvement.

It takes a systematic approach to reducing or eliminating process and product defects that impact things important to customers—designated as critical to quality. The customer focus of Six Sigma is a major strength—referred to as the voice of the customer (VOC). Customers are any person or group that is downstream in a process. So customers can be both internal and external to an organization.

Although its hard statistical and mathematical tools have been much touted, Six Sigma also applies softer problem-solving and facilitation tools that have proven to be effective as well. The key is knowing what combination of techniques to apply to a given situation. Six Sigma maintains the following:

- Continuous efforts to achieve stable and predictable process results by reducing process variations, which are essential to business success.

- Business processes have characteristics that can be measured, analyzed, improved, and controlled.

- Achieving sustained quality improvement requires commitment from the entire organization, particularly from top-level management.

TIPS AND TECHNIQUES

Why Some Six Sigma Projects Fail

Six Sigma projects that fail share similar issues with failed projects in general. Six Sigma projects often require behavioral change to overcome defenders of the status quo. Six Sigma's DMAIC process identifies the final control phase as important to prevent backsliding.

The problem comes from the nature of project management in general, not from Six Sigma. Project teams and budgets typically end upon project completion. The sustainability of most projects' deliverables is typically turned over to the users. It

Tips and Techniques (continued)

is not unusual for users to resent changes imposed by outsiders and regress unless the project has successfully addressed behavior change.

Behavioral change skills are not easily acquired and hard to measure. Project managers who excel at hard project management skills may lack the soft skills to sustain a project's deliverables once they roll off it. It is fair to criticize Six Sigma for its razor focus on data analysis and analytic tools at the expense of soft skills, which are not easily tested in a certification examination. This criticism applies to project management as well.

DMAIC and PPI in Risk Management Projects

DMAIC is a five-phase improvement and problem-solving methodology where D stands for define, M for measure, A for analyze, I for improve, and C for control.[1] Typically, D is the essential phase for achieving dramatic improvement quickly, and C is the most critical phase for realizing return on investment. DMAIC offers the advantages of a structured approach to risk management in the hands of well-trained problem-solving experts.

The success of the DMAIC in general and risk management in particular depends on selecting projects that offer the greatest rewards in risk reduction at the lowest cost and with the lowest chances of failure. The right project is the one that can result in a significant return on investment. Thus the first priority is to identify the right projects to work on that will have an impact on the bottom line and generate savings for the enterprise. A variety of potential risk management projects should be identified and evaluated based on a cost and benefit analysis.

Project Prioritization Index

Project Prioritization Index (PPI) is a simple metric that can be used to prioritize risk management projects according to the following equation:

$$PPI = (Benefits/cost) \times (Probability\ of\ success/ time\ to\ complete\ the\ project\ in\ years)$$

At a minimum, the PPI should exceed two (2) to ensure a return on investment. Initially, one can find many projects with PPI greater than four (4), thus making it somewhat easier to realize savings. Exhibit 4.1 is an example of the inputs to and calculations in a PPI.

Once the risk management project is selected, a cross-functional team can be formed to work on it. During the *Define* phase, the team develops a clear definition of the project, the project's scope, the process map, customer requirements, SIPOC (described below), and a project plan. In other words, in the Define phase, customer requirements are delineated and a process baseline is established.

The *Measure* phase establishes the sources of information, the performance baseline, and the opportunity's impact in terms of cost of quality.

The *Analyze* phase focuses on examining patterns, trends, and correlations between the process output and its inputs. A cross-functional team performs the cause-and-effect analysis using such tools as fishbone

---

EXHIBIT 4.1

Project Prioritization Index Example

Cost = $250,000
Benefit = $1 million
Probability of Success = 80%
Project Duration = 1 year
PPI = (1.0/0.25) × (0.8/1.0) = 3.2

diagrams. The purpose is to identify the root cause of the problem and necessary remedial actions to capitalize on the opportunity.

The first three phases of the DMAIC methodology help the team gain a better understanding of the process and learn the cause-and-effect relationship between the output and input variables.

The *Improve* phase enables the development of alternate solutions to achieve the desired process outcomes. The *Control* phase is employed to sustain the improvement utilizing effective documentation, training, process management, and process control techniques. The Control phase is also an opportunity to engage the senior management in the Six Sigma journey for support and aggressive goal-setting for identifying further opportunities for improvement.

TIPS AND TECHNIQUES

SIPOC Tool in Risk Assessments

SIPOC is a graphical tool that captures suppliers, their inputs to a process, a process, the outputs of a process, and the customers of the output process—Supplier, Input, Process, Output, Customer (SIPOC).

It is easy to use and with little effort provides a good overview of a process, with its boundaries. As such, it helps to define the scope of a project. It is helpful in the Define phase of the DMAIC process to identify processes at a high level—without excess and often time-consuming detail.

In creating a SIPOC diagram, it may be best to start in the middle with the process and work out to the suppliers and customers. This works well as a whiteboard and team exercise. Once completed, the team will be able to create detailed process maps in the Analyze phase.

The chart below is a sample SIPOC for an equipment lease.

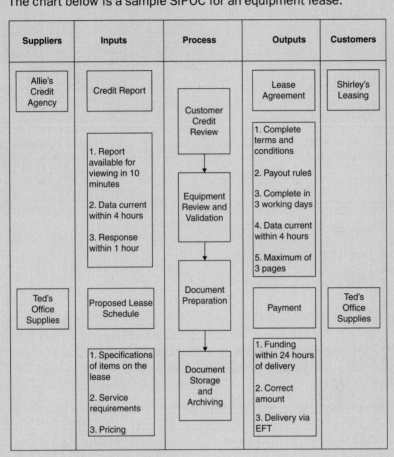

Suppliers	Inputs	Process	Outputs	Customers
Allie's Credit Agency	Credit Report	Customer Credit Review	Lease Agreement	Shirley's Leasing
	1. Report available for viewing in 10 minutes 2. Data current within 4 hours 3. Response within 1 hour	Equipment Review and Validation	1. Complete terms and conditions 2. Payout rules 3. Complete in 3 working days 4. Data current within 4 hours 5. Maximum of 3 pages	
Ted's Office Supplies	Proposed Lease Schedule	Document Preparation	Payment	Ted's Office Supplies
	1. Specifications of items on the lease 2. Service requirements 3. Pricing	Document Storage and Archiving	1. Funding within 24 hours of delivery 2. Correct amount 3. Delivery via EFT	

Voice of the Customer

Six Sigma's emphasis on listening to the voices of customers, all those who receive outputs from a process, is essential in successful risk management. Customers for risk management at an enterprise level include:

- Regulators
- Rating agencies

- Shareholders

- Executives and managers

- Employees

- Customers

- Suppliers

- News media

A traditional PPI does a good job of balancing cost versus benefits and duration versus risks, but does a poor job of capturing the voice of the customer. A simple means to add VOC to the PPI could be as basic as a high, medium, and low ranking for VOC.

- Low VOC impact $= 0.5$

- Medium VOC impact $= 1.0$

- High VOC impact $= 2.0$

$$PPI = (Benefits/cost) \times (Success\ probability/ Project\ duration\ [years]) \times VOC$$

Exhibit 4.2 shows the resulting formula and example.

EXHIBIT 4.2

Project Prioritization Index with VOC Example

Cost = \$250,000
Benefit = \$1 million
Probability of Success = 80%
Project Duration = 1 year
VOC = 0.5
PPI = (1/0.25) × (0.8/1) × 0.05 = 1.6

Listening to the Voice of Customer Too Literally

Thirty years of business experience and painful lessons learned suggest that listening to the voice of the customer is important, but may require judgment as to what the customer really desires. Customers with any problem typically know they have an issue that needs to be addressed, but usually do not know how to solve it themselves. If they did, they would not ask for help.

The problem stems from such customers directing you as a risk manager on how to solve the problem. This is where judgment, change management, and courage come into play. It is easy to take their marching orders literally and fail. It is more difficult to *do what your customer wants you to do,* rather than *what your customer tells you to do.*

This is not to suggest that you be disobedient or insubordinate, but that you use soft skills to contextualize the actions that will make your customer successful. This can be an iterative and subtle process as some executives (customers) may struggle in admitting judgmental flaws. If you are very good at this, customers will come to think it was their own idea.

Summary

Six Sigma is a proven problem-solving and process improvement technique that makes good sense in risk management. It provides well-established and documented tools and methodologies and does not require a major investment in bureaucracy or technology. The DMAIC approach to project management is helpful as a standardized framework for risk management projects. SIPOC (Supplier, Input, Process, Output, and Customer) is a simple tool to scope a risk management project, and VOC helps in considering all the stakeholders in the project.

The Project Prioritization Index (PPI) is also helpful as a means to rank the risk reduction opportunities that any organization faces. Risk assessments do work and will tend to identify more risks than an organization can effectively address. The probability/consequences matrix discussed in Chapter 3 will create the need to prioritize risks; the PPI will act as a tie breaker for projects that present roughly the same risk.

Note

1. This section extensively references Praveen Gupta, "Total Quality Management Using Lean Six Sigma," Chapter 4 in Anthony Tarantino and Deborah Cernauskas, *Risk Management in Finance* (Hoboken, NJ: John Wiley & Sons, 2009).

CHAPTER 5

Operational Risk

After reading this chapter, you will be able to:

- Identify the major categories of risk according to Basel.
- Comprehend the major qualitative and quantitative tools.
- Understand the need for a holistic approach to operational risk.
- Grasp the interconnections between operational risk failures and other types of risk.

Operational risk is caused by the failure of internal controls over people, process, technology, and external events. It can include a wide variety of problems: external fraud, internal fraud, inadvertent errors, technology failures, incorrect data entry, natural disasters, regulatory changes, terrorism, and so on.

Financial services industries are addressing operational risk through the Basel II accords for banking and the Solvency II accords for insurance. This is a major change from earlier versions of these risk frameworks, which were primarily focused on credit risk and gave little attention to operational risk. This is no academic exercise; it requires institutions to reserve capital to cover their operational risks. The Basel Committee of the Bank for International Settlements (BIS) and the Solvency Committee of the International Association of Insurance Supervisors (IAIS) define operational risk as the

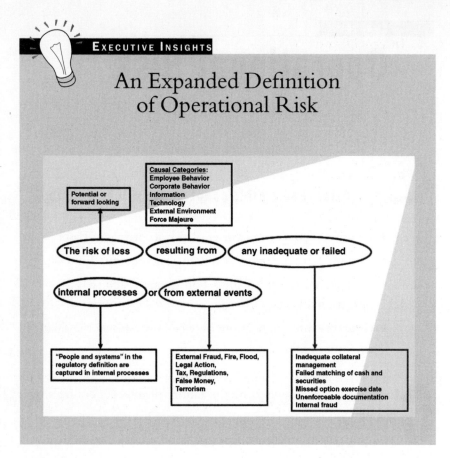

EXECUTIVE INSIGHTS

An Expanded Definition of Operational Risk

Causal Categories:
Employee Behavior
Corporate Behavior
Information
Technology
External Environment
Force Majeure

Potential or
forward looking

The risk of loss   resulting from   any inadequate or failed

internal processes or from external events

"People and systems" in the
regulatory definition are
captured in internal processes

External Fraud, Fire, Flood,
Legal Action,
Tax, Regulations,
False Money,
Terrorism

Inadequate collateral
management
Failed matching of cash and
securities
Missed option exercise date
Unenforceable documentation
Internal fraud

risk of losses resulting from inadequate or failed internal processes, people and systems, or external events. Although designed for financial institution, this definition should be applicable for any industry, institution, or individual.

Categories of Operational Risk

The Basel and Solvency approach to operational risk breaks it into 7 major categories, 20 secondary categories, and 64 subcategories. The great majority of these designations is not unique to financial services and can provide a good framework and checklist for addressing operational risk in any industry or organization. The three-level hierarchy is as follows:

1. Internal fraud

    a. Unauthorized activities

        i. Transactions not reported (informational)

        ii. Transaction type unauthorized (with monetary loss)

        iii. Mismarking of position (international)

    b. Theft and fraud

        i. Fraud/credit fraud/worthless deposits

        ii. Theft/extortion/embezzlement/robbery

        iii. Misappropriation of assets

        iv. Forgery

        v. Check kiting

        vi. Smuggling

        vii. Account takeover/impersonation/etc.

        viii. Tax noncompliance/evasion (willful)

        ix. Bribes/kickbacks

        x. Insider trading

2. External fraud

    a. Theft and fraud

        i. Theft/robbery

        ii. Forgery

        iii. Check kiting

    b. System security

        i. Hacking damage

        ii. Theft of information (with monetary loss)

3. Employment practices

    a. Employee relations

        i. Compensation, benefit, termination issues

        ii. Organized labor activities

   b. Safe environment

      i. General facility (e.g., slip and fall)

      ii. Employee health and safety rules, events

      iii. Workers' compensation

   c. Diversity and discrimination

      i. All discrimination types (racial, sexual, sexual orientation, religious, etc.)

4. Clients, products, and business processes

   a. Suitability, disclosure, and fiduciary

      i. Fiduciary breaches/guideline violations

      ii. Suitability/disclosure issues (know your customer, etc.)

      iii. Retail consumer disclosure violations

      iv. Breach of privacy

      v. Aggressive sales

      vi. Account churning (excessive buying and selling of securities by a broker to generate commissions)

      vii. Misuse of confidential information

      viii. Lender liability

   b. Improper business or market practices

      i. Antitrust

      ii. Improper trade/market practices

      iii. Market manipulation

      iv. Insider trading (on firm's account)

      v. Unlicensed activity

   c. Product flaws

      i. Product defects (unauthorized, etc.)

      ii. Model errors (poor design)

    d. Selection, sponsorship, and exposure

        i. Failure to investigate client as per guidelines

        ii. Exceeding client exposure limits

    e. Advisory activities

        i. Disputes over performance of advisory activities

5. Damage to physical assets

    a. Disaster and other events

        i. Natural disaster losses

        ii. Human losses from external sources (terrorism, vandalism)

6. Business disruptions and system failures

    a. Systems

        i. Hardware

        ii. Software and middleware

        iii. Telecommunications

        iv. Utility outage/disruptions (failures in business continuity)

7. Execution delivery and process management

    a. Transaction capture, execution, and maintenance

        i. Miscommunication

        ii. Data entry, maintenance, or loading error

        iii. Missed deadline or responsibility

        iv. Model/system misoperation

        v. Accounting error/entity attribution error

    b. Monitoring and reporting

        i. Failed mandatory reporting obligation

        ii. Inaccurate external report (loss incurred)

    c. Customer instate and documentation

        i. Client permissions/disclaimers missing

        ii. Legal documents missing/incomplete

    d. Customer/client account management

        i. Unapproved access given to accounts

        ii. Incorrect client record (loss incurred)

        iii. Negligent loss or damage of client assets

    e. Trade counterparties

        i. Nonclient counterparty performance

        ii. Miscellaneous nonclient counterparty disputes

    f. Vendors and suppliers

        i. Outsourcing

        ii. Vendor disputes

Strategic and Holistic Approach to Operational Risk

Organizations that take a strategic and holistic approach to operational risk management will enjoy an advantage over those that take a tactical and reactionary approach. Firefighting and crisis management are among the painful symptoms of a reactionary approach. Symptoms of a preventative and strategic organizational approach include:

- The organization's executives and board demonstrate the right tone-at-the-top, which supports and reinforces a moral and ethical culture including transparency and openness, and does not tolerate hiding mistakes or unethical behavior.

- The organization's executives and board have embraced operational risk management as a continuous process that is critical to meeting the organization's objectives, created a risk management committee that is chartered to perform active oversight of the firm's risk management framework, and ensured alignment among the organization's business objectives, revenue drivers, and risk exposure and appetite.

- The organization has embraced such risk management and problem-fixing frameworks as ISO 31000/31010 and Lean Six Sigma.

- The organization has defined operational risk management on an enterprise-wide level and is able to explain and defend its definition against peer organizations, regulations, and best practice frameworks.

- The organization has invested in a high-caliber chief risk officer and other needed resources that are chartered to conduct internal audits and assessments of operational risk efficiency.

- There is a management consensus as to the benefits in improving operational risk management, such as reducing operating costs and losses, improving pricing accuracy, lowering financing and insurance costs, improving competitive position in the marketplace, and achieving greater stability in earnings.

- The organization understands its constraints and weaknesses in improving operational risk management, such as budget constraints and inconsistent management support, and has compared them to its industry peers and best practices.

- The organization has a sound management control environment that includes segregation of duties, application and database controls over transactional and master-level data, and physical and logical controls over assets and data.

- The organization has instituted sound antifraud programs, such as active job rotation, forced vacation policies, whistleblower protections, and proactive investigations into suspicious employee behavior.

- The organization enforces strict documents and records life-cycle management that requires publication, access, and

version control of all sensitive information; document retention and destruction policies; and a focus on eliminating
paper documents.

- The organization exercises the same level of control over outsourced activities that impact financial reporting as it does over
internal activities.

- The organization has in place business resiliency plans (BRPs)
that include disaster recovery from natural and man-made disasters; resources, tasks, and costs to get the organization up
and running again; and an analysis of critical outsourced
processes.

EXECUTIVE INSIGHT

Business Resiliency Planning (BRP) on 9/11

Cantor Fitzgerald's New York City office, on the 101st to 105th floors of One World Trade Center (two to six floors above the impact zone of a hijacked airliner), was destroyed during the September 11, 2001 attacks. Cantor Fitzgerald lost 658 employees (all of the employees in the office that day), or about two-thirds of its workforce, considerably more than any other of the World Trade Center tenants or the New York City Police Department and New York City Fire Department.

The company was able to bring its trading markets back online within a week, and CEO and chairman Howard Lutnick, whose brother was among those killed, vowed to keep the company alive.

Cantor Fitzgerald's tragedy demonstrates that the scope of business resiliency planning must be much more than backup technology and systems and must include human factors that come with natural and man-made disasters.

Qualitative Tools

The collection and analysis of data are essential to gain an understanding of operational anticipated and actual losses. Although quantitative analysis will continue to grow in importance, qualitative analysis should remain the backbone of good operational risk management. Four main qualitative tools are emerging as leading industry practices:

1. Risk Control Self-Assessment (RCSA)
2. Scorecards
3. Key Risk Indicators (KRIs)
4. Scenarios

Risk Control Self-Assessment

The risk control self-assessment (RCSA) is a logical first step in determining operational risk exposure. The RCSA process assumes that the business owners and managers are closest to the issues and have the most expertise as to the source of the risk. It is a constructive process in compelling business owners to contemplate and then explain the issues at hand with the added benefit of increasing their accountability.

RCSA is typically a bottom-up process by business managers, but may also be a top-down process by senior stakeholders. It is a good blend—a granular view from the bottom up and an enterprise view from the top down. RCSA methods and tools include brainstorming sessions, interviews, facilitated workshops, scenario-building exercises, and questionnaires.

RCSA has its limitations in that it is subjective and can be perverted by a corporate culture unwilling to admit to mistakes or given to shifting blame. Therefore, executive management is vital in assuring RCSA participants that they will not suffer for speaking candidly and frankly.

Scorecards

Scorecards typically consist of generic questionnaires containing weighted risk-based questions with multiple-choice responses. They create qualitative assessments that can then be translated into quantitative measures, such as a ranking of risks, and used to adjust risk prioritization efforts. Scorecards weigh responses with preset numerical values by their importance and can be used to spread risk resources and capital across the appropriate business divisions and lines of business. In banking, problems can arise due to the subjective nature of scorecards and manipulation of the process to artificially lower capital charges.

Key Risk Indicators

Key risk indicators (KRIs) are used to alert the organization to critical changes in risk, especially as early-warning alerts to changes in the control environment. Improving KRIs beyond after-the-fact loss indicators to truly predictive KRIs will be challenging and KRIs cannot be expected to capture all potential losses.

Scenarios

Scenarios are a forward-looking process that can reflect risks for a given point of time. Scenarios are qualitative risk assessments in that they utilize expert opinion, but can be used to derive quantitative inputs into a capital model. There are four main steps in the scenario process:

1. Scenario generation.
2. Scenario assessment.
3. Review and validation of data quality.
4. Incorporation of scenarios into such advanced approaches to risk as the AMA.

In banking, the advanced measurement approach (AMA) to operational risk has to cover all significant operational risks, and as such, scenarios can be a useful tool. Scenarios can include internal data, external data, and key risk factors, but can be vulnerable to subjective inputs. The rating agencies are very supportive of scenarios in the AMA and suggest they be updated as required to remain relevant to the current state environment.

Quantitative Tools

Quantitative analysis can be seen as a major advance, but is not a magic bullet by any means, as the global financial crisis has demonstrated. Quantitative analysis seeks to expose underlying assumptions and tests empirical beliefs about the manageability and criticality of losses. Modeling is still evolving, with a number of mathematical models showing promise but restricted by limitations in data. Quantification tools use inputs from three main sources:

1. Internal data
2. External data
3. Scenarios

Internal Loss Data

Internal loss data are key to efforts to improve operational risk management. The biggest issue most organizations face, though, is the lack of reliable and consistent operational risk data. It may seem surprising, but many banks only started accumulating internal loss data in order to prepare for Basel II. Basel II requires a minimum of three years' worth of data to start and five years' worth of data on an ongoing basis as part of the AMA.

The quality of internal loss data will be a factor and must be available across all business lines and geographies. Ideally, it should also include near-loss data. It will be critical to capture all economic losses, not just major or material losses with a large impact on the bottom line. This is especially important in predicting expected losses (ELs), even though they typically represent less than 25 percent of all losses. Many loss events result from a variety and combination of factors, which makes their classification difficult. In theory, the same loss event could fall into credit, market, and operational risk buckets.

There is also an issue as to the organization's acceptance of risk. Many organizations are hesitant to capture operational risk losses as a negative reflection on their performance, but view market and credit risks as a cost of doing business and therefore more acceptable. One way to resolve these issues is for the organization to reconcile the general ledger with operational loss data. This will work for accounting losses, but will not capture lost opportunity costs. Few banks have bought into this as a solution, arguing that costs outweigh the benefits. It is difficult to see how operational loss data can be accepted by external auditors, regulators, and analysts over the long term if there is no tie to the general ledger.

External Data

Another method of validating internal loss data is to compare it with peer organizations via externally available data and then scale the data to reflect the organization's environment. External data is needed for the simple reason that there is typically a lack of internal data, especially data around unexpected losses, which represent the large majority of losses in most institutions. Issues in the use of external data stem from its sources—data providers or industry consortia. External data must be mapped, scaled, and adapted to each organization's business, legal, regulatory, technical, control, and cultural environment.

The Operational Risk Exchange (ORX) was created to support external loss data for banking. It is a nonprofit consortium of more than 50 banks. The member banks' internal loss data is anonymized and normalized and then shared in the ORX database for all banks to use. There are localization issues in using such a consortium; for example, customer and loss profiles from a Malaysian bank may look quite different from those of a Canadian bank.

Banks that are performing well may resist using external data, as they are dragged down by the greater losses suffered by their less successful peers.

Scenarios

Refer to the "Qualitative Tools" section for a description of scenarios.

TIPS AND TECHNIQUES

The Interconnected Nature of Operational Risk Failures

Toyota is a notable example of the relationship between multiple operational risk failures and their ability to create a chain reaction, or cascading effect, in other areas of risk.

Toyota took 30 years to develop brand recognition as a leader in quality and safety. This reputation was severely tarnished in 2009 and 2010 with a series of highly publicized quality failures. On the surface, this can be classified under product flaws, but Toyota's chairman admitted that it was caused by a fundamental change in philosophy and focus—aggressive growth over quality. In short, Toyota forgot what made them successful and pushed product introductions ahead of its ability to support them. This can be classified under aggressive sales or even fiduciary. It also leads to a huge legal risk in the form of hundreds of civil lawsuits.

Even more importantly, the operational risk failure has cascaded into a major reputational (brand) risk failure that will take years to repair. No amount of advertising and promotions could overcome the stream of negative news stories and jokes by late-night comedians.

Why Lindbergh Succeeded When So Many Others Died

Charles Lindbergh became one of the great heroes of the twentieth century in 1927 by flying nonstop for more than 32 hours from New York to Paris (without refueling stops in Nova Scotia or Ireland). The feat was even more amazing because he had no copilot, radio, or parachute. The aviators who attempted the crossing before him died in the effort as did those who immediately attempted to duplicate his feat. The other aviators were experienced flyers, using larger planes, copilots, and additional technology (i.e., radios).

Lindbergh's success is a great operational risk case study. So why was he successful when so many other competent pilots failed and died in the process? Some points in his favor:

❶ He reduced his risk by eliminating as many elements of risk as possible:

- One very reliable engine over twin engines.
- Monoplane design over biplane (less drag and greater lift with one wing).
- No copilot (no teamwork required).
- No radio (little help anyway and not reliable).

❷ He prepared for every detail of the flight himself—the devil is in the details:

- He oversaw the construction of his aircraft, the Spirit of Saint Louis, and thus knew the location and characteristics of even the smallest components.

❸ He had extensive experience flying solo in a wide variety of aircraft.

- As an airmail pilot in the Midwest, he knew how to fly in adverse conditions and navigate with only a compass (a solo pilot cannot use a sextant).

- In World War II in the Pacific, he taught pilots how to substantially increase the range of their bombers.

The lesson for risk managers is to eliminate as many elements of risk as possible; understand and mitigate the remaining risks with an obsession for training and practice for every possible contingency; and most importantly, know their own strengths and weaknesses. There are some situations in which discretion is the better part of valor—if the risk is too great, pass on the opportunity. There are few Lindberghs in the history of the world.

Summary

Operational risk is universal to all types and sizes of organizations. It is so varied that its treatment requires a wide variety of techniques and tools. Ironically, most organizations, including banking, have only recently begun to address operational risk in a formal and systematic manner.

Four areas of operational risk have received a great deal of attention: (1) legal risk, (2) financial crimes (fraud and corruption), (3) internal controls that impact financial reporting, and (4) data risk. Each of these areas will be addressed in the next four chapters. This is not to suggest that other risk subcategories are less important. It is typical for one area of operational risk failure to be interrelated to other areas and create a chain reaction.

CHAPTER 6

Legal Risk

After reading this chapter, you will be able to:

- Comprehend the scope of legal discovery.
- Appreciate the importance of the Federal Rules of Civil Procedure.
- Grasp why the United States' litigious nature is spreading to its trading partners.
- Understand how to mitigate your legal risk.

istorically the large umbrella of operational risk has included legal risk, but legal costs, especially those associated with the discovery process, have grown so large as to constitute the largest risk for many organizations based in the United States. The United States is arguably the most litigious society in history and America's sue-happy mentality has spread far beyond U.S. borders. This is because courts in Europe and the United States continue to rule that those companies and individuals that enjoy the benefits of doing business in a country must comply with that country's laws and regulations—regardless of the laws enforced at home. These issues go in both directions over the Atlantic Ocean, as Intel and Microsoft have discovered in the huge fines they have paid for their European business practices.

Here are some interesting factoids for those who do not accept just how big a risk legal issues present:

- Corporate legal discovery costs average over $1.2 million per case.

- Larger U.S. corporations (more than $1 billion in revenues) are typically fighting more than 500 legal actions at any given time.

- Legal discovery represents 75 percent of litigation costs in most major cases.

- The United States is home to more than 75 percent of the world's lawyers.

- 40,000 graduate from U.S. law schools every year, adding to the 1 million already in the field.

- In the United States, 30 million new lawsuits are filed every year.[1]

Legal Discovery

Legal discovery is the process of finding information that was not previously known. It is compulsory to share this information with other parties in a litigation case. Almost all this information is electronic (digital) in nature and includes electronic records, documents, and metadata. Electronic documents include e-mail, web pages, word processing files, computer databases, and virtually anything that is stored on a computer, along with their reference metadata. Technically, documents and data are electronic if they exist in a medium that can only be read through the use of computers. Such media include cache memory, magnetic disks (such as computer hard drives or floppy disks), optical disks (such as DVDs or CDs), and magnetic tapes.

Federal Rules of Civil Procedure—December 2006

The rules and methodology used in legal discovery were greatly clarified with the December 2006 approval by the Supreme Court and Congress of new Federal Rules of Civil Procedure (FRCP).[2] The FRCP govern civil procedure in U.S. district (federal) courts, dating back to 1938, and have been revised 10 times over the years. While U.S. states determine their own rules that apply in state courts, most states have adopted rules

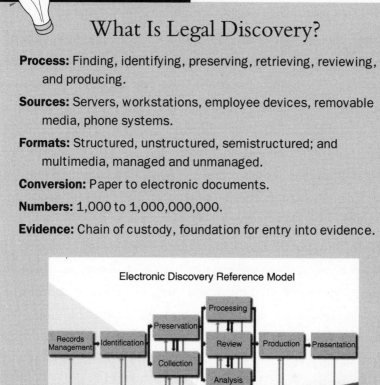

What Is Legal Discovery?

Process: Finding, identifying, preserving, retrieving, reviewing, and producing.

Sources: Servers, workstations, employee devices, removable media, phone systems.

Formats: Structured, unstructured, semistructured; and multimedia, managed and unmanaged.

Conversion: Paper to electronic documents.

Numbers: 1,000 to 1,000,000,000.

Evidence: Chain of custody, foundation for entry into evidence.

that are based on the FRCP. The FRCP introduced a new legal term, *electronically stored information* (ESI), and clearly indicated that there is no exclusion to ESI. A summary of some of the most relevant rules follows:

- **Rule 16(b)** makes provisions for litigants to meet in advance of the trial to discuss discovery issues related to electronically stored information.

- **Rule 26(a)(1)** states that litigants must provide the names of holders of its relevant information and a copy or description of the data it will use to the other parties in the litigation, without awaiting a

discovery request. This needs to be done in a timely manner, but
the determination of *timely* is left to judges.

- **Rule 26(b)(2)(B)** deals with the issues of the discovery of information that is not reasonably accessible because of undue burden
  or cost. There are protections from cost-prohibitive discovery,
  such as requesting all e-mail that a company generates rather than
  messages specific to a case. Litigants need not search or produce
  ESI (initially) from sources that are not reasonably accessible because of undue burden or cost. Judges can mandate cost shifting
  and/or cost sharing in cases where the information is needed but
  considered unduly costly to produce.

- **Rule 26(b)(5)(B)** states that privileged information is protected in
  what is called a *clawback* and safe harbor provision, in which litigants must promptly return, sequester, or destroy it upon its discovery. Judges may impose time limits to this process. Courts will
  look at five factors in considering a clawback: (1) the reasonable-
  ness of the precautions taken to prevent inadvertent disclosures, (2)
  the time to rectify the error, (3) the scope of the production, (4)
  the extent of disclosure, and (5) overriding issues of fairness.

- **Rule 26(f)** touches on a wide range of issues, including discussing
  any issues relating to preserving discoverable information at the
  pretrial meetings. As soon as practicable, litigants must confer and
  come to a consensus as to what is in scope and out of scope in what
  has become a critical meeting to develop a discovery plan. This
  includes the identification, sources, and forms of production for
  ESI, whether the ESI is reasonably accessible, the burden and cost
  of retrieving and reviewing such information, and finally, resolving
  issues relating to claims of privilege, including postproduction assertion of privilege or work-product protection. A discovery plan
  should include: knowing which data is where, actions taken to preserve it, time and effort to get to it, how it can be searched and

retrieved, what is privileged, what will not be searched, and in what format and media it can be provided.

- **Rule 37** is amended to address the problem of the destruction of records as a result of the routine, good-faith operation of an electronic information system. The rule is not intended "to provide a shield for the destruction of information related to a litigation." There is no penalty for purges as part of normal, routine, and good-faith operations, but once a suit is filed, litigants must stop the purge process or face sanctions. Rule 37 defines routine losses as "the ways in which such systems are generally designed, programmed, and implemented to meet the party's technical and business needs."

Legal Risk Case Law Examples

There are several legal case laws that demonstrate the impact of the FRCP and the current litigious environment. Many of these case law examples are now accepted as precedent setting and impact litigants beyond U.S. borders.[3,4,5]

Form of Production Impacted by Need for Metadata

If metadata is relevant and discoverable, production in TIFF or PDF format could be considered incomplete or inadequate. In *Hagenbuch v. 3B6 Sistemi Electronic Industrial*, a defendant decided (against the protests of the plaintiff) to convert all of the information on the original electronic media (that the plaintiff had designated for copying) into TIFF documents.

Clawbacks in a Timely Manner

In *Kuest Corp. v. Airtrol, Incorporated*, the courts denied clawback because the defendants were not timely in making their claims—less than three

---

TIPS AND TECHNIQUES

Metadata Is a Key Element in Every Electronic Business Record

Why Is Metadata important?

- It is often impossible to establish authenticity and relevancy of records without supporting metadata—the who, what, where, and when of data.

- Requesting parties are entitled to all metadata supporting records produced in discovery.

Application Metadata versus System Metadata

- Application metadata is embedded within the file; it describes the file and moves with the file when it is copied.

- System metadata is analogous to a library card catalog; it is stored and maintained external to the file. Every active file (no exception) in a computer system maintains system metadata used to track the file location and file demographics (i.e., file name, size, creation, modification, and usage).

MS Windows and MS Word example

- Supporting metadata may be larger than the file itself, with 80-plus application and system metadata fields tracked for MS Word .doc files.

---

months in this case. "Timely" is a relative concept and varies from judge to judge and case to case.

Sanctioned for Data Preservation Failures

In *Zubulake v. UBS Warburg LLC*, sanctions were imposed on the defendant for failing to preserve e-mail. In imposing sanctions, the court ruled that the defendant's counsel failed to communicate the litigation hold order to all key players. They also failed to ascertain each of the key players' document management habits. By the same token, UBS employees, for unknown reasons, ignored many of the instructions that counsel gave. This case represents a failure of communication, and that failure falls on counsel and client alike.

Discovery Cost Shifting

In two major cases, *Rowe Entertainment, Inc. v. William Morris Agency, Inc.* and *Zubulake v. UBS Warburg LLC*, courts introduced multifactor tests to determine when cost shifting is appropriate. In Rowe, the court concluded that the e-mail information sought by the plaintiffs was relevant and that a blanket order precluding its discovery was unjustified. However, balancing eight factors derived from case law, the court required the plaintiffs to pay for the recovery and production of the e-mail backups, except for the cost of screening for relevance and privilege.

Discovery of Backup Tapes

In Veeco Instruments Inc. securities litigation, the court permitted search of backup tapes, rejecting the argument that restoring and searching backup tapes would be unduly burdensome and costly.

High Costs Do Not Make It Inaccessible

In *AAB Joint Venture v. United States*, the court ruled that costs of several thousand dollars or tens of thousands of dollars do not make data inaccessible—requiring the government to produce e-mail from backup tapes.

Intentional Spoliation

Due to its intentional spoliation of ESI, Oved Construction Services was sanctioned, had a default judgment entered against it, and had to pay its adversary's attorneys' fees. In *EEOC v. EchoStar*, the company's practice of routinely disposing of e-mail, regardless of content, was deemed "risky and extraordinary," and Echostar was sanctioned for failing to preserve e-mail relevant to a former employee's EEOC claim.

Failure to Respond in a Timely Manner

A federal court in New York found that Strategic Resources was grossly negligent because it failed to timely produce 25 gigabytes of data, even though no evidence was destroyed.

Undue Burden

In *Ameriwood Industries, Inc. v. Paul Liberman*, the court ruled that providing information that is not reasonably accessible is satisfied by showing the efforts involved in copying a hard drive, recovering deleted information, and translating recovered data in searchable and reviewable format. But a defendant is not relieved of duty to produce records merely because they chose to preserve the evidence in a format that makes the ultimate production expensive.

Paying for Added Discovery Costs from Poor Due Diligence

In Bristol-Myers Squibb securities litigation, class-action plaintiffs agreed to pay for paper copies of documents that, unknown to them, were available in a less expensive electronic format. Litigants should be careful not to place a carte blanche order for something without knowing what is available and what potential cost may inhere. Conversely, the responding party has some responsibility to explain what is available and to present reasonable alternatives to the requesting party.[6]

Limits on the Scope of Discovery

In *Sallis v. University of Minnesota*, the plaintiff had sought university-wide discovery of the latter's central database. In affirming the denial of the request, the court of appeals ruled that Sallis's discovery requests had no limitation—he sought information on every allegation of discrimination against the university by all complainants in all departments. However, Sallis had spent the past 10 years working in just one department and his allegations of discrimination focused on the behavior of the supervisors there. The court found Sallis's request to be overly broad and unduly burdensome and limited discovery to one relevant department.

Sampling Discovery to Determine Reasonable Limits

In *McPeek v. Ashcroft* and *Hagemeyer v. Gateway Data Services*, the court supported the use of sampling to tailor the scope of further discovery. The requesting party may need discovery to test the assertion that the information is not reasonably accessible. Such discovery may involve taking depositions of those knowledgeable about the responding party's information systems, some form of inspection of the data sources, and requiring the responding party to conduct a sampling of information contained on the sources identified as not reasonably accessible. Sampling of the less-accessible source can help refine the search parameters and determine the benefits and burdens associated with a fuller search.[7]

Failure to Follow Data Retention Policies

In *EEOC v. Target Corporation*, the court cited 29 C.F.R. Part 1602, which requires employment applications for nonhires to be retained for one year. Target included this requirement in its records retention policies. The responsible Target manager was trained on the policy, but failed to follow it, trashing the applications. Even though the court ruled that the case had no merit, it was reversed because the deleted e-mail could have made the plaintiff's case.

Reasonably Accessible Data

In *Disability Rights Council (DRC) of Greater Washington v. Washington Metropolitan Transit Authority (MTA)*, the plaintiff, DRC, alleged that the Transit Authority failed to stop its e-mail system from deleting all e-mails older than 60 days, even two years after the lawsuit was filed. In its defense, the Transit Authority cited new Rule 37(f), which established a safe harbor provision for any electronic data lost as a result of the "routine, good faith" operation of an IT system. The court ruled the failure is indefensible, finding that the Transit Authority did not act in good faith when it continued to destroy the e-mail after the lawsuit was filed and that good cause existed to require the search and production of data from the Transit Authority backup tapes.

Following U.S. Laws Comes with Doing Business in the United States

In *Columbia Pictures v. Justin Bunnell*, Columbia, Disney, Universal, Warner, Paramount, and other major studios sued a Netherlands-based web site for copyright infringement. The court rejected the defendant's claims of protection under Dutch and European privacy laws, maintaining that a business doing business in the United States falls under U.S. laws.

Legal Risk Mitigation Techniques

There are six steps an organization can take to lower its legal discovery costs and improve its chances of prevailing in court:

1. **Implement workflows that control all electronic documents.** The technology has been available for many years and available for even the smallest organizations. End-to-end work or process flows automated processes and approvals while providing a transparent audit trail.

2. **Enforce document retention and destruction policies.** This is essential given the high costs of discovery and the many examples in which a majority of documents retrieved in litigation were retained beyond their retention requirements. A large portion of legal discovery costs are avoidable by destroying paper and electronic documents that are retained just in case.

3. **Implement an enterprise-wide records and document management system with federation capabilities.** Federation permits searching and retrieving content across disparate records repositories.

4. **Attack the number of siloed and disparate data repositories.** In many organizations this is a major task due to ongoing mergers and acquisitions, and it is complicated by the lack of standardized naming and classification methodologies.

5. **Digitize and classify all documents upon creation.** In a born-digital environment, the process is automated and paper originals are viewed as a liability. This includes capturing the metadata (the who, where, when, and what information about data) cross-references about data.

6. **Destroy all paper documents unless they are required by regulations and litigants.** There are few valid examples in which original paper documents are still required. Scanned and digital signatures are widely accepted by most regulatory agencies.

EXECUTIVE INSIGHT

The Inverse Negative Value of Paper Documents

A large portion of discovery costs are avoidable by destroying paper and electronic documents that are retained just in case. According to John Bace, vice president of research at Gartner, "Once required storage time for a record has expired, get rid of it. . . . The information quite often develops an *inverse negative value*. Some people say we'll keep everything forever. That is one of the worst ideas around, especially given the penalties and issues around the new discovery rules."*

*"Report: Records Management Still Sloppy," *Compliance Week*, October 16, 2007.

Summary

Some reforms are being discussed to reduce the size of punitive damages. There is almost virtual unanimity in most countries that a damaged party should be made whole—covering their direct costs. But U.S. juries have used punitive damages to cover pain and suffering and also to punish large and unpopular corporations. U.S. litigants have also used the courts to cover the gaps in regulatory enforcement and corporate governance. Since relief is, at best, years away, organizations must be prepared to face a very costly response process and lose law suits that can substantially damage reputations and financial viability.

Notes

1. See Chapter 16, "Reducing the Financial Risks in Litigation and Legal Discovery," in Anthony Tarantino, *Financial Risk Management, Six Sigma and Other Next Generation Techniques* (Hoboken, NJ: John Wiley & Sons, 2009).

2. The following link contains the new rules of Civil Procedure: www.supremecourtus.gov/orders/courtorders/frcv06p.pdf.

3. Timothy Carroll and Bruce Radke, "The Amendments to the Federal Rules of Civil Procedure Concerning eDiscovery Impact on Global Business Enterprises," http://busmanagement.com.

4. Barbara J. Rothstein, Ronald J. Hedges, and Elizabeth C. Wiggins, "Managing Discovery of Electronic Information: A Pocket Guide for Judges," (Federal Judicial Center, 2007).

5. See the eDiscovery and Analysis Group, "Electronic Discovery Law Blog," K&L Gates, www.ediscoverylaw.com/articles/case-summaries.

6. A. Blakley, ed., *Electronic Information* 14:62–63 (Federal Bar Association: 2002). In Dodge, Warren & Peters Insurance Services.

7. Barbara J. Rothstein, Ronald J. Hedges, and Elizabeth C. Wiggins, *Managing Discovery of Electronic Information: A Pocket Guide for Judges* (Federal Judicial Center, 2007).

CHAPTER 7

Financial Crimes— Fraud and Corruption

After reading this chapter, you will be able to:

- Comprehend the importance of the principal/agent problem.
- Use simple measures to reduce financial crimes.
- Grasp that corruption is a way of life in much of the world.
- Understand the basics of the major anticorruption and bribery standards.
- Appreciate the value of whistleblowers in a free society.

Our Executive Insight below is a role-playing exercise based on insider trading. It is insightful in demonstrating that those committing financial crimes are often individuals with no prior criminal record and who had led exemplary lives. In this chapter we also demonstrate that corruption is a way of life in many areas of the world and is not usually committed by people with sinister backgrounds. Fraud and corruption are the most well-known types of financial crimes that constitute a major source of operational risk to all types of organizations.

Financial crimes are defined as crimes against property, involving the unlawful conversion of property belonging to another to one's own personal use and benefit. Financial crimes often involve fraud. Exhibit 7.1 lists some of the more common types of financial crimes.

EXHIBIT 7.1

Types of Financial Crimes		
Check and credit card fraud	Health-care fraud	Identity theft
Mortgage fraud	Bank robbery	Cyber attacks
Medical fraud	Insider trading	Money laundering
Corporate fraud	Tax violations	Social engineering
Bank account fraud	Kickbacks	Burglary
Payment (point of sale) fraud	Embezzlement	Currency fraud

EXECUTIVE INSIGHT

Insider Trading Role Playing

Insider trading occurs when someone makes an investment decision based on information that is not available to the general public. In some cases, the information allows them to profit; in others, to avoid a loss. Insider trading was not considered illegal at the beginning of the twentieth century, but the abuses of the 1920s and subsequent depression of the 1930s led to its being banned with stiff civil and criminal penalties.

In our role-playing exercise, imagine that you are a new hire fresh out of school working for a leading hedge fund. The very charismatic president stops by your desk to welcome you to the firm. He is personally worth several million dollars and his top managers all make more than a million dollars per year. Your base salary is small, but the commission structure is generous. You owe more than $100,000 in loans for your Ivy League MBA.

The president asks you to develop strong relationships with a small list of senior vice presidents of influential firms with the goal of obtaining their insights as to potential mergers and acquisitions—the types of information they are forbidden to discuss outside of their firm. He authorizes you to pay up to $10,000 in cash for each hot tip. He also maintains that it is not your problem if they share restricted information and that you stand to make more than a million dollars in your first year. Those receiving payment will never be able to go public with their involvement. So there is nothing to worry about—or is there? Your colleagues have advised you that the president is not the type of person that takes no for an answer. So refusal will damage or end your career at the hedge fund.

So what do you do in this situation?

This case study demonstrates how the promise of huge financial rewards can become irresistible to anyone, no matter how strong their ethics and morals. In this case, it would be easy to rationalize following the boss's orders because of huge upside rewards and fear of job loss.

In the case of the Galleon Group, headed by Raj Rajaratnam, it is alleged that a few senior executives shared merger and acquisition information netting Mr. Rajaratnam several million dollars. As of this writing, seven individuals charged with insider trading have pleaded guilty to avoid the maximum penalty of 25 years in prison. None of these seven had any hint of scandals in their illustrious careers prior to their involvement with Galleon. Mr. Rajaratnam also faces 25 years in prison and is not likely to be able to make a deal with prosecutors. Ironically, he became a billionaire years before the scandal occurred, indicating that he was under no financial pressure to cut ethical corners.

Fraud is defined as deliberate deception designed for gain by hurting another person's interests. *Corruption* is defined as abuse of a position of trust for dishonest gain, such as taking a bribe. Ancient humans instinctively thought of fraud and corruption as immoral and therefore inconsistent with the material and spiritual well-being of citizens. Ancient philosophers often blamed crass materialism for fraud and corruption and therefore took an antiwealth stance to discourage cheating and a tendency to achieve material wealth by hook or by crook.

Arab-Islamic scholars were not antiwealth, but believed that money should be used only for ethical and moral purposes. The

Biblical statement that it is easier for a camel to pass through the eye of a needle than for a rich man to get into heaven is quite explicit. An open disdain for wealth may be read in some Jewish, Hindu, and Chinese philosophies. Major religions preach against fraud and corruption by pointing to the will of God and to natural law, and rarely through rational arguments.

Principal-Agent Problem in Fraud

The *principal-agent problem* is a name given by economists to a universal dilemma that arose when companies became too large for owners to do all the work themselves. Owners (principals) were compelled to hire outsiders, or employees who acted as agents on their behalf. The problem arose because the interests of principals and their agents are not aligned—employees receive compensation, but do not share in the profits of the organization. In many cases, they see no financial rewards for adding to the organization's growth and profitability.

Compensation plans attempt to reduce the misalignment, but can never eliminate it. In the worst of alignments, employees feel like suckers and are susceptible to double-dealing, fraud, bribery, and other financial crimes to achieve personal gains at the expense of the employer.

In the best of alignments, employees feel a greater sense of loyalty to their company, believing they will be rewarded for contributing to its profitability and growth. Unfortunately, many companies have lost the loyalty of their employees because of layoffs, plant closures, outsourcing, and role evolution. It is becoming rare in the United States to find multiple generations of family members who work for the same firm for their entire careers—this was common practice in prior generations.

Compensation Tied to Employer's Gain

There are a variety of techniques and tools used to improve the alignment of interests between principals and agents. One of the most popular is to make employee compensation directly proportional to the employer's gain. This includes profit sharing, commissions, and stock options. Stock options have grown in popularity over the past 20 years, but their abuse through earning management and backdating has become a major problem. Even when not abused, there is no evidence that share-based compensation plans have reduced financial crimes.[1]

In spite of efforts to align the interests of agents (employees) to their principals (owners), it can be argued that the principal-agent problem has never been larger than today. Increasing employee turnover rates, short-sighted layoffs, and share-based compensation plans all tend to make employees care little for the long-term interests of their employers and more prone to commit financial crimes.

TIPS AND TECHNIQUES

Common Sense and Low-Cost Measures to Combat Fraud

Société Générale, the large French bank, and Fry's Electronics, the multibillion-dollar retailer of consumer electronics, may have averted major cases of alleged fraud by following some common-sense and low-cost measures—measures that do not require a large investment in technology or overhead.

Jérôme Kerviel was the rough trader at Société Générale who is alleged to have nearly destroyed the huge French bank with unauthorized trades that resulted in €4.9 billion ($7 billion) in losses. Kerviel used a variety of techniques to avoid detection. One was known as a "mutating virus," in which hundreds of thousands of trades were hidden behind offsetting faked hedge trades. Kerviel was careful to close the trades in just two or three days, just before the trades' timed controls would trigger notice from the bank's internal control system, and Kerviel would then shift those older positions to newly initiated trades.*

Omar Siddiqui was a senior executive with Fry's Electronics, a major U.S. retailer of electronic components. Siddiqui is charged with demanding and receiving supplier kickbacks of more than $65 million. Siddiqui, who made $225,000 a year as a top executive, was a high roller and well known on the Las Vegas Strip—he once lost $8 million in a day. Court records indicate that the 43-year-old businessman gambled away as much as $167 million at casinos over the past decade. Yet even as he amassed huge IOUs, casinos around the country continued to lend him millions more. He owned a Ferrari, a Mercedes, and a town house in Palo Alto. But there were plenty of signs that something was amiss. Although Siddiqui may have won millions at the tables, at least seven casinos in Las Vegas, New Jersey, and Connecticut have sued him since 1999, seeking to recover at least $33 million.[†]

These are four countermeasures that would have helped to avoid the alleged misdeeds of Kerviel and Siddiqui:

❶ **Segregation of Duties (SOD) Over Time—*Mix Timing of Audits and Controls.*** Fraudsters become adept at working around regularly scheduled audits and control protocols. Consider changing schedules and frequencies and keep the changes secret as long as possible. (Kerviel knew Société Générale's schedules and worked them to his advantage.)

❷ **Vacation and Job Rotation—*Enforce Vacations and Job Rotation Policies.*** Europeans enjoy long employer-paid vacations and will rarely forgo the opportunity to take them. Fraudsters resist taking any time off for fear of discovery. Vacation policies should be enforced and those who do not take vacation may be worth investigating. (Kerviel was rare in not taking vacation days.) Customer or supplier account rotation serve the same purpose of keeping a potential fraudster off guard.

❸ **Credit and Background Checks—*Run on Existing Employees with Critical Responsibilities.*** Credit and criminal background checks are typical for new hires in many companies, but not typical for existing employees. (Fry's may have learned of Siddiqui's casino lawsuits and of his extravagant lifestyle through such an investigation.)

❹ **SOD over Procurement—*Prevent One Person from Having Exclusive Access to Critical Suppliers.*** Automating segregation of duties is a best practice in most situations, but a manual control may be required in dealing with sensitive supplier negotiations and contract administration. It is never desirable that one individual enjoy exclusive relationships with key suppliers. This can be prevented with the use of sourcing teams, enforcing vacation policies, and rotating account assignments—ideally on an unpublished schedule. (Siddiqui only got caught because another employee found spreadsheets in his unoccupied office. Ironically the company did not know about his lavish lifestyle.)

Both Kerviel and Siddiqui exhibited behavior that should have alerted their organizations of potential wrongdoing and double-dealing.

---

*"French Police Question Rogue Trader Kerviel," Reuters *National Post*, January 26, 2008, http://www.nationalpost.com/news/story.html?id=266900.
†Richard Paddock, "Debt Finally Topples a Las Vegas High Roller," *Los Angeles Times*, February 15, 2009.

Corruption

The fight against corruption requires a deeper understanding of the underlying malaise. Available data suggest that corruption accounts for a significant proportion of economic activity worldwide. Anwar Shah, lead economist for the World Bank, provides the following examples:

In Kenya, "questionable" public expenditures noted by the controller and auditor general in 1997 amounted to 7.6% of GDP. In Latvia, a World Bank survey found that more than 40% of households and enterprises agreed that "corruption is a natural part of our lives and helps solve many problems." In Tanzania, service delivery survey data suggests that bribes paid to officials in the police, courts, tax services, and land offices amounted to 62% of official public expenditures in these areas. In the Philippines, the Commission on Audit estimates that $4 billion is diverted annually because of public sector corruption.[2]

Public sector corruption can be viewed as a symptom of failed governance and as such cannot be adequately addressed until underlying governance issues are addressed. Issues include the quality of public sector management, the nature of accountability relations between the government and citizens, the legal framework, and the degree to which public sector processes are accompanied by transparency and dissemination of information. In this context, governance includes the norms, traditions, and institutions by which power and authority in a country are exercised.

Concern about corruption, the abuse of public office for private gain, is as old as the history of government. In 350 B.C.E., Aristotle suggested in *Politics* that in order to protect public funds in the treasury from fraud, all money should be openly issued before the city's entire population.

In recent years, concerns about corruption have mounted in tandem with growing evidence of its detrimental impact on development. Research indicates that corruption adversely affects GDP growth. Corruption has been shown to lower the quality of education, public infrastructure, health services, and to adversely affect capital accumulation. Corruption increases income inequality and poverty.[3]

Types of Corruption

Corruption comes in many forms:

- **Petty, administrative, or bureaucratic corruption.** Many corrupt acts are isolated transactions by individual public officials who abuse their offices, for example, by demanding bribes and kickbacks, diverting public funds, or awarding favors in return for personal considerations.

- **Grand corruption.** The theft or misuse of vast amounts of public resources by state officials—usually members of, or associated with, the political or administrative elite—constitutes grand corruption.

- **State or regulatory capture and influence peddling.** Collusion by private actors with public officials or politicians for their mutual, private benefit is referred to as state capture. That is, the private sector captures the state legislative, executive, and judicial apparatus for its own purposes.

- **Patronage/paternalism/clientelism and being a team player.** Using one's official position to provide assistance to clients having the same geographic, ethnic, and cultural origin so that they receive preferential treatment in their dealings with the public sector, including public sector employment, is another form of corruption, as is providing the same assistance on a quid pro quo basis to colleagues belonging to an informal network of friends and allies.

Root Causes of Corruption

World Bank research examined the root causes of corruption. The key corruption drivers identified by these studies include:

- The legitimacy of the state as the guardian of the public interest is contested. In highly corrupt countries, there is little public acceptance of the notion that the role of the state is to rise above private interests to protect the broader public interest.

- The rule of law is weakly embedded. Public-sector corruption thrives where laws apply to some but not to others, and where enforcement of the law is often used as a device for furthering private interests rather than protecting the public interest. A common symbol of the breakdown of the rule of law in highly corrupt countries is the police acting as lawbreakers rather than law enforcers.

- Institutions of participation and accountability are ineffective. In societies where the level of public-sector corruption is relatively low, one normally finds strong institutions of participation and accountability that control abuses of power by public officials.

- The commitment of national leaders to combat corruption is weak. Widespread corruption endures in the public sector when national authorities are either unwilling or unable to address it forcefully. In societies where public-sector corruption is endemic, it is reasonable to suspect that it touches the highest levels of government and that many senior officeholders will not be motivated to work against it.

Research reveals that because corruption is itself a symptom of fundamental governance failure, the higher the incidence of corruption, the less an anticorruption strategy should include tactics that are narrowly targeted to corrupt behaviors and the more it should focus on the broad underlying features of the governance environment. For example, support for anticorruption agencies and public awareness campaigns are likely to meet with limited success in environments where corruption is rampant and the governance environment is deeply flawed. In fact, in environments where governance is weak, anticorruption agencies are prone to being misused as tools of political victimization.[4]

The World Bank tracks and publishes six indicators of governance for more than 200 countries. The interactive charts and tables are free and available online. Exhibit 7.2 provides the Control of Corruption results for the 10 largest Gross Domestic Product (GDP) nations.[5] The World Bank chart captures "perceptions of the

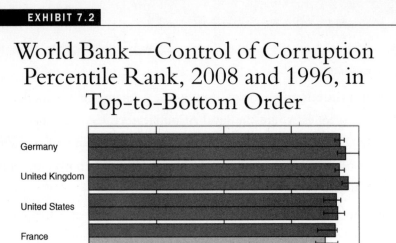

EXHIBIT 7.2

World Bank—Control of Corruption Percentile Rank, 2008 and 1996, in Top-to-Bottom Order

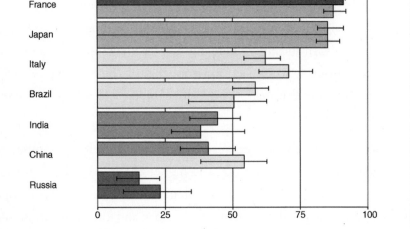

extent to which public power is exercised for private gain, including both petty and grand forms of corruption, as well as 'capture' of the state by elites and private interests," and is based on several indices, which are listed in their research paper *Governance Matters VIII.*[6]

Anticorruption and Bribery Laws and Standards

Over the past 30 years, a number of laws and standards have been enacted to combat corruption and bribery throughout the world. The challenge these efforts face is that widespread corruption is a symptom of an overall malaise that is not easily addressed at a tactical level—corruption will thrive until overall governance improves.

U.S. Foreign Corrupt Practices Act of 1977

The antibribery provisions of the Foreign Corrupt Practices Act (FCPA) prohibit issuers, domestic concerns, and any person from making use of interstate commerce corruptly, in furtherance of an offer or payment of anything of value to a foreign official, foreign political party, or candidate for political office, for the purpose of influencing any act of that foreign official in violation of the duty of that official, or to secure any improper advantage in order to obtain or retain business.[7] Persons subject to the FCPA include:

- **Issuers:** Includes any U.S. or foreign corporation that has a class of securities registered, or that is required to file reports under the Securities and Exchange Act of 1934.

- **Domestic concerns:** Refers to any individual who is a citizen, national, or resident of the United States and any corporation and other business entity organized under the laws of the United States or having its principal place of business in the United States.

- **Any person:** Covers both enterprises and individuals.

As a result of U.S. Securities and Exchange Commission investigations in the mid-1970s, more than 400 U.S. companies admitted making questionable or illegal payments in excess of $300 million to foreign government officials, politicians, and political parties. The abuses ran the gamut from bribery of high foreign officials to secure some type of favorable action by a foreign government to so-called facilitating payments that were made to ensure that government functionaries discharged certain ministerial or clerical duties.

OECD Antibribery Convention

The Organisation for Economic Co-operation and Development (OECD) established a legally binding standard to criminalize bribery of foreign public officials in international business transactions. It is the first and only international anticorruption instrument focused on the supply side of the bribery transaction. The 30 OECD member countries and eight nonmember countries—Argentina, Brazil, Bulgaria, Chile, Estonia, Israel, Slovenia, and South Africa—have adopted this convention.[8] It calls on its member states to:

- Adopt best practices for making companies liable for foreign bribery so that they cannot be misused as vehicles for bribing foreign public officials and so they cannot avoid detection, investigation, and prosecution for such bribery by using agents and intermediaries, including foreign subsidiaries, to bribe for them.

- Periodically review policies and approach on small facilitation payments. These are legal in some countries if the payment is made to a government employee to speed up an administrative process.

- Improve cooperation between countries for the sharing of information and evidence in foreign bribery investigations and prosecutions and the seizure, confiscation, and recovery of the proceeds of transnational bribery through, for instance, improved or new agreements between the states' parties for these purposes.

- Provide effective channels for public officials to report suspected foreign bribery internally within the public service and externally to the law enforcement authorities, and for protecting whistleblowers from retaliation.

- Work with the private sector to adopt more stringent internal controls, ethics, and compliance programs and measures to prevent and detect bribery.

The OECD has limited enforcement capabilities, relying on public pressure for nations that do not conform. If a country fails to implement the OECD antibribery instruments, the OECD's working group may send a high-level mission to the country in question, send a letter to the country's relevant ministers, or issue a formal public statement.

The World Bank's Control of Corruption statistics from 1996 to 2008 indicate a mixed bag of results with only France, Brazil, and India showing improvement out of the top 10 GDP nations, and Italy, China, and Russia suffering major declines. This is not to dismiss efforts to introduce and promote regulatory frameworks to fight corruption, but the results show they have a long way to go.

Know Your Customer

Know your customer (KYC) is the due diligence and regulation that financial institutions and other regulated companies must perform to identify their clients and ascertain relevant information pertinent to doing financial business with them. In the United States, KYC is typically a policy implemented to conform to a customer identification program mandated under the Bank Secrecy Act and USA PATRIOT Act. Know your customer policies are becoming increasingly important globally to prevent identity theft fraud, money laundering, and terrorist financing. In its simplest form, KYC rules may equate to answering a series of questions, but regulators may expect much more customer-specific information.

One aspect of KYC checking is to verify that the customer is not on any list of known fraudsters, terrorists, or money launderers, such as the Office of Foreign Assets Control's Specially Designated Nationals list. This list contains thousands of entries and is updated at least monthly. Beyond name matching, a key aspect of KYC controls is to monitor transactions of a customer against their recorded profile.

Banks doing KYC monitoring for anti–money laundering (AML) and Counter-Terrorism Financing (CTF) purposes increasingly use specialized transaction monitoring software, particularly names analysis software and trend monitoring software. The generated alerts identify unusual activity, which is then subject to due diligence or enhanced due diligence processes that use internal and external sources of information on the subject, including the Internet. This helps to determine whether a transaction or activity is suspicious and requires reporting to the authorities.

In the United States, suspicious activities would require Suspicious Activity Reporting (SAR) filing to Financial Crimes Enforcement Network (FinCEN).[9] In the United Kingdom, it would require a report to the Serious Organised Crime Agency (SOCA).[10]

Anti-Money Laundering

Money laundering is the practice of disguising illegally obtained funds so that they seem legal. It is a crime in many jurisdictions with varying definitions. It is a key operation of the underground economy. *Anti–money laundering* is a term mainly used in the financial and legal industries to describe the legal controls that require financial institutions and other regulated entities to prevent or report money laundering activities. AML activities increased dramatically after the September 11, 2001 attacks on the World Trade Center, which spawned the USA PATRIOT Act. Money laundering involves three independent and often simultaneous steps:

Step 1. Placement—physically placing bulk cash proceeds.

Step 2. Layering—separating the proceeds of criminal activity from their origins through layers of complex financial transactions.

Step 3. Integration—providing an apparently legitimate explanation for the illicit proceeds.

In U.S. law it is the practice of engaging in financial transactions to conceal the identity, source, or destination of illegally gained money. In U.K. law, the common law definition is wider. The act is defined as taking any action with property of any form that is wholly or in part the proceeds of a crime that will disguise the fact that the property is the proceeds of a crime or obscure the beneficial ownership of said property. Most global financial institutions, and many nonfinancial institutions, are required to identify and report transactions of a suspicious nature to the financial intelligence unit in the respective country. Banks must perform due diligence by ascertaining a customer's identity and monitor transactions for suspicious activity.

Whistleblowers

In the United States and many Western countries, governments have passed national and state laws to protect whistleblowers against retaliation by their employers for coming forward to expose wrongdoing. Exhibit 7.3 is an example of posters required to be posted in break rooms of public companies throughout the United States. The posters provide employees with assurances that they will be protected against employer retaliation.

EXHIBIT 7.3

Whistleblower Protection Poster

The Division of Labor Standards Enforcement believes that the sample posting below meets the requirements of Labor Code Section 1102.8(a). This document must be printed to 8.5 × 11 inch paper with margins no larger than one-half inch in order to conform to the statutory requirement that the lettering be larger than size 14 point type.

WHISTLEBLOWERS ARE PROTECTED

It is the public policy of the State of California to encourage employees to notify an appropriate government or law enforcement agency when they have reason to believe their employer is violating a state or federal statute, or violating or not complying with a state or federal rule or regulation.

Who is protected?

Pursuant to California Labor Code Section 1102.5, employees are the protected class of individuals. "Employee" means any person employed by an employer, private or public, including, but not limited to, individuals employed by the state or any subdivision thereof, any county, city, city and county, including any charter city or county, and any school district, community college district, municipal or public corporation, political subdivision, or the University of California. [California Labor Code Section 11061].

(continued)

(*continued*)
What is a whistleblower?

A "whistleblower" is an employee who discloses information to a government or law enforcement agency where the employee has reasonable cause to believe that the information discloses:

1. A violation of a state or federal statute,

2. A violation or noncompliance with a state or federal rule or regulation, or

3. With reference to employee safety or health, unsafe working conditions or work practices in the employee's employment or place of employment.

What protections are afforded to whistleblowers?

1. An employer may not make, adopt, or enforce any rule, regulation, or policy preventing an employee from being a whistleblower.

2. An employer may not retaliate against an employee who is a whistleblower.

3. An employer may not retaliate against an employee for refusing to participate in an activity that would result in a violation of a state or federal statute, or a violation or noncompliance with a state or federal rule or regulation.

4. An employer may not retaliate against an employee for having exercised his or her rights as a whistleblower in any former employment.

Under California Labor Code Section 98.6, if an employer retaliates against a whistleblower, the employer may be required to reinstate the employee's employment and work benefits, pay lost wages, and take other steps necessary to comply with the law.

How to report improper acts

If you have information regarding possible violations of state or federal statutes, rules, or regulations, or violations of fiduciary responsibility by a corporation or limited liability company to its shareholders, investors, or employees, **call the California State Attorney General's Whistleblower Hotline at 1-800-952-5225.** The Attorney General will refer your call to the appropriate government authority for review and possible investigation.

Unfortunately, there is compelling evidence that whistleblower legal protections have not worked, which is unfortunate because there is also compelling evidence that they expose much more fraud and corruption than any other source.

A PricewaterhouseCoopers (PWC) survey indicates whistleblowers detected 43 percent of known fraud—twice the level uncovered by regulators and auditors.[11] In spite of additional protections provided under the Sarbanes-Oxley Act, the number of whistleblowers coming forward declined 5 percent due to fear of retaliation, ostracism, and lack of rewards—45 percent decline to identify themselves. When whistleblowers do identify themselves, they allege that they were terminated, resigned under duress, or had significantly altered responsibilities more than 80 percent of the time. Many of them indicated that they would never blow the whistle again.[12]

A common misperception of whistleblowers is that they are typically disgruntled employees looking for a means to retaliate against employers for whom they hold a grudge. Although there is evidence of whistleblower abuse, they remain the most cost-effective means of identifying fraud.[13]

 Tips and Techniques

Rewards for Whistleblowers Work (Qui Tam)

There is an exception to the decline of whistleblowers coming forward—journalists in free societies involved in large cases and employees with access to qui tam suits. *Qui tam* is an English common law concept that those who identify theft of the king's property shall share in the rewards when the king's property is recovered. Qui tam established the precedent for rewarding whistleblowers.

Western societies rightfully claim to protect whistleblowers, but this is not the same as fostering a whistleblower environment—providing incentives for whistleblowers to risk retaliation by

TIPS AND TECHNIQUES (CONTINUED)

coming forward. Incentives are important because, even with legal protections, whistleblowers face discrimination or other forms of punishment from their friends and colleagues.

Rewards do work to overcome the fears of whistleblower retaliation. This can be seen in the health-care industry. The *Los Angeles Times* reported in September 2008 that whistleblowers in this industry helped authorities to recover more than $9 billion from 1996 to 2005. For their efforts, they received more than $1 billion in rewards, or between 15 and 25 percent of the total recovered.[14]

Dyck, Morse, and Zingales (2008) use health care as a good example for the positive relationship between financial rewards for whistleblowers and fraud detection. With the government accounting for a significant percentage of health-care revenue, 41 percent of frauds are identified by employees versus 14 percent in all other industries.[15]

A whistleblower can be either internal or external to an organization. The term comes from the London police known as Bobbies, who blew their whistles when confronting criminal behavior. They have knowledge of actions by other organization members that they believe to be unethical, illegal, and/or immoral, that are not in the interest of the public or shareholders. They become whistleblowers when they decide to speak out to company leaders, the media, government regulators, or other public forums.

The role of whistleblowers varies greatly from society to society depending on their level of human liberties and cultural traditions against speaking out against one's employer. Media journalists operating in a free environment are essential. In closed societies with few speech or press liberties, there is little tolerance for whistleblowers. Intolerance includes violence against courageous journalists in India, the Philippines, Russia, and other countries.

Paul Krugman's Examples of Double-Dealing

Noble Prize–winning economist Paul Krugman provides a comical example of double-dealing on the part of the owner of a money-losing ice-cream parlor.[16] He references infamous corporate scandals to show how it is possible, *but not ethical or legal*, to get rich in such a situation. Here are self-dealing strategies an unethical executive may consider:

Enron strategy. You begin by signing contracts providing customers with one ice-cream cone per day over the next 30 years. You then intentionally underestimate the ice cream's cost, booking all estimated profits on future ice-cream sales as part of the current year's bottom line. As a consequence, your business falsely appears to be highly profitable, resulting in an increased stock price.

Dynegy strategy. You convince your investors that the company will be profitable in the future. You then quietly enter into a deal with a second ice-cream parlor whereby you both falsely claim to buy hundreds of cones on a daily basis to give the appearance of being a big player in a coming business. With this image you are able to sell shares at inflated prices.

Adelphia strategy. You sign contracts with various customers, convincing investors to focus on the high contract volumes rather than the contracts' profitability. Rather than creating imaginary trades, you create imaginary customers. As a result, stock analysts give your company high ratings, enabling you to sell the stock at inflated prices.

WorldCom strategy. You manage to make real costs disappear by falsely claiming that operating expenses, such as sugar, milk, and chocolate syrup, are capital equipment expenditures, like a new refrigerator. It appears that the company is only borrowing for new equipment, which enables you to sell the stock at inflated prices.

Fictitious asset sale strategy (Enron, Harken Energy). You sell one of your ice-cream delivery trucks to ABC Company for a highly inflated price, claiming the capital gain as a profit. In reality, you own ABC Company secretly. Throughout this process your top managers get rich by exercising their stock options, Adelphia-style personal loans, and other unethical devices.

Professor Krugman wrote this before the global financial crisis. Undoubtedly, the list of examples will grow as the litigation and prosecutions go forward.

Summary

The battle against financial crimes is as old as man. There is an age-old cyclical nature to financial crimes as well. In periods of entrepreneurial enthusiasm, the common belief is that markets are the best means to fight financial crimes. In such periods, a disdain for regulations and oversight leads to excesses and abuse creating scandals and crisis. The pendulum then swings to a period of restrictive regulations and oversight. Unfortunately, regulations are often reactionary and do little to prevent future abuses. The reason for this is that cheaters are clever, sometimes powerful, and typically ahead of those who police them. Those in charge of policing are far too often bureaucratic, myopic, and lack imagination. The Bernard Madoff Ponzi scheme is only the most recent example.

Notes

1. See Anthony Tarantino, "The Root Cause of the Global Financial Crisis and Corporate Governance Reforms to Prevent Future Failures in Risk Management," Chapter 24 in Anthony Tarantino, *Risk Management in Finance: Six Sigma and Other Next Generation Techniques* (Hoboken, NJ: John Wiley & Sons, 2009).

2. See Anwar Shah, "Why Fighting Corruption Remains a Losing Battle," Chapter 10 in Anthony Tarantino, *Governance, Risk and Compliance Handbook* (Hoboken, NJ: John Wiley & Sons, 2008).

3. Ibid.

4. Ibid.

5. World Bank Interactive Governance and Corruption Charts, available at http://info.worldbank.org/governance/wgi/sc_country.asp.

6. Daniel Kaufmann, Aart Kraay, and Massimo Mastruzzi, *Governance Matters VIII: Aggregate and Individual Governance Indicators 1996– 2008* (policy research working paper 4978), http://papers.ssrn.com/sol3/papers.cfm?abstract_id=1424591##.

7. See U.S. Department of Justice web site: www.justice.gov/criminal/fraud/fcpa/.

8. See the OECD web site: www.oecd.org/document/20/0,3343, en_2649_34859_2017813_1_1_1_1,00.html.

9. See Comptroller of Currency web site: www.occ.treas.gov/sar .htm.

10. See Serious Organised Crime Agency web site: www.soca .gov.uk.

11. PriceWaterhouseCoopers, "Economic Crime: People, Culture and Controls," *The 4th Biennial Global Economic Crime Survey* (2008), www.whistleblowers.org/storage/whistleblowers/docu ments/pwc_survey.pdf.

12. A. Dyck, A. Morse, and L. Zingales, *Who Blows the Whistle On Corporate Fraud?* (Chicago: University of Chicago, Booth School of Business, October 2008), http://papers.ssrn.com/sol3/papers.cfm? abstract_id=891482.

13. M. T. Biegelman and J. T. Bartow, *Executive Roadmap to Fraud Prevention and Internal Control: Creating a Culture of Compliance* (Hoboken, NJ: John Wiley & Sons, 2006).

14. "Whistle-blowers Play Large Role in Uncovering Healthcare Fraud," *Los Angeles Times*, September 2, 2008, print edition, A-17.

15. A. Dyck, A. Morse, and L. Zingales, *Who Blows the Whistle on Corporate Fraud?*

16. Paul R. Krugman, *The Great Unraveling: Losing Our Way in the New Century* (New York: Norton, 2004).

CHAPTER 8

Internal Control Risks
U.S. and
International SOX

After reading this chapter, you will be able to:

- Grasp the globalization of Sarbanes-Oxley regulations.
- Comprehend the role of internal controls in operational risk.
- Appreciate the benefits of automating controls.
- Understand the international standards of auditing.
- Differentiate between the types of internal controls.

The financial reporting disciplines within a public company allow its stakeholders to value the organization by inspecting its revenue, profits, equity, costs, and other elements within its financial statements. Without assurances provided by internal controls over financial reporting, this financial assessment would not be possible. Without internal controls over operational risk, there is no assurance that an organization's financial performance is sustainable. Finally, the organization has a legal and cultural responsibility to conduct its financial operations in a manner that conforms to the country's accounting principles, such as Generally Accepted Accounting Principles (GAAP) in the United States, and the International Financial Reporting Standards (IFRS) in much of the rest of the world.

At a basic level, internal controls ensure that an organization is being run in accordance with the overall plan, that the financial statements and management reporting present an accurate view of the operations, and that all activities (including reporting) that are covered by statutory regulations are being carried out within the constraints of those regulations.[1]

Internal control can be defined as the process designed, implemented, and maintained by those charged with governance, management, and other personnel to provide reasonable assurance about the achievement of an entity's objectives with regard to reliability of financial reporting, effectiveness and efficiency of operations, and compliance with applicable laws and regulations. The term "controls" refers to any aspect of one or more of the components of internal control.

Operational risks arise when internal controls fail and bring into question the validity of statutorily mandated financial reports, typically issued on a quarterly and annual basis. Financial reports that cannot demonstrate viable internal controls are useless to investors, regulators, rating agencies, and analysts.

Regulations over Internal Controls

The Sarbanes-Oxley Act of 2002 (SOX) is the best-known set of laws and regulations to improve internal controls over financial reporting.[2] SOX requires public companies to demonstrate a robust discipline to protect any area that impacts its financial reports. In the last decade, similar COSO-based legislation has been enacted globally to improve internal controls, including:

- The European Union (Euro SOX—EU Directives 4, 7, and 8)
- China (China SOX—Basic Standard for Enterprise Internal Control)
- Japan (J-SOX—The new Corporate Law and the Financial Instruments and Exchange Law)

- Canada (Ontario Securities Commission, Multilateral Instruments 52–109 and 52–111)
- Australia (AX10 Principles)
- India (Clause 49)

SOX and SOX-like regulations and their associated audit standards exist to assure investors and other stakeholders that financial reports represent the real financial position of public companies at a specific point in time. To accomplish this they follow a COSO-like framework with five control elements:

1. Internal environment
2. Risk assessment
3. Control activities
4. Information and communication
5. Internal monitoring

Common to many of these regulations are requirements for companies to clearly demonstrate a robust and enterprise-wide internal control framework. Companies need to:

- Include the five control elements in their internal control processes and procedures.
- Create, implement, and publish clearly defined internal control policies and procedures.
- Deploy a viable information technology (IT) infrastructure, including application and database controls, typically following a COBIT or ITIL framework.
- Conduct periodic internal control self-assessments, including written assessments as to their effectiveness.
- Maintain the independence of the selected audit firms by prohibiting them from also providing consulting services.

U.S. Auditing Standards over Internal Controls

Common to many of these regulations is a system of audit standards, which internal and external auditors apply to test the validity of internal controls. The Public Company Accounting Oversight Board (PCAOB) was created under Section 101 of the SOX as a nonprofit corporation whose board members and employees are not considered government employees. The PCAOB currently has audit standards that all public companies must adhere to in order to attest to their internal controls.[3] They include:

- U.S. Auditing Standard Number Three (AS3)—Audit Documentation

- U.S. Auditing Standard Number Four (AS4)—Reporting on Whether a Previously Reported Material Weakness Continues to Exist

- U.S. Audit Standard Number 5 (AS5)—An Audit of Internal Control Over Financial Reporting That Is Integrated with an Audit of Financial Statements (replaces the much-criticized AS2)

AS2 was the source of much of the criticism of U.S. SOX. AS2 was replaced by AS5, which addresses many of these criticisms with such reforms as:

- Permitting auditors to rely on the work of others (Paragraphs 16–19)—A company's internal auditors, IT, and business professionals can conduct their own audits.

- Permitting the benchmarking of automated controls (Appendixes B28–B33)—Automated controls need not be audited on an annual basis.

- Changing from location-based to risk-based audits (Appendix B10)—Reduces or eliminates audits for locations that have a minor impact on financial reports.

International Auditing Standards over Internal Controls

The International Auditing and Assurance Standards Board (IAASB)[4] has published 36 International Standards on Auditing (ISAs) and approximately 20 International Auditing Practice Statements (IAPSs) and other pronouncements on topics such as quality control. The ISAs have been developed over the IAASB's 30-year history with increasing input from the public to ensure that auditors have the necessary guidance to address those issues of greatest concern to the public as well as the markets. More than 100 countries are now using or in the process of adopting or incorporating ISAs into their national auditing standards. More and more national regulatory bodies are accepting financial statements audited using ISAs.

Of the 36 ISAs, 5 support SOX-related audit activities. Many of these are similar to the U.S. PCAOB's Auditing Standards:

- ISA 240: The Auditor's Responsibilities Relating to Fraud in an Audit of Financial Statements
- ISA 300: Planning an Audit of Financial Statements
- ISA 315: Identifying and Assessing the Risks of Material Misstatement through Understanding the Entity and Its Environment
- ISA 320: Materiality in Planning and Performing an Audit
- ISA 330: The Auditor's Responses to Assessed Risks

Internal Controls

On a basic level, internal controls can be classified as either manual or automated. Examples of manual controls may include approvals and reviews of transactions, reconciliations, and follow-up of reconciling items. Examples of automated controls include initiating, recording, processing, and reporting transactions and are accompanied with electronic forms instead of paper documents.

Automated controls can be classified as either detective or preventative. Detective controls are typically after-the-fact monitoring and review of transactions for signs of controls violations. Preventative controls stop the violations from occurring. When designed properly they also provide alerts as to the attempted violation. Therefore, preventative controls with a system of dashboard alerts are preferred by auditors. Automated preventative controls also benefit organizations by reducing the risks of fraud and errors and lowering processing and compliance costs.

Another major benefit to fully automated preventative controls over manual and detective controls is that they require less auditing effort to certify their adequacy. It is especially helpful when electronic workflows are in place and are auditable and transparent from end-to-end. Promoting the benefits of automation over manual controls is a common theme in the PCAOB's AS5 and the IAASB's ISAs.

Manual internal controls may be less reliable than their automated counterparts because they can be more easily ignored, bypassed, or overridden, and they are also more prone to simple errors and mistakes. Therefore, the consistent application of manual controls cannot be assumed. Manual controls are typically less than ideal in the following situations:

- Recurring or high volume transactions.

- Where errors can be anticipated, detected, and corrected by control parameters that are automated.

- Control activities where the specific ways to perform the control can be adequately designed and automated.

Access Controls and Segregation of Duties

The major financial scandals of the past 10 years has brought about a revolution in the audit industry with new risks to address, new audit procedures to develop, new training for their auditors, and new

Benchmarking Automated Controls Can Substantially Reduce Audit Costs

The PCAOB's Auditing Standard No. 5 (AS5—Appendices B28 to B33) includes a provision for benchmarking automated controls. Benchmarking in this context does not mean comparing your organization with industry peers or leaders, but saving time and money with auditing controls that are fully automated with well-accepted software tools—those with strong controls to prevent unauthorized and undocumented program changes. AS5 makes the following case for benchmarking of automated controls.

Entity-level automated application controls are generally not subject to breakdowns due to human failure, which allows auditors to use a "benchmarking" strategy.

"If general controls over program changes, access to programs, and computer operations are effective and continue to be tested, and if the auditor verifies that the automated application control has not changed since the auditor established a baseline (i.e., last tested the application control), then the auditor may conclude that the automated application control continues to be effective without repeating the prior year's specific tests of the operation of the automated application control."[*]

To determine whether to use a benchmarking strategy, the auditor should assess the following risk factors. These factors include the extent to which the application control can be matched to a defined program within an application, the extent to which the application is stable, and the availability and reliability of a report of the compilation dates of the programs placed in production.

---

[*]PCAOB, *Auditing Standard No. 5—An Audit of Internal Control Over Financial Reporting That Is Integrated with an Audit of Financial Statements*, June 12, 2007.

regulations and auditing standards. One of implications of these changes is a greater focus on segregation of duties (SOD).[5]

Virtually all protocols to improve internal controls include provisions to enforce SOD. SOD should include the assurance that no individual has the physical and system access to control all phases of a business process or transaction from authorization to custody, and to record keeping. When conflicts exist in SOD, organizations can be exposed to significant risks. Auditors are looking for conflicts in SOD in which one individual has access to responsibilities that are inherently in conflict with one another, such as purchasing and accounts payable, purchasing and receiving, general ledger, and supply management. The conflicts can be caused by innocent and unintentional errors or by intentional and criminal fraud.

Internal and external auditors have tested for conflicts in SOD over the years. Most audit firms have created a matrix of conflicting duties where functions such as accounts payable (AP), accounts receivable (A/R), and inventory control are at odds. Complicating SOD is the trend to expand the responsibilities within application software where so-called *super users* can access functions beyond traditional business models. This trend has been accelerated by wave after wave of downsizing and outsourcing to the point that wearing multiple functional hats has become the norm. Examples of violations of segregation of duties include:

- **Order management.** An individual may have the ability to release customer orders while creating and maintaining customer master information. This creates the risk that one user could release sales orders to customers who have unacceptable credit and then enter invalid or fraudulent sales orders.

- **Accounts receivable.** An individual may have the ability to enter A/R receipts, credit memos, and invoices while entering and maintaining customer master information. This creates the risk that one user could create fraudulent or erroneous sales and A/R transactions.

- **General ledger (G/L).** An individual may have the ability to maintain G/L setups while entering and posting journals. This creates the risk that one user could modify setup financial configurations, input invalid and unauthorized journal entries, make erroneous consolidation mappings resulting in erroneous financial statement consolidations, and approve unauthorized intercompany transactions.

- **Accounts payable.** An individual may have the ability to enter and approve invoices while entering and maintaining employee master information. This creates the risk that users could commit fraud by setting themselves up as a supplier and then entering and approving fraudulent invoices to their fraudulent supplier.

- **Purchasing.** An individual may have the ability to enter and maintain purchase order (PO) transactions while maintaining supplier master information and entering receiving/inventory transactions. This creates the risk that one user could commit fraud by creating fraudulent suppliers, purchase orders to the fraudulent supplier, and fraudulent receipts against fraudulent purchase orders.

- **Procure-to-pay.** In organizations with a materials or supply chain management approach, an individual may have the ability to access and control inventory, purchasing, receiving, and supplier master information. This creates the risk that one user could commit fraud in many ways. A successful SOD would typically segregate the following functions: inventory control, purchasing, receiving, and supply master.

EXECUTIVE INSIGHT

Is Auditable Segregation of Duties Much Ado about Nothing?

SOD controls are considered a critical element to the prevention of fraud and a major focus of virtually all internal control audit protocols. During the first few years under U.S. SOX, many U.S. companies were commonly cited by auditors as lacking proper SOD. U.S. companies made major efforts and took on considerable costs to improve their SOD with a combination of manual and automated tools.

In Chapter 7, we cited the Fry's Electronics scandal in which a powerful executive is alleged to have received millions of dollars of kickbacks from suppliers. Additional controls at Fry's could have helped to prevent the alleged abuse, but it is doubtful that Fry's violated traditional SOD controls, which demand a separation of duties between procurement, accounts payable, and inventory control. Therefore, it can be argued that Fry's would have passed SOD audit standards—if it were a public company. (Fry's is a privately held U.S. company.)

In the other case study of financial crimes, there is no evidence that Société Générale's alleged rogue trader Jérôme Kerviel violated auditable segregation of duty controls. (Kerviel is accused of using his coworker's passwords and insider's knowledge to violate controls.)

Ironically, there is little evidence that failure in internal controls in general and SOD in particular contributed to the marquee scandals and crises of the last decade. The fraud of Enron and World-Com and crises at Bear Stearns and Lehman Brothers were caused by major fraud, double-dealing, and stupidity that exist above the level that internal controls and SOD are designed to prevent.

TIPS AND TECHNIQUES

Hierarchical Segregation of Duties

Hierarchical, or multilevel, approvals refer to a concept whereby authorizations are attached to positions in a hierarchy, rather than to individual users. With hierarchical approvals, you can determine how authorizations are to be passed up and down within an organization.

Further complicating the ability to maintain SOD and provide viable checks and balances, consider the same reporting relationship in a global organization in which each functional area is in a different time zone or even on a different continent, with users speaking different languages in many of these locations.

To prevent hierarchical violations of SOD, consider the following:

- Identify individual conflicts in segregation of duties.
- Identify the roles and responsibilities of the individuals involved.

Summary

Internal controls are an essential component in operational risk management. Although it can be argued that the regulatory reforms focused on improved internal controls may have been an overreaction and somewhat misdirected, there is no sign that internal control laws, regulations, and auditing practices will ever return to the pre-Enron era.

Improved internal controls do help prevent fraud and unintentional errors, but they also help to standardize processes, policies, and procedures beyond regulatory requirements to provide for a more transparent, auditable, and cost-effective means of conducting operations.

Notes

1. This section extensively references Ian Rodgers, "Internal Control Best Practices," Chapter 22 in Anthony Tarantino, *Governance, Risk, and Compliance Handbook* (Hoboken, NJ: John Wiley & Sons, 2008).
2. This section extensively references "The Globalization of SOX Regulations," Chapter 8 in Anthony Tarantino and Sanjay Anand, *Sarbanes-Oxley in Leading Economies* (Upper Saddle River, NJ: Prentice Hall, 2010).

3. This section extensively references "The Globalization of SOX Audit Standards," Chapter 9 in Anthony Tarantino and Sanjay Anand, *Sarbanes-Oxley in Leading Economies* (Upper Saddle River, NJ: Prentice Hall, 2010).

4. Ibid.

5. See Jeff Hare, "Beyond Segregation of Duties: Next Generation Techniques in Evaluating User Access Control Risks," Chapter 25 in Anthony Tarantino and Deborah Cernauskas, *Financial Risk Management: Six Sigma and Other Next Generation Techniques* (Hoboken, NJ: John Wiley & Sons, 2009).

CHAPTER 9

Environmental and Product Risks— Sustainability

with Shirley Cui Tarantino

After reading this chapter, you will be able to:

- Grasp why the sustainability movement is irreversible.
- Add sustainability to financial reporting.
- Argue the pros and cons of cap and trade.
- Understand the basics of RoHS and WEEE.
- Comprehend the major impact REACH will bring to the EU.

Many leading organizations have recognized the need to manage environmental risks and demonstrate a commitment to sustainability and related environmental compliance. The pressure to do so is unrelenting in the United States and European Union, where children and young adults are committed to the green/sustainable revolution. This mind-set is bound to expand to the rest of the world.[1]

In the West, there is no going back to the time of industrialization without regard to environmental issues. Countries like China that have been obsessed with industrial expansion regardless of the environmental consequences are likely to modify their behaviors to support sustainably, just as has occurred in the West over the past 20 years. (This can be explained by Kuznets's curve theory, discussed later in this chapter.)

A major change in Western economic theory is the idea that economic development and environmental goals can be aligned and are not divergent or in conflict. Historically, the common perception was that pursuing environmental goals hurt profitability and growth and was an added cost of doing business. The concept of sustainable development changed this, arguing that economic and environmental goals are neither mutually exclusive nor necessarily conflicting. Sustainability is now widely accepted by both liberal and conservative policy makers. The differences are more about the pace of change to support sustainability. Most global corporations have embraced sustainability as a means to enhance their reputations and as a good investment—in some cases they have voluntarily enacted sustainable policies ahead of regulatory requirements.

After decades of end-of-pipe treatment and controls on industrial releases to the environment, attention has shifted to including elimination of potential pollution at its source, design with environmental factors in mind, and sustainable manufacturing. These efforts have incorporated engineering attempts to redesign products and processes, incentives to encourage pollution reduction, and pollution prevention, while focusing on sustainable development.

Many studies in the early 1990s showed that appropriate environmental policy and government regulation are the most important catalysts in leading organizations to consider environmental issues today. Forces such as customer pressure, shareholder pressure, and minimizing financial and social risks may also play a significant role in the development of an environmental plan at the firm level. Since various empirical studies suggest that most firms already spend between 1 and 2 percent of their revenues as a response to environmental concerns, it is becoming increasingly essential for firms to develop a corporate environmental policy.[2]

Inherent in the sustainability movement are growing environmental regulations, which present both risks and opportunities. The risk comes in failing to calibrate the impact of such regulations on product costs, cycle times, markets, and organizational reputations. The opportunities come in beating the competition in sustainability and bragging about your achievements. Increasingly, sustainability will become a tie-breaker in determining purchasing decisions.

Being perceived as anti-environment and anti-sustainability is unacceptable in today's corporate world. Regulators, analysts, and scientists will prevent major organizations from only providing lip service to green initiatives, a practice sometimes called greenwashing. In short, the major environmental and product risks that major organizations face are not embracing sustainability in a proactive manner. Laggards will suffer in a variety of ways—from lost business, fines, litigation, employee defections, and brand erosion. The leaders should enjoy enhanced reputations, lower legal costs, increased employee loyalty, and additional business.

Sustainability

The mission of sustainable development is to equilibrate economy with resources and natural ecosystems.[3] Sustainable development is a concept that requires restructuring of social, economic, technological, and industrial policies and practices. Sustainability goals can be achieved through *environmentally desirable changes* in industrial production: eliminating waste, changing production processes, redesigning products, fostering profitable innovation, promoting energy conservation, and so forth.

Decades of review of industrial performance suggest that organizations can gain competitive advantage from redesigning production processes to pollute less, substituting less-polluting inputs, recycling by-products of processes, and instituting less-polluting processes. Such approaches reduce the cost of production by increasing the efficiency of production processes and reducing input and waste disposal costs.

The relationship between the economy and the environment has been the focus of many studies. Materialist and postmaterialist approaches suggest that economic needs must be satisfied before environmental goals are pursued. The sustainable development perspective, however, stresses that economic and environmental goals are neither mutually exclusive nor necessarily conflicting.

Maslow's Theory of Motivation

Theories of motivation illustrate reasons for pursuing green production and sustainability. Maslow's theory of motivation (1970), suggests that economic fulfillment is a necessity while environmental concerns are higher needs related to association and the quality of life. Accordingly, societies pursue basic needs, such as economic satisfaction, before considering higher goals, such as environmental protection.[4]

Kuznets's Curve Theory

Simon Kuznets's curve theory and Grossman and Krueger (1993, 1995) suggest an inverted U-shaped relationship between income inequality, economic growth, the size of an industry or economy and environmental pollution.[5] According to Kuznets's curve theory, as income increases, pollution also increases to a point (win–lose situation), after which it decreases with increase in income (win–win situation). The Environmental Kuznets Curve (EKC) suggests an approximated link between environmental change and income growth. The most popular indicator of the EKC is the inverted U-shaped curve found between local air pollutants and per capita income. Despite many findings, including studies relying on the application of sophisticated econometric techniques to explain this theory, there is still no clear-cut evidence to support the existence of the EKC.[6]

Sustainability in Financial Reporting

In the European Union and the United States, annual financial statements are now required to include the impact of a public company's operations on climate change and the environment. These reporting requirements are bound to become more and more demanding and spread to other leading economies. Major environmental disasters, such as the April 2010 Gulf of Mexico drilling platform explosion and massive oil spill, will tend to hasten this trend.

EC Directive 2003/51/EC

The Accounting Modernization Directive 2003/51/EC requests public companies in member states to include nonfinancial information in their annual reports and consolidated annual reports. "The information should not be restricted to the financial aspects of the company's business. It is expected that, where appropriate, this should lead to an analysis of environmental and social aspects necessary for an understanding of the company's development, performance, or position."[7]

SEC 2010 Guidance Regarding Disclosure Related to Climate Change

Effective February 8, 2010, the Securities and Exchange Commission (SEC) has clarified that publicly held companies have a responsibility to report on the following environmental areas:

- The direct effects of existing and pending environmental regulation, legislation, and international treaties on the company's business, operations, risk factors, and in Management's Discussion and Analysis (MD&A) of Financial Condition and Results of Operations.

- The indirect effects of such legislation and regulation on a company's business, such as changes in demand for products that create or reduce greenhouse gas emissions.

- The effect on a company's business and operations related to the physical changes to our planet caused by climate change—such as rising seas, stronger storms, and increased drought conditions.

The SEC maintains that these changes to the environment could have a number of material effects on corporations, such as impairing the distribution and production of goods and damaging property, plant, and equipment.

In announcing the clarification around environmental reporting, SEC Commissioner Luis A. Aguilar stated that the SEC will begin to be far more proactive on environmental reporting. He noted that this action is a first step in an area where the SEC will play a more proactive role, consistent with its mandate under the National Environmental Policy Act of 1969, to consider the environment in its regulatory action. The National Environmental Policy Act charged the federal government to use all practicable means to fulfill the responsibilities of each generation as trustee of the environment for succeeding generations.[8]

The SEC and European Commission well understand the rising interest of investors and other stakeholders around companies' environmental risk reporting who are asking companies to provide more information about their environmental risks and mitigants to those risks. Investors are concerned that their investments will disappear in an environmental disaster such as the one facing British Petroleum (BP) over its Gulf of Mexico drilling platform. While BP is so large it will most likely recover from this environmental disaster, investors realize the events in the Gulf will impact company operations and profitability for years to come. Its green marketing campaign and reputation were shattered overnight, and the cost of and regulation over offshore operations will undoubtedly increase for the entire industry.

Emissions Trading

Emissions trading (or cap and trade) is a much debated approach to limiting greenhouse pollution by providing economic incentives for achieving reductions in the emissions of pollutants. Typically a national governmental agency sets a limit, known as the cap, on the amount of a pollutant that can be emitted. Once the cap is established, companies are issued emission allowances, credits that can be traded. The debate is whether cap and trade is the most cost-effective means to reduce greenhouse gas emissions, or yet another burden on business growth and profitability.

The goal of cap and trade is to reduce overall emissions by continuing to reduce the emission cap each year. This rewards those who reduce emissions through the sale of credits, which will continue to increase in value as the cap is reduced, and allows heavier polluters to buy credits rather than simply going out of business. The hope is that heavier polluters will then have the time to invest in greener processes. In short, the buyer of credits is paying a charge for polluting, while the seller of credits is being rewarded for having reduced emissions by more than was needed. The theory is that those who can reduce emissions most cheaply will do so, achieving pollution reduction at the lowest cost to society.

EC Directive 2003/87/EC and Emission Trading Scheme

There are trading programs for several air pollutants. For greenhouse gases, the largest is the European Union Emission Trading Scheme (ETS) based on the EC Directive 2003/87/EC, which establishes a scheme for greenhouse gas emission allowance trading.[9] The European Commission (EC) argues that ETS is "a cornerstone in the fight against climate change, and the first international trading system for CO^2 emissions in the world. It covers more than 11,500 energy-intensive installations across the European Union (EU), representing close to half of Europe's emissions of carbon dioxide (CO^2). These installations include combustion plants, oil refineries, coke ovens, iron and steel plants, and factories making cement, glass, lime, brick, ceramics, pulp, and paper."[10]

The EC also advocates ETS as a means for its member states to achieve compliance with their commitments under the Kyoto Protocol. "Emissions trading does not imply new environmental targets, but allows for cheaper compliance with existing targets under the Kyoto Protocol. Letting participating companies buy or sell emission allowances means that the targets can be achieved at least cost. If the Emissions Trading Scheme had not been adopted, other—more costly—measures would have had to be implemented."

According to the question and answer section of the Directorate General Communication's web site, under the ETS, emission credit prices are:

> a function of supply and demand as in any other free market. Market intermediaries quote prices for allowances offered or bid for. The Commission will not intervene in the allowance market. Should distortions occur, competition law would be applicable as with any other market . . . . The National Allocation Plans (NAPs) determine the total quantity of CO^2 emissions that Member States grant to their companies, which can then be sold or bought by the companies themselves . . . . The idea is that Member States limit CO^2 emissions from the energy and industrial sectors through the allocation of allowances, thereby creating scarcity, so that a functioning market can develop later and overall emissions are then reduced.[11]

In the United States there is a national market to reduce acid rain and several regional markets in nitrogen oxides.[12] The Environmental Protection Agency (EPA) advocates cap and trade as a tool that delivers results with a mandatory cap on emissions while providing sources flexibility in how they comply. The EPA argues that successful cap and trade programs reward innovation, efficiency, and early action and provide strict environmental accountability without inhibiting economic growth.

Acid Rain Program

The EPA cites as an example of a successful cap and trade program the nationwide Acid Rain Program. It created an allowance trading system for utility companies that provided "low-cost rules of exchange that minimize government intrusion and make allowance trading a viable compliance strategy for reducing SO^2 (sulfur dioxide). The Acid Rain Program represents a dramatic departure from traditional command and control regulatory methods that establish specific, inflexible emissions limitations with which all affected sources must comply. Instead, the Acid Rain Program introduces an allowance trading system that harnesses the incentives of the free market to reduce pollution."[13]

According to the EPA, the Acid Rain Program creates allocated allowances based on an individual utility company's "historic fuel consumption and a specific emissions rate. Each allowance permits a unit to emit one ton of sulfur dioxide (SO^2) during or after a specified year. For each ton of SO^2 emitted in a given year, one allowance is retired, that is, it can no longer be used. Allowances may be bought, sold, or banked. Anyone may acquire allowances and participate in the trading system. However, regardless of the number of allowances a source holds, it may not emit at levels that would violate federal or state limits set under Title I of the Clean Air Act to protect public health."[14]

Although the debate over the cost versus effectiveness of emission trading will continue, its inclusion in the Kyoto Accords and its embrace in the European Union indicates its use will expand. A key to its success is that regulators thoroughly understand the existing emission levels by industry down to individual companies. Historically, this data was not captured or was captured inconsistently. Without very precise data, cap levels will not be accepted by environmentalists, industries, or other stakeholders.

Restriction of Hazardous Substances Directive

A broad range of environmental regulations is spreading over the globe that will compel manufacturers and distributors to standardize their products to meet the most stringent standards. The alternative is not very attractive—to build to a variety of standards. It will become even less attractive as sustainability spreads throughout the world. China and Korea are examples of Asian countries that have adopted stringent green product regulations in order to meet the highest international standards, even though there was little domestic pressure for adoption.

EC Directive 2002/95/EC (RoHS)

EC Directive 2002/95/EC on the restriction of the use of certain hazardous substances in electrical and electronic equipment took effect in July 2006, and is required to be enforced and become law in each European Union member state.[15] The directive restricts the use of six hazardous materials in the manufacture of various types of electronic and electrical equipment. The Restriction of Hazardous Substances Directive is often referred to as the Lead-Free Directive, but it restricts the use of all the following six substances:

1. Lead (Pb)
2. Mercury (Hg)
3. Cadmium (Cd)
4. Hexavalent chromium (Cr6+)
5. Polybrominated biphenyls (PBB)—flame retardant
6. Polybrominated diphenyl ether (PBDE)—flame retardant

Compliance is the responsibility of the company that puts the product on the market, as defined—the regulation is applied at the homogeneous material level. Therefore, data on substance concentrations needs to be transferred through the supply chain to the final producer. RoHS applies to these products in the EU whether made within the EU or imported. Certain exemptions apply, and these are updated on occasion by the EU.

RoHS restricted substances have been used in a broad array of consumer electronics products. Examples of leaded components include:

- Paints and pigments
- PVC (vinyl) cables as a stabilizer (e.g., power cords, USB cables)
- Solders
- Printed circuit board finishes, leads, internal and external interconnects
- Glass in television and photographic products (e.g., CRT television screens and camera lenses)
- Metal parts
- Lamps and bulbs
- Batteries

Cadmium is found in many of the above components; examples include plastic pigmentation, nickel-cadmium (NiCd) batteries, and CdS photocells (used in night lights). Mercury is used in lighting applications and automotive switches; examples include fluorescent lamps (used in laptops for backlighting) and mercury tilt switches (these are rarely used nowadays). Hexavalent chromium is used for metal finishes to prevent corrosion. Polybrominated biphenyls and diphenyl ethers/oxides are used primarily as flame retardants.

RoHS Product Category 8 and 9 Exclusions

Medical devices and monitoring and control instruments comprise RoHS Category 8 and Category 9 products respectively. The EU recognizes that these products are manufactured in small numbers and generally have a long product life. Furthermore, these products are often used in mission-critical applications where their failure can reasonably be expected to be extremely disruptive, if not catastrophic. The long-term effects of lead-free solder, a primary RoHS objective, cannot be known for a period of at least five years following the directive's application to the remaining eight categories. Therefore, the EU has established at least a temporary moratorium for Category 8 and 9 products.

China Order No. 39 (China RoHS)

China Order No. 39: Final Measures for the Administration of the Pollution Control and Electronic Information Products has the stated intent to establish similar restrictions, but takes a very different approach. Unlike EU RoHS, where products in specified categories are included unless specifically excluded, there will be a list of included products, known as the catalog. Initially, products that fall under the covered scope must provide markings and disclosure as to the presence of certain substances, while the substances themselves are not (yet) prohibited. Some products are considered electronic information products (EIPs), which are not in scope for EU RoHS; for example, radar systems, semiconductor-manufacturing equipment, and photomasks. The list of EIPs is available in Chinese and English. The marking and disclosure aspects of the regulation became effective on March 1, 2007. There is no timeline for the catalog yet.[16]

California Electronic Waste Recycling Act (California RoHS)

California Senate Bill SB 20: Electronic Waste Recycling Act of 2003, or EWRA, has prohibited the sale of electronic devices since January 1, 2007 that are prohibited from being sold under the EU RoHS directive. But items are across a much narrower scope, such as liquid crystal displays (LCDs) and cathode ray tubes (CRTs), only covering the four heavy metals restricted by RoHS. EWRA also has a restricted material disclosure requirement. Effective January 2010, the California Lighting Efficiency and Toxics Reduction Act applies RoHS to general purpose lights. Other U.S. states and cities are likely to follow California's lead and eventually sustainability pressures will bring about RoHS on a national level.[17]

RoHS in its various forms has been criticized for its high cost of compliance, particularly for small to mid-size enterprises. Restrictions on cadmium and lead do not apply to some of the largest applications and are unduly expensive to the electronics industry. For example, the total lead used in electronics makes up only 2 percent of world lead consumption, while 90 percent of lead is used for batteries (covered by battery directives, which require recycling and limit the use of mercury and cadmium, but do not restrict lead). Another criticism is that less than 4 percent of lead in landfills comes from electronic components or circuit boards, while approximately 36 percent comes from leaded glass in monitors and televisions, which can contain up to 4.4 pounds per screen.[18]

EXECUTIVE INSIGHT

You Cannot Outsource Your Responsibilities under RoHS and Other Green Regulations

The desktop PC chart below is a bill of material, a list of parts and their relationships to one another in the manufacture of a desktop personal computer (PC). Many large PC sellers have outsourced manufacturing, supply chain, and logistics to multiple third parties. In our example, the computer is assembled and tested by a contract manufacturer who buys the harness assembly from another supplier who buys connectors and wires from a variety of suppliers.

Under RoHS, the seller and distributor of the PC must certify that their product is lead-free. This requires the seller to obtain certifications down through the supply chain, including assemblies and basic components, from each connector and wire supplier in our example.

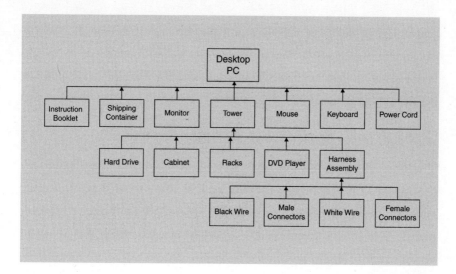

Advocates for RoHS argue that it reduces damage to workers and their local environments in third-world countries where the great majority of high-tech manufacturing and waste resides. They maintain that lead-free solders and components have provided immediate health benefits to workers in the electronics industry who are exposed to solder paste.[19]

EC Directive 2002/96/EC (WEEE)

European Commission Directive 2002/96/EC covers waste of electronic and electrical equipment. Electronic waste includes all entertainment device electronics, secondary computers, mobile phones, and other items such as refrigerators and television sets, whether sold, donated, or discarded by their original owners. Known as the Waste Electrical and Electronic Equipment (WEEE) Directive, it became effective in most European countries over the last three years. WEEE calls for the collection, recycling, and recovery of all types of electrical goods. The responsibility for the disposal of waste electrical and electronic equipment is placed on the manufacturers of such equipment, requiring them to establish an infrastructure for collecting WEEE in such a way that the consumers of electrical and electronic equipment can return them without incurring a fee. Manufacturers are compelled to treat the recovered waste in an ecologically friendly manner, either by ecological disposal or by recycling.[20]

Individual versus Collective Responsibility

There is a distinction in WEEE between individual and collective responsibility for accepting products back at the end of their useful life and then managing them in a manner to meet WEEE directive requirements. The distinction depends on whether end-of-life management systems reward organizations for designing products that are more reusable or recyclable. Individual responsibility includes organizations paying to manage their own products and benefiting from designs that use recyclable materials and facilitate disassembly. It also typically includes the costly process of sorting or tracking waste products by brand. Collective responsibility includes organizations sharing end-of-life product costs based on their market share, so they do not benefit from environmentally friendly design changes.

The directive permits collective responsibility for waste from products produced and sold before August 13, 2005, but requires individual producer responsibility for products produced and sold after August 13, 2005. At a minimum, WEEE makes producers responsible for recovering waste electrical and electronic equipment from collection points, but not from individual households. This may translate into governments paying to transport waste to collection points.

As with RoHS, WEEE is spreading beyond the EU. China enacted its own WEEE, which becomes effective on January 1, 2011.[21] Four U.S. states have passed laws targeting e-waste: California, Maine, Maryland, and Washington. Only California has a substance restriction law focused on the use of certain substances in electronics. California's Electronic Waste Recycling Act was passed in 2003, requiring a recycling fee at the point of retail sale for covered electronic devices such as CRTs, computer monitors containing CRTs, laptop computers with LCD screens, LCD-containing desktop monitors, televisions containing CRTs, plasma and LCD TVs, and portable DVD players.[22]

Ec Directive 1907/2006/EC (REACH)

EC Directive 1907/2006/EC: Registration, Evaluation, Authorisation, and Restriction of Chemicals is a European Union regulation that addresses chemical substance production and use along with their potential environmental impact. Unlike RoHS and WEEE, it is not a directive—when it passed it became a regulation at the EU level and was immediately in effect in all EU member states. A European Chemicals Agency was established to oversee its implementation. REACH became effective on June 1, 2007.[23]

RoHS targeted only six classes of substances, which equates to about 100 substances and chemical compounds. REACH addresses the thousands of substances used in electronic products, many of which are known or suspected to be toxic to people and/or the environment. REACH is a proposal to replace Europe's current systems used in assessing risks with a single regulatory framework. Today, existing substances in the EU can be used without testing and are virtually unregulated. This class of substances totals more than 30,000 chemicals. Assessing the risks that these chemical substances pose rests with the member states.

REACH targets chemical substances, not products, and requires registration of all chemical substances put on the market in the EU in excess of 1 ton per year. It also moves the responsibility for assessing the safety of substances from the government to the chemical industry.

Compliance is achieved by randomly testing at least 5 percent of all dossiers registered. Substances may also be evaluated in case of a suspicion that the substance presents a risk to human health or the environment. As of December 2008, more than 140,000 chemical substances marketed in the EU were preregistered. Supplying substances to the European market that have not been preregistered or registered is illegal.

REACH applies to all chemicals imported or produced in the EU, in contrast to the U.S. Toxic Substances Control Act, which only applies to chemicals newly coming into use. The European Chemicals Agency will manage the technical, scientific, and administrative aspects of the REACH system.

Criticism of REACH within the EU has argued that the regulation's high compliance costs would drive industry outside of the region. Criticism of REACH has come from both the Bush and Obama Administrations. The following is from the Office of the U.S. Trade Representative (Executive Office of the President):

> While supportive of the EU's objectives of protecting human health and the environment, the United States has raised numerous trade-related concerns with respect to REACH, which impacts virtually every U.S. industrial sector—from automobiles, cosmetics, and plastics, to steel, household cleaners, and textiles. REACH, which regulates chemicals as a substance, in preparations, and in products, imposes extensive registration requirements on tens of thousands of chemicals even before any scientific analysis has been conducted by the Commission. Further, several U.S. industry sectors have reported that REACH's registration provisions and their implementation make it more difficult for them to comply with the measure than for their European competitors. The first registration deadline is November 30, 2010, with U.S. industry reporting that many companies, particularly Small to Mid-sized Enterprises (SMEs), will be unable to meet the deadline and, consequently, will lose access to the EU market. The United States will continue to monitor closely REACH implementation, as well as Member State-level implementation and enforcement regimes, in the coming year and intends to participate in the REACH review process that the Commission has recently begun and will complete by June 1, 2012.[24]

Ec Directive 2006/66/EC (Batteries)

The latest version of RoHS added lead to its list of restricted substances, but it did not address the largest use of lead in the environment—batteries. EC Directive 2006/66/EC seeks to minimize the negative impact of batteries and accumulators on the environment and to harmonize requirements for the smooth functioning of the internal market. To achieve these objectives, the directive introduces measures to prohibit the marketing of some batteries containing hazardous substances. It contains measures for establishing schemes aiming at high levels of collection and recycling of batteries with quantified collection and recycling targets. The directive sets out minimum rules for producer responsibility and provisions with regard to labeling of batteries and their removability from equipment. Collection rates of at least 25 percent and 45 percent have to be reached by September 26, 2012 and September 26, 2016, respectively.[25]

The directive applies to all types of batteries and accumulators, apart from those used in equipment to protect member states' security or for military purposes, or in equipment designed to be sent into space. It therefore covers a wider range of products than Directive 91/157/EEC, which applied only to batteries containing mercury, lead, or cadmium, and excluded small button batteries.

Directive 2006/66/EC prohibits:

- Batteries and accumulators, whether or not incorporated in appliances, containing more than 0.0005 percent by weight of mercury (except for button cells, which must have mercury content of less than 2 percent by weight).

- Portable batteries and accumulators, including those incorporated in appliances, with cadmium content by weight of more than 0.002 percent (except for portable batteries and accumulators for use in emergency and alarm systems, medical equipment, or cordless power tools).

- Batteries or accumulators that do not meet the requirements of this Directive that were placed on the market after September 26, 2008.[26]

To ensure that a high proportion of spent batteries and accumulators are recycled, member states must take whatever measures are needed (including economic instruments) to promote and maximize separate waste collections and prevent batteries and accumulators from being thrown away as unsorted municipal refuse. They have to make arrangements enabling end-users to discard spent batteries and accumulators at collection points in their vicinity and have them taken back at no charge by the producers.

In principle, it must be possible to remove batteries and accumulators readily and safely. It is for member states to ensure that manufacturers design their appliances accordingly. Member states also have to ensure that, since September 26, 2009, batteries and accumulators that have been collected are treated and recycled using the best available techniques. Recycling must exclude energy recovery. As a minimum, treatment must include removal of all fluids and acids. Batteries and accumulators must be treated and stored (even if only temporarily) in sites with impermeable surfaces and weatherproof covering, or in suitable containers.

As with RoHS and WEEE, Europe has taken the lead in efforts to control batteries, and it can be expected that the United States and other leading economies will follow with similar initiatives.

EXECUTIVE INSIGHT

How Sustainability Impacts Various Functions

Design and engineering. Historically design engineers have been concerned with the form and function of their products. Products must now be designed to meet environmental and end-of-life requirements (disassembly, disposal, and recycling).

Purchasing and supply chain. Purchasing managers must ensure that component suppliers test and certify their products to meet environmental requirements.

Manufacturing. Manufacturing and quality managers will be audited to assure that products are free of chemical contaminants and that their facilities are not violating pollution laws.

Finance and accounting. Financial managers will now include comprehensive sustainability assessments in their annual reports. Undoubtedly they will be called on to calculate the costs versus benefits of capital investments to meet regulatory requirements to engage in emission trading.

Sales and marketing. Sales and marketing managers will need to factor in the green image of their organizations and brands in their marketing and sales campaigns.

Summary

Sustainability has created a fundamental change in business operations that creates risks and opportunities impacting every aspect of operations. The highest risk will come for laggards who do not take a strategic and holistic approach to environmental issues and plan accordingly.

Notes

1. This section extensively references Nasrin Khalili, "Reducing Liability Risk Through Best Environmental Practices," Chapter 29 in Anthony Tarantino and Deborah Cernauskas, *Financial Risk Management: Six Sigma and Other Next Generation Techniques* (Hoboken, NJ: John Wiley & Sons, 2009).
2. Ibid.

3. Ibid.

4. Ronald Inglehart, *The American Political Science Review* 75, no. 4 (1981): 880–900.

5. G. M. Grossman and A. B. Kruger, *Quarterly Journal of Economics* 110 (1995): 353–377.

6. T. Kronenberg and S. Fuss, *Proceedings, SSES Annual Meeting* (Zurich 2005).

7. See Directive 2003/51/EC of the European Parliament and of the Council of 18 June 2003, amending Directives 78/660/EEC, 83/349/EEC, 86/635/EEC and 91/674/EEC on the annual and consolidated accounts of certain types of companies, banks, and other financial institutions and insurance undertakings, http://eur-lex.europa.eu/LexUriServ/LexUriServ.do?uri=OJ:L:2003:178:0016:0022:en:pdf.

8. See Securities and Exchange Commission (SEC), 17 CFR PARTS 211, 231 and 241 [Release Nos. 33-9106; 34-61469; FR-82] Commission Guidance Regarding Disclosure Related to Climate Change, Effective date: February 8, 2010, www.sec.gov/rules/interp/2010/33-9106.pdf.

9. See Directive 2003/87/EC of the European Parliament and of the Council of 13 October 2003, establishing a scheme for greenhouse gas emission allowance trading within the Community and amending Council Directive 96/61/EC, http://eur-lex.europa.eu/LexUriServ/LexUriServ.do?uri=OJ:L:2003:275:0032:0046:en:pdf.

10. See the European Commission Emission Trading System web site: http://ec.europa.eu/environment/climat/emission/index_en.htm.

11. See the ETS Question and Answer web site: http://europa.eu/rapid/pressReleasesAction.do?reference=MEMO/05/84&format=HTML&aged=1&language=EN&guiLanguage=en.

12. See the Environmental Protection Agency's Clean Air Markets web sites: www.epa.gov/airmarkets and www.epa.gov/captrade.

13. See the EPA's Acid Rain Program web site: www.epa.gov/air markets/progsregs/arp/basic.html#phases.

14. See the EPA's Acid Rain Fact Sheet web site: www.epa.gov/air markets/trading/factsheet.html.

15. See Directive 2002/95/EC of the European Parliament and of the Council of 27 January 2003, on the restriction of the use of certain hazardous substances in electrical and electronic equipment, http:// eur-lex.europa.eu/LexUriServ/LexUriServ.do?uri=OJ: L:2003:037:0019:0023:en:PDF.

16. See the China Trade in Services web site: http://tradeinservices .mofcom.gov.cn/en/b/2006-02-28/8967.shtml.

17. See the California State web site: www.calrecycle.ca.gov/ electronics/act2003.

18. European Power Supply Manufacturers Association, "The Status of Lead-Free Electronics and its Impact on Power Electronics," Summary, February 26, 2003, www.epsma.org/pdf/Report%20on %20Lead%20free%20Electronics_June%2030%202003_summary% 20article.pdf.

19. Ogunseitan, Oladele A. "Health and Environmental Benefits of Adopting Lead-Free Solders," *Journal of Materials* 59, no. 7 (2007): 12–17. www.tms.org/pubs/journals/jom/0707/ogunseitan-0707 .html.

20. Directive 2002/96/EC of the European Parliament and of the Council of 27 January 2003, on waste electrical and electronic equipment (WEEE): http://eur-lex.europa.eu/LexUriServ/Lex UriServ.do?uri=OJ:L:2003:037:0024:0038:en:pdf.

21. See the China Environmental Law web site: www.chinaenviron-mentallaw.com/2009/03/17/china-weee-the-regulation.

22. See the Cal Recycle web site: www.calrecycle.ca.gov/electronics/ ACT2003.

23. See the European Commission's REACH web site: http://ec .europa.eu/enterprise/sectors/chemicals/reach/index_en.htm.

24. See Office of the U.S. Trade Representative, Key Technical Barriers to American Exports, accessed on May 20, 2010 from www.ustr.gov/about-us/press-office/fact-sheets/2010/march/key-technical-barriers-american-exports.

25. Directive 2006/66/EC of the European Parliament and of the Council of 6 September 2006, on batteries and accumulators and waste batteries and accumulators and repealing Directive, http://europa.eu/legislation_summaries/environment/waste_management/l21202_en.htm.

26. Ibid.

CHAPTER 10

Data Governance and Risk

After reading this chapter, you will learn how to:

- Conduct a data governance assessment.
- Apply a data governance maturity model.
- Apply best practices in data governance.
- Use data analytics.

The governance of data is critical to all organizations. Without robust controls over data, an organization is exposed to high levels of financial risk. The leaders in data governance will enjoy an advantage in managing risks and opportunities over the laggards. *Governance* in business and information technology can be defined as the processes and audited internal controls required to ensure meeting business objectives. *Data* is a type of information captured within a computerized system, which can be represented in graphical, text, or speech form. *Data governance* is the governance of the people, process, and technology applied to data used by an organization to ensure its definition, validity, consistency, quality, timeliness, and availability to the appropriate owners and users of the data.

The risks around data come in a variety of forms—it can be incomplete, incorrect, inconsistent, delayed, encrypted, duplicated, or nonstandard, to name a few. Banks worry about moving the right data at the right time to the right users. Health-care companies worry about patient data and maintaining its privacy. Pharmaceutical companies worry about documenting their compliance with complex regulations. Manufacturing and distribution companies worry about inventory and bills of material accuracy. Retailers worry about capturing point of sales in real time. All firms should worry about consolidating financial information to their general ledgers to support period end closes and audits.

Complicating data governance is the issue of paper documents. In today's organizations, it is rare for paper documents not to originate in some sort of electronic or digital format. This is becoming a major issue in litigation and regulatory audits. Litigants, regulators, and auditors are less and less willing to accept paper documents without its electronic metadata references as to ownership, access and change controls, time stamps, and so on. The reason is simple; it is easy to fake a paper document. So, by extension, data governance is not just over digital data, but all data—paper and electronic.

Data governance is not the same as data management. Data management is a subcomponent of data governance and includes the management of data and metadata access points. Documents and records management can be seen as a subset of data governance as well and includes the technologies used to capture, manage, store, preserve, and deliver content and documents related to organizational processes. It is typically a process to control unstructured data, while data governance controls all types of data—structured, semistructured, unstructured, metadata, registries, ontologies, and taxonomies.

Unstructured data creates headaches for most organizations in achieving data governance. Even its definition is debatable. Unstructured data is typically said to be data that is not readily readable by computers, such as e-mail, instant messages, word processor documents, audio, and video. It typically represents the great majority of all data in any organization and the trend is accelerating with the growth of instant messages and e-mail. Data with some type of structure may also be classified as unstructured if its structure does not support the needed processing task. For instance, while an HTML web page is tagged, the tag supports its format and not its meaning.

Data Governance Assessment

For an organization to understand its data governance current state, and the gaps it needs to fill to achieve its desired end state, it is helpful to conduct an assessment. This is a traditional process in problem solving widely used by consultants and process improvement teams.

It begins by capturing the current state of data governance across the enterprise. This is typically no minor task in decentralized organizations with heterogeneous IT environments and multiple silos of data in which many practices are not documented or are poorly understood outside of the business units and geographic locations. It is important to capture both the strengths and weaknesses as islands of strengths can be used as role models for the rest of the organization.

Next, it is necessary to survey the business owners as to how they would define data governance success. It is unlikely that there will be a great deal of consistency in their definition of success and the desired end state. It makes sense to first charter a data governance center of excellence (DG CoE; described later in this chapter) to take ownership of defining the desired end state. The alternative would be to present a variety of disparate and confusing ideas to an organization's executive management. The desired end state should not be made in isolation, but should leverage best practice frameworks such as COBIT, ITIL, NIST 800, and related ISO standards. There is no need to start with a blank sheet.

Once the desired end state is agreed on, the next step is to perform a gap analysis. The gap analysis should incorporate the risks of doing nothing and the risks, costs, and benefits of closing the gaps.

The final phase is to prepare a proposed action plan to achieve the end state, including a prioritization of each objective. Achieving best practices and next generation techniques in data governance is a daunting task. Some goals will take years to achieve while others are short term. Overwhelming an organization with unattainable or excessive stretch goals will backfire and create more problems than doing nothing.

TIPS AND TECHNIQUES

Data Governance Maturity Model

The assessment process can be enhanced by rating the organization against a data governance maturity model. In this model, the least mature organizations are in a reactive and firefighting mode. As organizations improve, they begin to move from a project to an enterprise-wide approach. Ultimately they use qualitative and quantitative metrics to continuously monitor and improve their people, processes, and technologies.

Unfortunately, many organizations are at the lowest levels of the maturity model. Characteristics of immature organization include:

- Data governance ownership and accountability are not clearly defined, understood, or adhered to.
- Enterprise-wide policies, procedures, guidelines, and standards are lacking.
- Data governance is viewed by business owners and stakeholders as an IT issue.
- IT addresses data governance in application and business silos.
- IT infrastructure is overly complex—applications are silo-driven.
- Data accuracy is typically inconsistent in and across the lines of business.

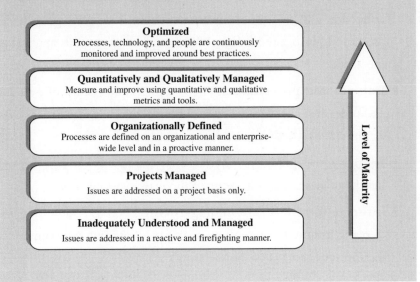

- IT initiatives are sometimes redundant and poorly coordinated; consistent enforcement of data retention and destruction is lacking.

Optimized
Processes, technology, and people are continuously monitored and improved around best practices.

Quantitatively and Qualitatively Managed
Measure and improve using quantitative and qualitative metrics and tools.

Organizationally Defined
Processes are defined on an organizational and enterprise-wide level and in a proactive manner.

Projects Managed
Issues are addressed on a project basis only.

Inadequately Understood and Managed
Issues are addressed in a reactive and firefighting manner.

Level of Maturity

The unfortunate reality is that many organizations are at the lowest levels of the maturity model. These are some of the characteristics to look for in an organization that is challenged by its data governance:

- **Data quality.** Data governance ownership and accountability are not clearly defined, understood, or adhered to. Enterprise-wide policies, procedures, guidelines, and standards are lacking. Data governance is viewed by business owners and stakeholders as an IT issue. IT addresses data governance in application and business silos.

- **Data architecture.** An enterprise-wide data architecture is not in place and each application and database owner has its own definition of data and applicable standards. There is typically little sharing of data or efforts to find a common framework.

- **General IT environment.** The IT infrastructure is overly complex, applications are silo-driven, data accuracy is typically inconsistent in and across the lines of business, and IT initiatives are sometimes redundant and poorly coordinated.

- **Metadata.** There is a lack of consistency and standardization in the collection and storage of metadata. There is no enterprise-wide program to associate all digital data upon creation of its applicable metadata.

- **Policies and procedures.** There is no viable system of policies and procedures in force to control the data governance process. As a consequence, activities are reactive and ad hoc.

- **Security and privacy.** There is a lack of adherence to accepted best practice standards in security and privacy protection.

- **Information life-cycle management.** There are some policies in place around data retention and destruction, but enforcement is inconsistent and not well understood.

- **Tone-at-the-top.** The organization understands the basics of the regulatory, risk, and legal discovery drivers behind data governance, but lacks the executive sponsorship, or tone-at-the-top, to instill the critical importance of data organization to the well-being and survival of the organization.

EXECUTIVE INSIGHT

Data Governance Best Practices

These are best practices that transcend industries, regions, and organization complexity.

- **Determine the value and risk of the data.** Prioritize data in order of its value to the organization. Once its value is determined, calculate the risks associated with it. Now determine what to budget in terms of finances and resources to manage it.

- **Digitize all content on origination.** Given the masses of disparate data that all organizations must address, it is critical to digitize all data on its origination. This includes classifying and indexing data to its metadata references. This tags all data on origination as to ownership; date of creation, revision, or access; and nature. Without this, data is not easily searched or accessed, making for a painfully expensive and tedious audit and legal discovery process.

- **Reduce the number of content repositories.** Data governance is simplified with the reduction of the number and types of data repositories and the standardization of the data in those that remain.

- **Federate content across repositories.** Federation of content provides the means to access multiple data repositories and create a virtual data repository. More complex federation permits cross-referencing and accessing all documents and records that are related, that is, all records related to a given customer or supplier.

- **Expand the use of data quality tools.** Data quality tools compare data against a data quality standard. Outputs can include the identification of duplicated master level data (supplier, customer, item, commodity code, etc.). Some commodity coding tools will attempt to assign the proper code based on an item's description. The problem arises in that any given item can be described in many ways.

Data Governance Council or Center of Excellence

A good first step in achieving data governance (DG) is to create a council or center of excellence (CoE) to champion good data governance. Some organizations have established data governance councils as a focal point of data governance activity, and a DG CoE can take this beyond a group that coordinates activities to a group that owns and communicates the organization's vision of data governance. Without a council or CoE, an organization may have a different vision for each of its lines of business, regions, and/or IT environments. A DG council or CoE should have the following responsibilities:

- It fully understands the organization's current state of DG. This includes periodic surveys of all lines of business, locations, and IT environments.

- It develops a desired DG end state based on the desires and business requirements of all the organization's DG stakeholders. The desired end state is approved by the organization's executive management, external auditors, and applicable regulatory agencies. Once approved, the desired end state is communicated to the entire organization and its stakeholders.

- It coordinates periodic DG assessments, which include a current state, desired end state, gap analysis, and cost/benefit analysis.

- It reviews, coordinates, and approves all enterprise-wide data governance guidelines, policies, procedures, audit procedures, risk-control matrices, and workflows. This is not to say that they usurp local controls, only that they provide oversight that captures the organization's DG vision.

- It strives to eliminate disparate DG practices and move the organization to enterprise-wide practices based on industry-accepted best practice frameworks.

The DG CoE should include representatives of each line of business, information technology (IT), legal, and internal audit. It need not be a large organization and can include only a small dedicated staff.

Data Analytics—Business Intelligence

The growing volumes of information and the speed of its spread create significant risks and opportunities to all organizations. Data analytics technologies,[1] such as text data mining, show promise in enabling organizations to effectively utilize vast amounts of information for business insights and value.

There are a set of key analytics technologies, especially in the text analytics space, that have emerged in the past decade. They include social media mining solutions that mine blogs, message boards, news, and web content in order to protect organizational reputations, improve brand image, increase market share, and gain consumer insights.

Information Overload

Information overload is a major issue with the continuing growth of electronic information of all types. Today's volume and velocity of information suggest that an organization may be compelled to ignore a significant amount of it to avoid getting drowned. Therefore, the notion of ignoring vast amounts of information may have some wisdom to it. Yet, this is only valid if an organization knows what data to ignore and what data to evaluate—obviously an unrealistic choice for most organizations. A more viable approach is to make a serious effort to use analytics in a manner that is appropriate for the size and complexity of the organization and appropriate to the marketplace within which it operates.

The emergence of the Internet and other advances in information technologies changed the world completely—to an information age. Information storage capacity and speed of access have advanced rapidly at ever lower costs. Even terabyte storage is easily affordable by all enterprises and many individuals. As a result, virtually everyone has easy access to all types of information at all times through the Internet.

The concept of business intelligence (BI) came into its own when data mining evolved from an academic exercise to a real-world practice. BI mined structured data stored in rational databases to find hidden associations; for example, the relationship between the sales of a given product and the buyer's gender, location of purchase, and time of purchase. Online Analytical Processing (OLAP) and BI solutions are now addressing challenges in many aspects of business, ranging from customer relationship management (CRM) to financial performance analytics and optimization.

Structured information accounts for only a small fraction of the total information population.

The prominence of unstructured data, such as e-mail, instant messages, and various forms of documents, demands even more advanced information analytics approaches. In the past decade, a wide variety of text mining techniques for unstructured data have been developed.

Data and Text Mining

Structured data is data that can be shared electronically because the structure and meaning of data has been standardized and usually determined by a data model. *Unstructured data* is data whose meaning has to be elaborated in order to be used by a computer, such as word processing documents, e-mail messages, pictures, digital audio, and video. Typically, data mining addresses structured data while text mining addresses unstructured data.

Data Mining

Data mining refers to the process of using computer-based computational algorithms or statistical techniques to analyze large volumes of data, typically structured data, in order to determine trend, patterns, and relationships. Many data mining applications involve partitioning data items into related subsets.

Data mining has become an important tool in transforming data into information. It is commonly used in a wide range of profiling practices, such as marketing, surveillance, fraud detection, and legal discovery.

Text Mining

Text mining, sometimes alternately referred to as text data mining or text analytics, is the process of deriving high-quality information from text, typically unstructured data. High-quality information is typically derived through the divining of patterns and trends through means such as statistical pattern learning. Typically, text mining involves the process of structuring text by parsing and then inserting it into a database, deriving patterns within the structured data, and then evaluating and interpreting the output. Text mining is an interdisciplinary field that draws on data mining, machine learning, information retrieval, statistics, and computational linguistics.

As the relational databases grow in size and table relationships become increasingly complex, data mining techniques emerged. Although less prominent than traditional BI and OLAP technologies, text mining technologies are now providing key insights in many business functions. Data mining aims at finding hidden patterns in data and relationships by mining large relationships in databases. Typically data mining solutions require three key technology suites:

1. Extract, transform, and load (ETL) solutions for data processing, cleansing, and data warehouse building.

2. Data mining analytics algorithms that identify hidden patterns and relationships.

3. Visualization and reporting front-end technologies that allow end-users to quickly review analytics results and compose analytical reports.

EXECUTIVE INSIGHT

Case Study: Text Analytics
Saves Company Reputation

The following case study is courtesy of Dr. Ying Chen and shows the effectiveness of text analytics in a real-world situation to

EXECUTIVE INSIGHT (CONTINUED)

repair a reputation damaged by a botched product introduction.*
The company in our case study was able use a text mining and
analytics solution to quickly detect significant, very negative,
consumer blog buzz after a product launch. The company was
able to analyze where the buzz was coming from and how the
buzz was evolving over the Internet. Their monitoring and analysis resulted in the change of company actions regarding a product launch in about one week. This was the sequence of events:

Day 1. The company's marketing team announced products with
specific ingredients that, unbeknownst to marketing, are
forbidden in certain ethnic communities.

Days 1 and 2. Blogswarm is a situation in which thousands of
bloggers comment on the same story or news event and can
make it the day's hot topic in both the blogosphere and
mainstream media. A blogswarm of protest was observed by
the company's analysts, who identified where the buzz came
from and determined that many ethnic communities were
outraged by the product announcements.

Days 3–6. These ethnic communities sent e-mails and made
phone calls threatening to boycott the company's products
and stop consuming them altogether.

Day 7. The company reversed the decision and apologized to the
community.

Key to the case study is how quickly the reputational and brand
damage spread. The company was able to resolve the problem by
intervening in a few business days. Without text analytics, the
company may not have responded quickly enough to prevent a
product launch disaster and may have opened the door for its
competitors to offer their own nonoffending products.

---

*Ying Chen, "Analytics: Secrets to Deriving Business Value and Insights out
of Information," Chapter 14 in Anthony Tarantino and Deborah Cernauskas,
Risk Management in Finance: Six Sigma and Other Next Generation Techniques
(Hoboken, NJ: John Wiley & Sons, 2009).

Summary

The risks from all types of data are quite profound, yet many organizations do not make the necessary commitments and investments to provide the data they need to compete and excel in the marketplace.

One of the reasons is that this is never an easy or painless process. The example of content and records management application software is telling. Viable enterprise-level content and records management application programs have been available for years, but many organizations resist implementing them, not due to the software cost but because of the painful process of standardizing data, eliminating duplicates, and enforcing their own retention and destruction policies. The argument for inertia is that there is not a strong business case with a good return on investment. Unfortunately, these are the kinds of organizations destined to suffer from major litigation, reputation, and operational risk losses.

Information and data are key to any well-run organization and require a strategic approach and executive-level commitment to their management.

Note

1. See Ying Chen, "Analytics: Secrets to Deriving Business Value and Insights out of Information," Chapter 14 in Anthony Tarantino and Deborah Cernauskas, *Risk Management in Finance: Six Sigma and Other Next Generation Techniques* (Hoboken, NJ: John Wiley & Sons, 2009).

CHAPTER 11

Market Risk—From Value at Risk to Black Swans

with Deborah Cernauskas, PhD

After reading this chapter, you will learn how to:

- Differentiate between qualitative and quantitative techniques.
- Apply three approaches to value at risk (VaR).
- Understand the limitations of VaR.
- Prepare for Black Swans.

Market risk is a universal concern to all types of public and private organizations. It can be defined as the risk that the value of financial instruments or contracts will decrease due to changes in market prices. The Basel Committee of the Bank for International Settlements (BIS) recognized the importance of market risk in 1997 by requiring banks to measure and apply capital charges in respect to their market risks in addition to their credit risks. The Basel committee defined market risk as the risk of losses in on- and off-balance-sheet positions arising from movements in market prices.

The Basel committee separates the market risk of assets of financial institutions into four categories:

1. Equities—stocks and stock options.

2. Interest rate products—bonds and bond options.

3. Foreign currencies.

4. Commodities—for example, oil, coffee, and metals.

Although market risk affects every firm, outside of the financial services industry, no regulations or standards exist for the management of market risk.

Basel II provides for two methods of measuring market risk—the simpler standardized approach and the more complex internal models approach, which uses qualitative and quantitative standards, specifications to market risk factors, and stress testing. Value at risk (VaR) is the most popular and accepted internal model approach to market risk within banking, investment firms, and corporations in general. It has been successfully applied in many situations but cannot capture the risk of rare outlier events known as *Black Swans*—such as the stock market crash of 1987 and the global financial crisis of 2008.

EXECUTIVE INSIGHT

The Quantitative versus Qualitative Debate

In 1999, Peter L. Bernstein described the ongoing debate between advocates of quantitative analytics and modeling and advocates of a more subjective and qualitative approach. "The story that I have to tell is marked all the way through by a persistent tension between those who assert that the best decisions are based on quantification and numbers, determined by the patterns of the past, and those who base their decisions on more

EXECUTIVE INSIGHT (CONTINUED)

subjective degrees of belief about the uncertain future. This is a controversy that has never been resolved.''*

This is a critical issue in market and credit risks, which are very much related. Changes in market prices have a major impact on credit default rates. The global financial crisis has seriously challenged the wisdom of overrelying on VaR analytics in financial services in general and portfolio management in particular. More troublesome is the lack of moves by regulators to revisit the use of these tools. To the contrary, the Basel II banking accords mandate their use.

---

*Peter L. Bernstein, *Against the Gods: The Remarkable Story of Risk* (New York: John Wiley & Sons, 1996).

Measuring Market Risk with Value at Risk

Typically, market risk is measured using a value-at-risk (VaR) methodology. Value at risk asks a simple question: How bad can things get? More specifically, it answers the question of how much can one lose, typically with a 95 or 99 percentile probability, over a preset time horizon.

VaR is not a single model but a group of related models that have in common a shared mathematical framework. VaR typically measures a portfolio's risk boundaries over periods of time. For example, a $100,000 weekly VaR at a 95 percent confidence level indicates that there is a 95 percent chance over the next week that a portfolio will not lose more than $100,000. Stated another way, there is a 5 percent chance of a portfolio loss of $100,000 or more over the next week.

Therefore, the great appeal of VaR, for those who are not PhD-level modelers, is that it expresses risk over multiple asset classes in a single dollar value. It is also popular because it is able to measure both enterprise-level risk (a combined and weighted VaR that nets all of an organization's trading desk positions) and individual risks (the risk contained in a single investor's portfolio). With high–speed computers, executives in large organizations are able to view their daily VaR within a few minutes of a market's close.[1]

From a mathematical point of view, VaR is simply a quantile of a return distribution function that focuses on measuring and quantifying outcomes that occur in the lower tail of a statistical probability distribution of returns. Investors and risk managers are interested in the tail of the distribution because that is where the negative returns or losses occur.

VaR has five main uses in finance:

1. Risk measurement

2. Risk management

3. Financial control

4. Financial reporting

5. Computing regulatory capital in banking

VaR is sometimes used in nonfinancial applications as well.[2]

The greatest benefit of VaR may come from its imposition of a structured methodology to risk management and the ability to measure the combined risk over multiple asset classes. Organizations that compute their VaR are compelled to confront their exposure to financial risks and to set up a proper risk management function, so the process of getting to VaR may be as important as the number itself.

VaR did not emerge as a distinct concept until the stock market crash of 1987. This was the first major financial crisis in which a large number of PhD-level quantitative analysts, known as *quants*, were employed by banks and investment firms. The crash raised their concerns about their firms' survival. The statistical models in use at the time failed to predict the crash, bringing into question the basis for quantitative finance. Some quants came to believe that a more advanced approach was indicated—one that would work for day-to-day events and for the rare outlier events that impacted many markets at once, including some that were usually not correlated. These rare outlier events were named "Black Swans" by Nassim Nicholas Taleb in 1997 and the concept has been extended far beyond finance.[3]

J.P. Morgan led in the development and promotion of VaR starting in the early 1990s. A 1995 Institutional Investor survey found that 32 percent of all firms used VaR as a measure of market risk, and 60 percent of pension funds responding to a survey by the New York University Stern School of Business reported using VaR.[4]

In 1997, the SEC mandated public companies to disclose quantitative information about their derivatives activity. Banks and investment companies chose VaR as their favorite means to meet the SEC requirement.[5] The Basel II capital accords for large global banks gave further impetus to the acceptance of VaR.

Three Methods of Calculating Value at Risk

There are three popular methods in use to calculate value at risk:

1. Historical data

2. Normal probability distribution

3. Monte Carlo simulation

Here are the advantages and disadvantages of each.

Historical Data Method

The *historical data method* is a popular VaR approach that directly uses historical data to estimate what may happen in the future. Current portfolio weights are applied to historical asset returns by going back in time, such as over the past 252 trading days (the average number of trading days in a year).

A distribution of portfolio returns is then obtained and the corresponding quantile of the distribution is determined, resulting in a one-day VaR by the historical simulation method.

The historical data method has the advantage of being simple to use and allows for non-normal distributions and nonlinearities. The historical simulation method does not rely on valuation models and is not subjected to the risk that the models are wrong.[6] There are many weaknesses to this approach, including (but not limited to):

- The availability of sufficient historical price data, in that some assets may have a short history or, in some cases, no history at all.

- Assuming the past is the best predictor of the immediate future.

- The return correlations between asset classes will not change.

Historical simulation can become cumbersome for large portfolios with complicated structures.

TIPS AND TECHNIQUES

Historical Data Method of Calculating VaR Using Microsoft Excel

It is relatively simple to calculate historical data VaR using Microsoft Excel for a publicly traded company. Investment firms use very powerful computers to calculate updates to VaR in near–real time, but this example for calculating the VaR for one stock will show the mechanics of how it works.

Using this methodology, the VaR for the one stock can be compared over time and against other stocks.

❶ Begin by downloading the daily stock price for a period of time (such as the last year, which equates to 252 trading days).

	A	B	C	D
1	Date	Adj Close	Daily Return	
2	5/20/2010	51.30		
3	5/19/2010	53.04	-0.032805430	=(B2-B3)/B3
4	5/18/2010	53.71	-0.012474400	
5	5/17/2010	52.73	0.018585246	
251	5/26/2009	48.92	-0.01369583	
252	5/22/2009	48.18	0.01535907	
253	5/21/2009	48.05	0.002705515	

❷ Calculate the daily stock return for each day using the arithmetic or geometric return.

$$\text{Return} = \frac{B2 - B3}{B3} \ \text{or} \ \ln\left(\frac{B2}{B3}\right)$$

Note the adjusted closing price already takes into account the dividend payment.

❸ Use Excel's percentile function to calculate historical simulation VaR in both percent and in dollars (using the last closing price on 5/20/201X). Percentile returns the kth percentile of a data set.

❹ In our example, the value at risk, as of May 20, 201X, over the past year is 1.40 percent or $0.72 per share.

	A	B	C
280		-1.40%	$ (0.72)
283		Percentile(D2:D274,0.05)	B280*51.3

Normal Probability Distribution Method

Sometimes known as the variance/covariance method, the *normal probability distribution method* assumes that stock returns are normally distributed and requires only two factors to be calculated: (1) an expected (or average) return and (2) a standard deviation. The main weakness of this method is that the probability distribution of return data is fat-tailed and non-normal.

Financial returns data are generally *leptokurtotic*—fat-tailed and peaked. Fat tails refers to heavy-tailed distributions that exhibit more observations in the tails of the distribution than a normal distribution. Peakedness refers to a higher peak than a normal distribution. Fat-tailed distributions occur whenever there are many events or values that stray widely from the average, giving more frequent high and low values. Exhibit 11.1 illustrates the difference between a normal distribution ($\mu = 0.03\%$, $\sigma = 0.892\%$) and a typical

EXHIBIT 11.1

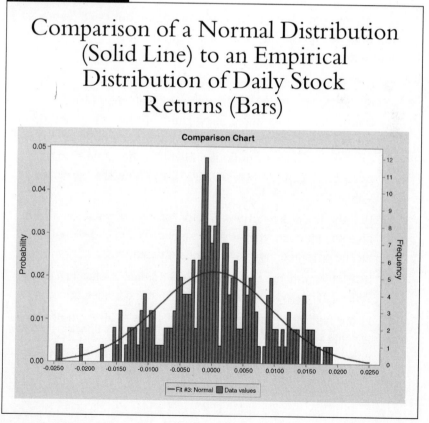

Comparison of a Normal Distribution (Solid Line) to an Empirical Distribution of Daily Stock Returns (Bars)

empirical stock price return distribution with the same mean and standard deviation.

When VaR is based on the assumption of normal return distributions, the resulting risk measurement is underestimated. Another problem is that this method inadequately measures the risk of nonlinear instruments such as options or mortgages.

TIPS AND TECHNIQUES

Normal Probability Distribution Method of Calculating VaR Using Microsoft Excel

Using the same stock data as our historical data example, we can also use Microsoft Excel to calculate a normal probability distribution VaR.

1 Use the same downloaded daily stock price in our first example and the same 95 percent confidence level. Unlike our first example using the historical data method, we need to determine the mean and standard deviation for the 252 daily returns. We also use the same closing price of $51.30 on May 20, 201X to calculate the dollar VaR.

2 Use the Excel's functions STDEV (standard deviation based on a sample) and NORMINV (normal cumulative distribution for the specified mean and standard deviation).

3 NORMINV requires three inputs: (1) confidence level (0.05 = 95%), (2) mean (or average), and (3) standard deviation.

4 In our historical data example, the value at risk, as of May 20, 201X, over the last year is 1.40 percent or $0.72 per share. The normal distribution VaR is very similar at 1.44 percent or $0.75 per share.

	B	C	D	E
264	Mean	51.33	0.0299%	
265		=AVERAGE(C3:C254)	=AVERAGE(D3:D254)	
266	Std Deviation	2.52	0.8918%	
269		=STDEV(C3:C254)	=STDEV(D3:D254)	
270	Norminv	47.1942	-1.44%	-$0.74
272		=NORMINV(.05,C264,C266)	=NORMINV(.05,D264,D265)	=D270*51.3
273			Value at Risk	

Monte Carlo Simulation Method

Monte Carlo simulation is a statistical sampling technique used to approximate solutions to quantitative problems. The methodology's goal is to solve problems by directly simulating their underlying (physical) processes and then calculating the average result of the processes. It is considered a valid approach in a variety of fields, such as electrical engineering, computer sciences, physics, and finance.

Monte Carlo simulations consist of three steps. First, a stochastic (random variable) process is specified for the financial variables. Second, fictitious price paths are simulated for all financial variables of interest. Third, each of these pseudo-realizations is then used to compile a distribution of returns from which a VaR can be determined.

The Monte Carlo method has the advantage of incorporating non-normal distributions, nonlinear positions, implied parameters, and even user-defined scenarios. Its popularity and usage has increased with the advent of high-speed computers due to its large computational demands. For example, if 1,000 sample paths are generated with a portfolio of 500 assets, the total number of valuations amounts to 500,000. A disadvantage of Monte Carlo simulations is that they are subject to the risk of model errors.

Developing forecasting models that plan for future events requires making assumptions such as returns on an investment, price changes in a commodity critical to a business, the time needed to complete a specific task, and the costs of a project. As these are future projections, the best we can do is to estimate an expected value based on prior experience, historical data, and subject matter expertise. Although this estimate is useful for developing a model, it contains some inherent uncertainty and risk because it is an estimate of an unknown value.

In some cases, it is possible to estimate a range of values, such as the distribution of possible values through the standard, the mean, and the deviation of returns in a commodity market. Creating a range of possible values over one guess should provide a more realistic future projection.

When a model is based on a range of value estimates, the model's outputs will also be a range. A normal forecasting model is different in that it starts with fixed estimates, such as the duration of four project tasks, and estimates the project's total duration time. If the same model were based on ranges of estimates for each of the four project tasks, the resulting estimate would be a range of duration times to complete the project. When each of the four parts has an estimated minimum and maximum, it is possible to apply those values to estimated total minimum and maximum project durations.

When you have a range of values as a result, you are beginning to understand the risk and uncertainty in the model. The key feature of a Monte Carlo simulation is that it can tell you—based on how you create the ranges of estimates—how likely the resulting outcomes are.

In a Monte Carlo simulation, a random value is selected for each of the tasks, based on the range of estimates. The model is calculated based on this random value. The result of the model is recorded, and the process is repeated. A typical Monte Carlo simulation calculates the model hundreds or thousands of times, each time using different randomly selected values. When the simulation is complete, we have a large number of results from the model, each based on random input values. These results are used to describe the likelihood, or probability, of reaching various results in the model.

Monte Carlo Simulation Method of Calculating VaR Using a Microsoft Excel Add-On

The following Monte Carlo example is provided by RiskAMP, a Monte Carlo simulation engine that works with Microsoft Excel spreadsheets by creating comprehensive probability simulation to spreadsheet models and Excel applications.

Phase	Time Estimate
Phase 1	5 Months
Phase 2	4 Months
Phase 3	5 Months
Total	14 Months

In this example, the goal is to estimate the total time to complete a software project that contains three phases that must be done sequentially, not in parallel. This model provides only one estimate for each of the three tasks. Since there is no minimum or maximum value, the risk cannot be calculated. Therefore our estimate is 14 months to complete the software project without using a Monte Carlo simulation.

Phase	Minimum	Most Likely	Maximum
Phase 1	4 Months	5 Months	7 Months
Phase 2	3 Months	4 Months	6 Months
Phase 3	4 Months	5 Months	6 Months
Total	11 Months	14 Months	19 Months

In a Monte Carlo simulation, a minimum and maximum time are added, providing a range of possible outcomes—11 to 19 months.

TIPS AND TECHNIQUES (CONTINUED)

Time	No. of Times (Out of 500)	Percent of Total (Rounded)
12 Months	1	0%
13 Months	31	6%
14 Months	171	34%
15 Months	394	79%
16 Months	482	96%
17 Months	499	100%
18 Months	500	100%

A Monte Carlo simulation generates values for each of the phases, then calculates the total time to completion. In this example the simulation will be run 500 times. Based on simulation results, it is possible to describe some of the risk characteristics in the model. Counting the times a particular result occurred tests its likelihood of occurring.

Using Monte Carlo, we see our original 14-month estimate has only about a one in three chance of occurring, but about a four in five chance of occurring in 15 months. For the extremes, there is a virtually 100 percent chance of it occurring between 12 and 18 months, and virtually no chance of occurring in less than 12 months.

Source: See the RiskAMP web site, www.riskamp.com. Exhibit is located at www.riskamp.com/files/RiskAMP%20–%20Monte %20Carlo%20Simulation.pdf.

As our first example demonstrates, Monte Carlo simulations can be useful when you look at the result of a number of random variables. Exhibit 11.2, also courtesy of Riskamp.com, is for a 10-year stock

EXHIBIT 11.2			
Ten-Year Stock Portfolio			
Opening Balance			**$1,000,000**
Year	**Return**	**Gain (Loss)**	**Closing Balance**
1	9.8%	97,503	$1,097,503
2	−11.2%	(122,860)	$ 974,643
3	4.8%	47,042	$1,021,685
4	7.5%	76,740	$1,098,424
5	7.3%	80,731	$1,179,155
6	18.6%	219,845	$1,399,001
7	1.9%	27,175	$1,426,176
8	17.4%	248,192	$1,674,368
9	12.1%	202,140	$1,876,508
10	−19.0%	(357,368)	$1,519,140
Closing Balance			$1,519,140
Average Closing Balance			$1,691,748
Minimum Closing Balance			$ 684,461
Maximum Closing Balance			$3,083,306

From	To	Result	Analysis
400,000	600,000	0%	Probability closing balance under $1 million = 4%
600,000	800,000	0%	
800,000	1,000,000	3%	
1,000,000	1,200,000	7%	
1,200,000	1,400,000	17%	
1,400,000	1,600,000	18%	
1,600,000	1,800,000	19%	
1,800,000	2,000,000	14%	
2,000,000	2,200,000	9%	Probability closing balance over $2 million = 22%
2,200,000	2,400,000	5%	
2,400,000	2,600,000	4%	
2,600,000	2,800,000	1%	
2,800,000	3,000,000	1%	
3,000,000	3,200,000	1%	

portfolio. It contains a starting and ending balance and a normally distributed value for the annual return. Using a Monte Carlo simulation, we can look at distributed returns to understand the risk involved in the portfolio, such as the likelihood of a closing balance falling below the opening balance, or the likelihood of a closing balance of more than $2 million. The simulation suggests that the probability of a closing balance under $1 million is small (4 percent), while there is more than a one in five chance of a close over $2 million.

Like any forecasting model, a Monte Carlo simulation will only be as good as the estimates that go into it. It's important to remember that the simulation only represents estimates and not certainty. Nevertheless, Monte Carlo simulation can be a useful tool when forecasting.

Criticism of Value at Risk

The widespread institutional reliance on VaR and its acknowledged failure in the global financial crisis, is now calling into question whether its use was a major mistake. VaR-based risk modeling did little to warn of a financial meltdown. Aaron Brown, formerly a risk manager at Morgan Stanley, noted: "Risk modeling didn't help as much as it should have." A similar sentiment was voiced by David Einhorn, the founder of a leading hedge fund, Greenlight Capital, who stated that VaR was "relatively useless as a risk-management tool and potentially catastrophic when its use creates a false sense of security among senior managers and watchdogs. This is like an air bag that works all the time, except when you have a car accident."[7]

There were early warnings to the severe limitations of VaR. Long-Term Capital Management (LTCM) was a very successful hedge fund that fully embraced VaR as its investment strategy of choice, then collapsed in 1998. Rather than accepting the limitations of VaR, Wall Street rationalized the collapse as an example of LTCM getting their comeuppance, in spite of Nobel laureates on their board.

Some of the commonly cited limitations of VaR as a market risk measure include:

- The measure provides a probability that losses will exceed a threshold value within a specified timeframe, but does not provide any guidance on the magnitude of the loss when the threshold is exceeded.

- For fat-tailed distributions, the aforementioned normal probability distribution method may give little practical guidance as to the true risk exposure.

- VaR calculations do not enlighten us as to the shape of the tail. Two distributions can have the same 1 percent VaR but vastly different 0.5 percent VaRs.

- VaR does not take into account liquidity issues.

- The VaR measure is not coherent; that is, portfolios that are more risky are not always assigned a higher risk value.

- Parameter estimation error may be significant but is generally ignored—increasing the length of the historical sample will not provide more accurate parameter estimates for financial returns or operating losses.

- VaR is a forward-looking measure of potential losses only under the assumption of the status quo.

- VaR is not subadditive; the VaR of a combined portfolio can be larger than the sum of the VaRs of its components.

Black Swans

Black Swan Event is a term coined by Nassim Nicholas Taleb to describe very rare but catastrophic events.[8] It was a commonly used expression in London of the 1500s to describe impossibility, originating from the assumption that all swans must be white.[9] According to Taleb, a Black Swan event has three characteristics:

1. It is an outlier and surprise event, as it lies outside the realm of regular expectations, because nothing in the past can convincingly point to its possibility.

2. It carries an extreme impact.

3. In spite of its outlier status, the event is rationalized in hindsight, as if it had been expected.

Taleb's is a concept based on opacity and skepticism, arguing that rare events are not predictable using quantitative modeling and other forecasting tools, which overestimate the value of rational explanations of past data and underestimate the prevalence of unexplainable randomness in those data. Core to Taleb's Black Swan concept is that we know much less than we think we do, and that the past should not be used naively to predict the future.

Taleb suggests that most people ignore Black Swan events because they are more comfortable seeing the world as something structured, ordinary, and comprehensible. Taleb describes this as a type of blindness and opacity consisting of:

- An illusion of understanding of current events.

- A retrospective distortion of historical events.

- An overestimation of factual information, combined with an overvalue of the intellectual elite.

Warning of the global banking crisis—in his 2007 book, *The Black Swan*, and prior to the global financial crisis—Taleb cautioned that globalization creates interlocking fragility, while reducing volatility and giving the appearance of stability. As such it creates catastrophic Black Swans, which can threaten global collapse.[10] The highly interrelated nature of financial markets means that the small economy of a Greece or Portugal can threaten the well-being of some of the largest economies of the world—namely Germany, France, and England.

EXECUTIVE INSIGHT

Black Swans Are Not as Rare as You Might Think

Nicholas Taleb's notion that nothing in the past can convincingly point to the possibility of a Black Swan event makes sense—unless you are a student of history. Throughout history, markets have waxed and waned, boomed and crashed. Twentieth-century history is full of panics, crises, and major wars that will frustrate any modeling regime. The nature of markets is never a straight line of steady growth—a concept that many market followers seem to embrace.

The real estate crash of 2008 is hardly a Black Swan beyond expectation, as the graph below indicates. Common sense would suggest that the most recent huge spike was not sustainable, as it would price all but the richest of buyers out of the housing market. The graph also shows nothing like a straight line of

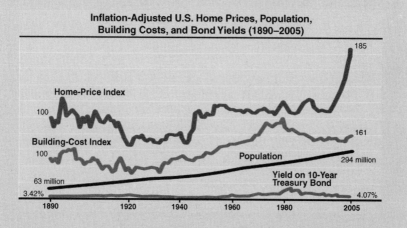

Inflation-Adjusted U.S. Home Prices, Population, Building Costs, and Bond Yields (1890–2005)

Source: Data from Figure 2.1 in Robert J. Shiller, *Irrational Exuberance, Second Edition* (Princeton, NJ: Princeton University Press, 2005).

Executive Insight (continued)

steady growth, but rather several peaks and valleys over the last century. It could be argued that the real Black Swan was the spike that began in 2004. For the prior 50 years, housing prices, adjusted for inflation, had been relatively flat.

The lesson from Black Swan events for risk managers is that rare events with major consequences are poorly dealt with by conventional statistics, forecasting, and modeling techniques, but are not as unpredictable as many believe, especially for students of history. The lesson from quantitative modeling is that models can become a crutch and a rationalization for taking on excessive risk. Models are only as good as the data they use and the objectivity of their creators.

Summary

Value at risk and other modeling tools can be useful during periods of normal market fluctuations, but need to be in the hands of skeptical risk managers and used as a check and balance against taking on excessive risk. Tragically, VaR has been widely used by investment managers to give even the most sophisticated of investors a false sense of security.

Notes

1. Joe Nocera, "Risk Management," *New York Times*, January 4, 2009.

2. Alexander McNeil, Rüdiger Frey, and Paul Embrechts, *Quantitative Risk Management: Concepts Techniques and Tools* (Princeton, NJ: Princeton University Press, 2005).

3. Nassim Nicholas Taleb, *The Black Swan: The Impact of the Highly Improbable* (New York: Random House, 2007).

4. Philippe Jorion, *Value at Risk: The New Benchmark for Controlling Market Risk* (New York: McGraw-Hill, 1996).

5. Philippe Jorion, *Value at Risk: The New Benchmark for Managing Financial Risk*, 3rd ed. (New York: McGraw-Hill, 2006).

6. Ibid.

7. Nocera, "Risk Management."

8. Taleb, *The Black Swan*.

9. Stephanie Baker-Said, "Taleb Outsells Greenspan as Black Swan Gives Worst Turbulence," (Bloomberg, March 27, 2008), available online at http://bloomberg.com/apps/news?pid=20601109&sid=aHfkhe8.C._8&refer=home.

10. Taleb, *The Black Swan*.

CHAPTER 12

Volatility, Risk Aversion, and Portfolio Management

with Deborah Cernauskas, PhD

After reading this chapter, you will learn how to:

- Calculate volatility.
- Understand the relationship between utility and risk aversion.
- Apply the processes and tools of portfolio management.
- Avoid the landmines of portfolio management.

The concepts of volatility, risk aversion, and investment-based portfolio management are interconnected in some interesting ways. Most portfolio management strategies are based on the notions of volatility and risk aversion. Many approaches to portfolio management, such as modern portfolio theory (MPT) and the efficient market hypothesis (EMH), use volatility as their measure of risk. Most portfolio management models share the following underlying assumptions around volatility and risk aversion:

- Investors are typically risk adverse.

- Investors rate and rank investment opportunities by their risk-weighted returns.

- Investors will accept lower returns from less risky and less volatile investments.

- Investors will accept more risky and volatile investments promising greater returns.

Volatility, Utility, and Risk Aversion

Volatility, utility (or economic value), and risk aversion are major and interconnected themes in portfolio management.

Volatility

Typically, *volatility* in investments refers to the standard deviation of continuously compounded returns of financial instruments over a given period of time. It is typically expressed in annualized terms as a fraction of the mean (10 percent) or an absolute number ($10). Volatility is usually seen as representing uncertainty and risk, which can be either positive or negative, depending on the investment strategy. In certain markets, volatility is directly traded through such derivative instruments as options and variance swaps.

Standard deviation is a common means of calculating volatility. The standard deviation of a data set is the square root of its variance. It shows how much variation there is from the mean or average. A low standard deviation indicates that the data points tend to be very close to the mean, whereas high standard deviation indicates that the data are spread out over a large range of values. The wider the standard deviation, the greater the volatility.

In calculating standard deviations, all differences are squared, so that negative and positive differences are combined into one quantity.

Therefore, volatility does not measure the direction of price changes, merely how dispersed they are expected to be. Annualized volatility σ is the standard deviation of an instrument's logarithmic returns over a year. Volatility σ_T for time horizon T in years is expressed as:

$$\sigma_T = \sigma\sqrt{T}$$

Consider a stock with an annual volatility of 25 percent (i.e., $\sigma = .25$). The six-month volatility is found by multiplying the annual volatility by the square root of time.

$$\sigma_{6month} = \sigma_{annual} x\sqrt{T} = .25x\sqrt{0.5} = 0.1768$$

If the daily logarithmic returns of a stock have a standard deviation of σ_{SD} and the time period of returns is P, the annualized volatility is expressed as:

$$\sigma = \frac{\sigma_{SD}}{\sqrt{P}}$$

Markowitz, Sharpe, and others decided to define risk as volatility, assuming the greater a portfolio's volatility, the greater its risk.[1] As such, volatility would be measured either in terms of beta or standard deviation. Many economists favored this definition of risk, because it is based on the assumption that investors should be risk averse and act in a rational manner—not taking on risks unless justified by a preponderance of supporting evidence pointing to greater rewards.

There are problems with the acceptance of volatility as a definition of risk. Investors are concerned about downside volatility, but few of them show concerns over upside volatility. According to Haugen and Heins and Murphy, there is no compelling evidence that high volatility yields better returns or that lower volatility yields lower returns; that is, there is no significant correlation between risk, as defined as volatility, and returns.[2,3]

Utility

In economics, *utility* is a measure of relative satisfaction. A straight-line utility function reflects a risk-neutral profile while a concave utility function reflects risk aversion. Daniel Bernoulli proposed an expected utility hypothesis that investors' acceptance of risk should factor not just potential losses but also the utility, or intrinsic value, of the investment itself. Bernoulli's hypothesis is similar to the notion of diminishing marginal returns, and maintains that investors not accept a highly risky investment choice if the potential returns will provide little utility, or value.[4]

Risk Aversion

In finance, *risk aversion* (risk tolerance) is the general reluctance of an investor to accept the promise of a higher return that comes with greater risk, an uncertain payoff. A risk-averse investor might choose to put his or her money into treasury bills with a very low, but guaranteed, interest rate, rather than into stocks offering higher returns that come with the risk of becoming worthless. Applied to portfolio management, risk aversion is the additional marginal reward an investor requires to accept additional risk. The curvature of the investor's utility function portrays the investor's risk attitude.

Risk aversion versus risk acceptance can change with the age of investors. Younger investors who still have their highest income-earning years ahead of them can be expected to accept greater volatility and risks for investments offering higher potential returns. Conversely, older investors with adequate savings will be unwilling to accept higher volatility and risks because the potential rewards are not likely to be worth the risk.

Risk aversion can wax and wane during economic cycles as well. The global financial crisis of 2008 has traumatized many investors who will resist coming back into markets, regardless of how good the news of a recovery is. As in past cycles, such risk aversion will melt away after a few good years of recovery—memories can be short for those who are optimistic about the future.

EXECUTIVE INSIGHT

Limitations of Volatility in Portfolio Management

The standard deviation or volatility of asset returns is generally accepted as a measure of risk. This has been the case since the early 1950s, when Harry Markowitz defined risk in this manner. In spite of this, volatility does have some limitations.

- Volatility is not constant over time and is characterized by clustering; that is, large price changes typically are found in clusters. This feature indicates that asset returns are not independent across time.

- Volatility does not differentiate between prices falling or prices rising in value.

- Volatility is not additive across assets or time.

Are there alternatives to using the standard deviation as a risk measure?

- Semivariance uses only the returns below the mean in the calculation of the standard deviation.

- Shortfall probability is the probability that a return will fall below a target amount.

- Value at risk, as described in Chapter 11, is well accepted and widely applied to measure a portfolio's risk boundaries over periods of time.

Sources: See Eugene F. Fama and Kenneth R. French, "Common risk factors in the returns on stocks and bonds," *Journal of Financial Economics*, vol. 33, Issue 1, (February 1993) 3–56, and Eugene F. Fama and Kenneth R. French, "The Cross-Section of Expected Stock Returns," *Journal of Finance*, 67 (1992), 427–465.

Portfolio Management

In finance, a *portfolio* is an appropriate mix or collection of investments held by institutions or a private individual. Diversification is a key component in most approaches to portfolio management, as creating a diversified portfolio of investments reduces risks. It is the simple notion of not putting all your eggs in one basket—by owning several assets, certain types of risk can be reduced. The portfolio's assets can include real estate, gold certificates, bonds, stocks, warrants, futures contracts, production facilities, or other items that are expected to retain their value over the investment period.

Portfolio management is a three-step process:

Step 1. Investment analysis. This is the process of conducting your own investment analysis or relying on a third party, such as a financial institution, or financial advisor that offers investment research and advice.

Step 2. Portfolio management. This is the process of deciding which assets to include in the portfolio, in what proportion, and in what time, in order to meet the goals of the portfolio owner.

Step 3. Performance measurement. This is the process of selecting performance metrics and tracking the portfolio against them. Typically this includes the return on the portfolio against its risk, and comparing expected portfolios returns for different asset bundles.

Portfolio management typically includes the following features and processes:

- **Asset allocation.** This is the process of distributing asset holdings among various asset classes, such as money markets, equities, and bonds, with the goal of constraining the portfolio's risk.

- **Real time.** For many financial instruments, it is necessary to maintain portfolios in real or near–real time. For sophisticated traders, real time has come down to computer-generated transactions that react in less than a millisecond.

- **Reconciliation.** For many investors, it is essential to capture and reconcile actual positions on a daily basis. Before the advent of high-speed computers, this was a much more challenging task.

- **Completeness.** This is the ability to capture and display the value of all securities holdings plus any associated unrealized and/or realized profit and loss. It can also include capturing currency balances.

- **Cross asset class.** This is the process of classifying and marketing funds under such asset classes as fixed income, specialist equity, or foreign exchange (FX).

- **Historical data.** Beyond capturing near-term history and real-time transaction data, it is critical to accurately and easily capture historical portfolio data. Ideally, the historical data will be normalized and standardized. Without robust historical data, it is not possible to calculate value at risk (VaR), Sharpe ratios, and volatility.

Alpha

Alpha, also known as *Jensen's Performance Index*, is used to determine the abnormal return of an investment security or portfolio of securities over its theoretical expected return. A positive alpha is the extra return awarded to an investor for taking a risk, instead of accepting the market return (as measured by an index). For example, an alpha of 0.4 means the fund outperformed the market-based return estimate by 0.4 percent. An alpha of −0.6 means a fund's monthly return was 0.6 percent less than would have been predicted from the change in the market alone—the more positive the alpha, the better the return against the market.

The expected return is predicted by an investment model, such as the capital asset pricing model (CAPM), discussed below. The market model uses statistical methods to predict the appropriate risk-adjusted return of an asset. In the case of CAPM, beta is used as a multiplier.

In the CAPM, returns are risk-adjusted so as to factor the relative riskiness of an asset. The assumption is that riskier assets will generate higher returns than less risky assets. A high positive alpha is an indication of abnormally high returns relative to the market. Therefore, investors seek investments with the highest alphas.

Calculating alpha requires the following inputs:

- Market return
- Realized return of the portfolio
- Risk-free rate of return
- The beta of the portfolio (discussed in the next section)

Jensen's alpha = Portfolio Return − [Risk-Free Rate + Portfolio Beta × (Market Return − Risk-Free Rate)]

$$\alpha_J = R_i - \left[R_f + \beta_{iM} \cdot \left(R_M - R_f \right) \right]$$

Jensen's alpha can be negative, positive, or zero. If the alpha is positive, the portfolio is outperforming the market.

Although there is criticism of Jensen's alpha, it is still widely used to evaluate portfolio performance, often in conjunction with the Treynor ratio and Sharpe ratio (both described later in this chapter.)

Beta

The *beta* of a stock or portfolio is an index of the systematic risk[5] due to general market conditions that cannot be diversified away. It is the measure of a fund's or stock's risk in relation to the market. If an asset has a beta of 0, this means that its price has no correlation to the market. A positive beta means that the asset generally follows the market. A negative beta shows that an asset inversely follows the market; that is, the asset typically decreases in value if the market goes up, and vice versa. For example, a beta of 0.7 means the fund's total return is likely to move up or down 70 percent of the market change (as measured by an index); a beta of 1.3 means total return is likely to move up or down 30 percent more than the market.

Put another way, the market, as measured by the S&P 500 or other popular indices, has a beta of 1.0, and individual equities are measured by how much they deviate from the macro market.

Therefore, the larger the beta, the greater the dependency on market movements. For example, a stock with a beta of 2 will follow the market in an overall growth or decline, but will do so by a factor of 2. This means if markets decline by 4 percent, stocks with a beta of 2 will fall by 8 percent.

Beta is also an input to the CAPM, discussed below, by measuring an asset's statistical variance that cannot be mitigated by the portfolio's diversification. The formula for the beta of an asset within a portfolio is:

$$\beta_p = \frac{Cov(r_p, r_M)}{Var(r_M)}$$

where $Cov(r_p, r_M)$ = the covariance between the rates of return
            r_p = the rate of return of the portfolio
            r_M = the rate of return of the market

The calculation of beta is sensitive to the data frequency and the number of observations included.

Betas for portfolios will tend to be more stable than betas for individual assets.

Limitations of Beta in Portfolio Management

Beta views risk solely from the perspective of market prices, and fails to consider economic developments or specific business fundamentals. Beta has the limitation of ignoring price, as if GE selling at $15 per share would not be a lower-risk investment than GE selling at $30 dollars per share.

Beta also does not consider the impact investors, especially large institutional investors, can exert on the volatility and riskiness of their holdings. This can come from proxy fights, shareholder resolutions and lawsuits, or from large stock purchases or sales.

Another beta weakness is its assumption that downside risk and upside growth potential for any asset are fundamentally equal—a function of its volatility compared to the market as a whole. History tells us that past security price volatility can be a poor predictor of future risk.

There is research indicating that beta has poor predictive powers. Fama and French examined 9,500 stocks between 1963 and 1990, concluding that a stock's risk, measured by beta, was not a reliable predictor of performance. Fama stated that "beta as the sole variable in explaining returns on stocks . . . is dead. . . . What we are saying is that over the last 50 years, knowing the volatility of an equity doesn't tell you much about the stock's return."[*]

Beta gives the appearance of a highly sophisticated mathematical formula, but in reality it is data mining. Looking at history, you can find a number of factors that seem to be correlated, but these correlations are more often than not sheer coincidence. It is not unusual for investors to confuse correlation with causation, and to assume correlations can be extrapolated into the future.

[*]Eugene F. Fama and Kenneth R. French, "Common Risk Factors in the Returns on Stocks and Bonds," *Journal of Financial Economics*, 33(1) (February 1993): 3–56.

Models Used in Portfolio Management

Portfolio management can be approached with a variety of models that help in selecting, valuing, and managing a portfolio of investments. They include:

- Single-index model
- Capital asset pricing model—developed independently by Jack Treynor, William Sharpe, John Linter, Jan Mossin, and Harry Markowitz in the 1960s
- Arbitrage pricing theory/model—developed by Stephen Ross in 1976
- Modern portfolio theory—developed by Harry Markowitz in the 1960s
- The Treynor index, also known as the reward-to-volatility ratio—developed by Jack L. Treynor
- The Sharpe ratio/index—developed by William Forsyth Sharpe in 1966
- The Sortino ratio—created by Brian M. Rom in 1986
- Post-modern portfolio theory
- Value at risk (VaR) model

Single-Index Model

The *single-index model* (SIM) is a fairly simple financial asset pricing model commonly used to measure the return and risk of a stock. The formula is expressed as follows:

$$r_{it} - r_f = \alpha_i + \beta_i(r_{mt} - r_f) + \varepsilon_{it}$$
$$\varepsilon_{it} \sim N(0, \sigma_i)$$

where: r_{it} = return to a stock i in period t

r_f = the risk-free investment return rate, such as the interest rate from U.S. Treasury Bills

r_{mt} = the return to the market portfolio in period t

α_i = the stock's alpha, or its abnormal return

β_i = the stock's beta, or its responsiveness to the market return

ε_{it} = the unsystematic or diversifiable risk of the stock

The logic behind SIM is that a stock's return is influenced by the market (beta), but has a company-specific anticipated value (alpha), as well as a company-specific unexpected component (residual). As a means of simplification, SIM assumes only one macroeconomic factor that causes systematic risk impacting all stock returns. This factor can be captured by market index's return rate, such as the FTSE 100 or S&P 500. Using SIM, a stock's return can be broken out into its anticipated excess returns due to company-specific factors, usually referred to as its alpha coefficient (α), anticipated returns due to macroeconomic forces impacting the entire market, and unexpected microeconomic forces impacting only the company.

The single-index model assumes the following:

- Most companies respond similarly to macroeconomic factors, and therefore have a positive covariance.

- Some companies are more sensitive to these macroeconomic factors than others, creating a company-specific variance known as its beta (β).

- The covariance among stocks in a portfolio can be calculated by multiplying their market variance and their betas.

Capital Asset Pricing Model

The *capital asset pricing model* (CAPM) is used to calculate the desired rate of return of an asset to justify its inclusion into a well-diversified portfolio, factoring in its nondiversifiable (systemic or market) risk—often known as its beta (β). CAPM also factors in anticipated returns for a theoretical risk-free asset and anticipated returns for the market.

Working independently in the 1960s, Jack Treynor, William Sharpe, John Lintner, Jan Mossin, and Harry Markowitz all contributed to CAPM's development. Sharpe, Markowitz, and Merton Miller shared the Nobel Prize in Economics for this contribution to the field of financial economics. This gave CAPM a great deal of credibility.

CAPM can be used to predict the expected return of an individual stock or an entire portfolio. For individual stocks, security market line (SML) is used to calculate reward-to-risk ratios for any security in relation to that of the overall market. The formula for CAPM is expressed as:

$$E(R_i) = R_f + \beta_i\big(E(R_m) - R_f\big)$$

where:　$E(R_i)$ = expected return on a capital asset

R_f = the risk-free rate of interest, such as on short-term U.S. Treasury Bills

β_i = the sensitivity of the expected excess asset returns to the expected excess market returns, or also

$$\beta_i = \frac{Cov(R_i, R_m)}{Var(R_m)}$$

$E(R_m)$ = the expected return of the market

$E(R_m) - R_f$ = the *market premium* or *risk premium* (the difference between the expected market rate of return and the risk-free rate of return)

CAPM comes with major shortcomings. It makes assumptions about investors that do not stand up to the light of day. It assumes all investors:

- Are widely diversified across a range of investment categories.
- Are rational and risk-adverse.

- Aim to maximize economic utility.

- Cannot influence market prices.

- Can borrow and lend unlimited amounts under a risk-free interest rate.

- Trade without taxation or transaction costs.

- Have access to the same information as all other investors and at the same time.[6,7]

Arbitrage Pricing Theory

Arbitrage pricing theory (APT) is a general theory of asset pricing. It is based on the law of one price, which states that identical items should be offered at the same price. Otherwise, a riskless profit can be earned by selling the higher-priced item and buying the lower-priced item. Hence, any two assets or portfolios should be priced the same if their risks on return are identical.

APT argues that systematic risk is caused by macroeconomic factors, such as changes in interest rates, and expected returns for a given financial asset can be modeled as a linear function of an unspecified number of macroeconomic forces. In APT, each factor's sensitivity to changes is expressed by its beta coefficient. This will be used to price assets correctly—their price should equal the expected price at the end of a given period, discounted at the rate suggested by the model.

According to this theory, if prices diverge, arbitrage will bring them back into line. Arbitrage is the practice of taking advantage of a state of imbalance between two or more markets and to make a risk-free profit—trading in two assets where one of the assets is mispriced. The arbitrageur sells an asset that is relatively too expensive and uses those proceeds to buy one that is relatively too cheap.

With APT, risky asset returns are said to follow a *factor structure* if they can be expressed as:

$$r_j = E(r_j) + b_{j1}F_1 + b_{j2}F_2 + \ldots b_{jn}F_n + \varepsilon_j$$

where: $E(r_j)$ = the jth asset's expected return

F_k = a systematic factor which is assumed to have mean of zero

b_{jk} = the sensitivity of the jth asset to factor k, also known as *factor loading*

ε_j = the risky asset's idiosyncratic random shock with a mean of zero

APT and CAPM are two influential theories on asset pricing. APT is less restrictive than CAPM by allowing for an explanatory, versus a statistical, model of asset returns. CAPM may be considered a subset of APT in that its securities market line (SML) represents a single-factor model of asset pricing, where beta is exposed to changes in value of the market.

Modern Portfolio Theory

Modern portfolio theory (MPT) is a widely recognized approach to investment based on diversification as a means to maximize returns while minimizing risks. Developed in the 1960s and early 1970s by Harry Markowitz, it was considered an important advance in financial modeling by establishing a formal risk/return framework for investment decision making.

MPT models an asset's return as a random variable, and models a portfolio as a weighted combination of assets so that the return of a portfolio is the weighted combination of the assets' returns. The return on a portfolio can be expressed as:

$$r_p = \sum_{i=1}^{n} w_i r_i$$

where: w_i = the weight of asset i in the portfolio

r_i = the return on asset i

MPT's mathematical concept of investment diversification has the goal of selecting a portfolio of assets that has the maximum expected return at its level of risk, or alternatively, the minimum risk at a selected expected return level. Portfolio diversification is the key. The variance of the returns of a portfolio takes into account how assets move in relation to each other. Consider a portfolio composed of two assets. The variance of the portfolio is given by:

$$\sigma_p^2 = w_i^2 \sigma_i^2 + w_j^2 \sigma_j^2 + 2w_i w_j \sigma_{ij}$$

where: σ_i^2 is the variance of asset i

w_i is the proportion of wealth held in asset i

σ_{ij} is the covariance of assets i and j

An undiversified portfolio will have a positive covariance term in the above equation, which will serve to increase the portfolio variance. For example, a portfolio comprised of HP and IBM will be undiversified with a positive covariance term and a high portfolio variance, that is, a high risk. Alternatively, a portfolio comprised of any two assets with a zero or negative covariance will be diversified. As the number of assets in the portfolio increases, the variance of individual assets representing firm-specific risk can be diversified away. The main risk left facing the portfolio investor is the covariance risk.

EXECUTIVE INSIGHT

Limitations of Modern Portfolio Theory

MPT makes several assumptions about investors and markets that are not entirely true, limiting its effectiveness. MPT assumes the following:

- **Asset returns are normally distributed random variables.** In reality, equity returns typically are not normally distributed—

sometimes they exhibit large swings in standard deviations from the mean.[*]

- **Correlations between assets are fixed and constant.** In reality, correlations depend on systemic relationships between their underlying assets, and change when these relationships change.

- **All investors are rational and risk-averse.** The global financial crisis is just the latest example of how irrational and reckless investors can be. Even more disturbing were the many examples of sophisticated and institutional investors who followed a herd mentality.

- **All investors have access to the same information at the same time.** In fact, there exists a major asymmetry in market information based on access to massive computing technology, real-time positions, and market expertise, as well as a variety of other factors.

- **Investors have an accurate conception of possible returns.** Unfortunately, an investor's expectations may be biased and unrealistic, possibly causing market prices to be inefficient.[†]

- **There are no transaction or tax costs.** Of course, all financial products are subject to both transaction and tax costs.

- **Investors' actions do not influence prices.** In reality, large purchases or sales of a given asset can shift its market price or the market price of a class of assets.

- **Investors can borrow or lend unlimited amounts at a risk-free rate of interest.** Of course, all investors have credit limits.

Note: CAPM makes many of these same assumptions.

---

[*]Mandelbrot, B., and Hudson, R. L. (2004). *The (Mis)Behaviour of Markets: A Fractal View of Risk, Ruin, and Reward*. London: Profile Books.

[†]Kent D. Daniel, David Hirshleifer and Avanidhar Subrahmanyam. "Overconfidence, Arbitrage, and Equilibrium Asset Pricing," *Journal of Finance*, 56(3) (June, 2001): 921–965.

Treynor Ratio

The *Treynor ratio*, also known as the *reward-to-volatility ratio*, is a measurement of the returns earned in excess of that which could have been earned on an investment that has no diversifiable risk, such as U.S. Treasury Bills, or on a completely diversified portfolio. Treynor's ratio relates excess returns over risk-free rates to the additional systemic risks taken. Accordingly, the higher the Treynor ratio, the higher the portfolio's return. The Treynor ratio, like the Sharpe ratio (discussed in the next section), does not quantify the value added by active portfolio management. It is simply a ranking criterion and typically only useful for subportfolios of a broader and more fully diversified portfolio.

The formula is:

$$T = \frac{r_i - r_f}{\beta_i}$$

where T = Treynor ratio
r_i = portfolio i's return
r_f = risk-free rate of return
β_I = Portfolio i's Beta

Sharpe Ratio

The *Sharpe ratio*, also known as the *reward-to-variability ratio*, is a measure of an investment fund's excess return (or risk premium) relative to the total variability of the fund's holdings. Therefore, the higher the Sharpe ratio, the better the fund's historical risk-adjusted performance. Since an asset with a higher Sharpe ratio gives a greater return for the same risk, investors are often advised to select investments with higher Sharpe ratios. Sharpe ratios, along with Jensen's alpha and Treynor ratios, are often used to rank the performance of portfolios and fund managers.

In its current configuration, its formula is:

$$S = \frac{R - R_f}{\sigma} = \frac{E[R - R_f]}{\sqrt{var[R - R_f]}},$$

where $R =$ the asset return

$R_f =$ the return on a benchmark asset, such as the risk-free rate of return,

$E[R - R_f] =$ the expected value of the excess of the asset return over the benchmark return

$\sigma =$ the standard deviation of the asset[8]

Sortino Ratio

The *Sortino ratio* measures the risk-adjusted return of a portfolio or individual asset. It is a modification of, and improvement over, the Sharpe ratio, as it only penalizes those returns falling below a required rate of return, or a user-defined target. The Sharpe ratio has a major weakness in that it penalizes both downside and upside volatility equally. Advocates of the Sortino ratio argue that it is a more realistic measure of risk-adjusted returns then the Sharpe ratio. The Sortino ratio was created by Brian M. Rom in 1986 as a component of post-modern portfolio theory, discussed in the next section.[9]

The Sortino ratio is calculated as:

$$S = \frac{R - T}{DR}$$

where: $R =$ the asset or portfolio realized return

$T =$ the target or required rate of return for the investment strategy under consideration

$DR =$ the downside risk

Post-Modern Portfolio Theory

Post-modern portfolio theory (PMPT) is a modification of, and expansion on, modern portfolio theory (MPT). They have in common the goal of demonstrating how investors can use diversification to optimize their portfolios, and how risky assets should be priced. PMPT attempts to address two major weaknesses in MPT:

1. MPT assumes variance of portfolio returns is the correct measure of investment risk.

2. Investment returns for all individual assets and portfolios can be represented by their normal distribution.

MPT is limited by measures of returns and risks that do not always represent the realities of the investment markets. Using standard deviation has the limitation of implying that better-than-expected returns are just as risky as those returns that are worse than expected. Most investors believe that risk involves negative outcomes and therefore do not view returns above a minimum as risky.[10]

Recent advances in finance and portfolio theory, along with high-speed computers, have overcome the limitations of MPT. The result is an expanded risk/return paradigm known as post-modern portfolio theory. Advocates of PMPT argue that it improves on MPT by accepting that investors prefer upside volatility over downside volatility and creating the three-parameter log-normal distribution, a more robust investment model.

Value at Risk Method

Value at risk is a very popular tool used in portfolio risk management and market risk management. The VaR techniques described in Chapter 11, "Market Risk," are applied to portfolio risk as well as market risk.

Landmines to Avoid in Portfolio Management

In this chapter, we provide brief introductions to a variety of portfolio management techniques and include Executive Insights warning as to their limitations. This is a critical point for any investor or risk manager.

Even the most sophisticated modeling scheme relies on a combination of historical data and then applies assumptions to project future developments. The massive failures of the big investment firms and global banks are the best evidence of just how fragile these models can be.

Our tip here is to always proceed with a great deal of caution. Do not become so emotionally involved that you jump into a hot market that is actually a bubble—sometimes the best strategy is to sit on the sidelines. Finally, do not be intimidated by those with prestigious credentials advocating for their pet modeling techniques. Far too often, those using these models have failed the common sense and common decency test.

Summary

The area of portfolio management will continue to receive a great deal of attention as investors look for a breakthrough technique or technology that will provide an edge in making wise buying and selling decisions. The science and math have advanced in significant ways over the past 30 years. This creates an opportunity and a risk. Technology can improve decision making, but the risk comes in an overreliance on the technology at the expense of qualitative factors, including subject matter expertise, experience, and the lessons of history.

Notes

1. Bob Seawright, "The Limits of Modern Portfolio Theory," *The Signal*, January 12, 2009, http://thesignalinthenoise.blogspot.com/2009/01/limits-of-modern-portfolio-theory.html.

2. J. Michael Murphy, "Efficient Markets, Index Funds, Illusion, and Reality," *Journal of Portfolio Management* (Fall 1977): 5–20.

3. Haugen and Heins, "Risk and the Rate of Return on Financial Assets: Some Old Wine in New Bottles," *Journal of Financial and Quantitative Analysis* (December 1975): 775–784.

4. K. J. Arrow, "The theory of risk aversion," in *Aspects of the Theory of Risk Bearing*, by Yrjo Jahnssonin Saatio (Chicago: Markham, 1971), 90–110.

5. In this context, total risk = systematic risk + nonsystematic (diversifiable) risk.

6. See Benoit Mandelbrot and Richard Hudson, *The Misbehavior of Markets: A Fractal View of Risk, Ruin, and Reward* (London: Profile Books, 2004).

7. See Kent D. Daniel, David Hirshleifer, and Avanidhar Subrahmanyam, "Overconfidence, Arbitrage, and Equilibrium Asset Pricing," *Journal of Finance*, 56(3) (June 2001): 921–965.

8. William F. Sharpe, "The Sharpe Ratio," *Journal of Portfolio Management* 21(1) (1994): 49–58.

9. Stephen Satchel and Christian S. Pedersen, "On the Foundation of Performance Measures under Asymmetric Returns," February 12, 2002, www.sortino.com/htm/satchell.pdf.

10. Ashraf Chaudhry and Helen L. Johnson, "The Efficacy of the Sortino Ratio and Other Benchmarked Performance Measures under Skewed Return Distributions," *Australian Journal of Management*, 32(3), March 2008.

CHAPTER 13

Credit Risk

with Deborah Cernauskas, PhD

After reading this chapter, you will learn how to:

- Differentiate the major types of credit risk.
- Calculate expected losses.
- Grasp the pivotal role Basel II plays in global banking.
- Consider sovereign risk in investment decisions.

Credit risk is the potential that a borrower or counterparty will fail to meet its obligations to a lender or other creditors in accordance with agreed-on terms. The goal of credit risk management is to maximize a bank or other creditor's risk-adjusted rate of return by maintaining credit risk exposure within acceptable parameters.

While liquidity, operational, and market risk are addressed by the Bank for International Settlements (BIS) in its Basel II accords, financial institutions continue to be most concerned about counterparty credit risk for their individual retail and wholesale customers, and for entire portfolios. The major causes of their problems continue to be directly related to credit risk:

- Lax credit standards for borrowers and counterparties.
- Poor portfolio risk management.

- Lack of attention to changes in economic or other circumstances that can lead to deterioration in the credit standing of a bank's counterparties.

Financial institutions also need to consider the relationships between credit risk and other risks.

Market risk and credit risk are very much interdependent, as was demonstrated in the mortgage crisis. As markets declined, more borrowers delayed payments, defaulted on their loans, or simply walked away from their homes.

Because of its importance, banks and other lenders need to measure credit risk for the following reasons:

- **Risk-based pricing**—Rates are higher for high-risk borrowers.

- **Risk-sensitive capital allocation**—This is needed for prudent and realistic allowances to cover credit risk defaults and other problems.

- **Risk-based reporting**—There are regulatory, market disclosure, and external rating requirements that mandate an accurate portrayal of credit risk exposure.

For many banks, loans are the largest and most obvious source of credit risk; however, other sources of credit risk exist throughout the activities of a bank, including:

- In their banking and trading book.

- On and off the balance sheet.

- Various financial instruments other than loans, including acceptances, interbank transactions, trade financing, foreign exchange transactions, financial futures, swaps, bonds, equities, options, in the extension of commitments and guarantees, and the settlement of transactions.

There are three major types of credit risk: counterparty risk, sovereign (country) risk, and foreign exchange (settlement) risk.

Counterparty Risk

Counterparty risk is the risk that a bank or other lender's counterparty will fail to perform during the life of the credit/loan transaction. In most cases, failure to perform is caused by financial deterioration or collapse, although some failures may also be willful, such as mortgage borrowers who walked away because they were underwater (i.e., they owed more than the property was worth).

Sovereign or Country Risk

Sovereign or country risk is the risk that an investor faces when a country's economic conditions deteriorate, it suffers political and social upheaval, it nationalizes and expropriates assets, the government defaults on its debts, or it significantly depreciates or devalues its currencies. In some cases, it can be a combination of these factors; for example, Greece in 2010.

Foreign Exchange Risk

Foreign exchange (FX) risk, also known as *replacement* or *settlement* risk, is the exposure to the potential impact of movements in foreign exchange rates. The risk is that adverse fluctuations in exchange rates may result in a loss in local currency to a financial institution. It can arise from two factors: currency mismatches in an institution's assets and liabilities—both on- and off-balance-sheet—that are not subject to a fixed exchange rate, and currency cash flow mismatches.

Basic Components of and Factors in Credit Risk

There are five basic components to credit risk management that form the foundation to even the most advanced approaches:

1. Probability of default
2. Exposure at default

3. Loss given default

4. Expected loss

5. Unexpected losses

Probability of Default

Probability of default (PD) is the probability that a borrower will default, typically over the next 12 months. Under the more demanding regulatory requirements, such as Basel II, lenders are required to internally estimate the probability of default associated with each borrower grade. Each risk ratings grade is mapped to an appropriate estimate of PD.

Exposure at Default

Exposure at default (EAD) is defined as the economic value of the exposure upon default of the borrower. In most cases the EAD will equal the nominal amount of the loan facility. (In finance, a facility is a loan extended to a borrower in need of operating capital.) Under the more demanding regulatory approaches, exposure at default is calculated as the outstanding balance plus a portion of the undrawn amount. All other things being equal, the higher the exposure at default, the higher the risk to the borrower, and hence the higher a bank's capital charges for the exposure. Commitments that have not been fully drawn require empirically derived estimates based on future lending prior to default. National regulators may provide supervisory estimates for undrawn commitments in the event of a transition from the foundation approach to the advanced approach.

Loss Given Default

Loss given default (LGD) is expressed as a percentage and applies to a specific loan or facility. LGD estimates the portion of the loan or facility that would be lost in the event of a default. For example, an LGD of 45 percent would mean that 45 percent of the outstanding loan balance is expected to be lost if the borrower defaults. The LGD percentage would be lowered if the loan were to be collateralized, guaranteed, or risk-mitigated in some way. In the more demanding regulatory regimes, such as Basel II, the effect of collateral on loans is captured through the LGD. Hence, the higher the collateral value, the lower the LGD and the lower the capital charge for the exposure represented by the loan.

Expected Loss

Basel II's advanced approach to credit risk allows lenders to internally estimate the three major risk components in an exposure (PD, LGD, and EAD) as a means to calculate their expected losses. The probability of default (PD) of a borrower or group of borrowers is the central measurable concept on which Basel's most advanced approach to credit risk, the Internal Ratings-Based (IRB) Approach, is based, but lenders also need to measure how much they could lose should a borrower default on an obligation. This is contingent on two elements: (1) LGD providing an estimate of the magnitude of likely loss, and (2) EAD providing an estimate of the amount of the exposure to the borrower at the time of default. Expected loss is thus calculated as follows, with PD and LDG as a percentage and EAD as a dollar or other financial amount:

Unexpected Losses

One of the functions of bank capital is to provide a buffer to protect a bank's debt holders against peak losses that exceed expected levels. Peak losses do not occur every year, but when they occur, they can be very large. Losses above expected levels are usually referred to as unexpected losses and include Black Swans, rare but catastrophic events that challenge even the most prudent risk management regimes. Financial institutions know they will occur now and then, but they cannot know in advance their timing or severity. Ego, arrogance, and ignorance can all play a role in contributing to unexpected losses or Black Swans. Many investment firms well understood that the credit bubble of the past decade could not continue unabated, but believed they would be able to jump out in time to avoid disaster. History proved them wrong.

There are four basic factors that go into credit risks. They can be characterized as external and internal factors and consist of:

1. **Industry Risk (External)**—Industry characteristics and financials.
2. **Business Risk (Internal)**—Market positions, operating efficiencies.
3. **Management Risk (Internal)**—Track record, creditability, payment record.
4. **Financial Risk (Internal)**—Existing and future financial position, financial flexibility, accounting quality.

Basel II's Treatment of Credit Risk

In 2004, the Basel Committee of the Bank for International Settlements introduced an update to its earlier Basel Capital Accord. Known as Basel II, it included:

- A three pillar approach:

  Pillar 1—Capital calculation

  Pillar 2—Regulatory oversight

  Pillar 3—Market disclosure

- The introduction of operational risk, based on indicators (Basic or Standardized) or on a comprehensive approach (Advanced Measurement)

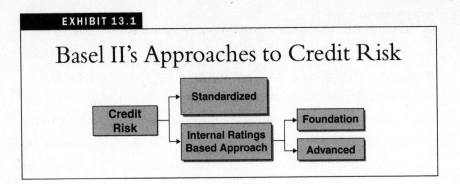

EXHIBIT 13.1

Basel II's Approaches to Credit Risk

- Two approaches to credit risk (see Exhibit 13.1):

  1. Standardized Approach, which is similar to Basel I but uses credit ratings to distinguish between risks

  2. IRB approaches, which are closer to economic capital appro aches based on expected losses (loss estimates based on internal ratings of each bank), referred to as Foundation and Advanced Approaches

Basel II's Standardized Approach

The Standardized Approach under Basel I and Basel II uses the concept of risk-weighted assets to measure a bank's on-balance-sheet credit risk. Each asset class (sovereign debt, interbank assets, residential mortgages and all other on-balance-sheet exposures) is assigned a risk weighting. The total risk-weighted asset value is calculated by multiplying the risk weights by the asset class value.

At a high level, Basel II differs from Basel I in the following ways:

- Basel II utilizes more asset classes (sovereign debt; corporate and commercial mortgages; residential mortgages; other retail loans; past due loans; securitized issues; and all others) than Basel I.

- The risk weights are assigned based on asset class and credit rating grade (ratings from an independent credit rating agency).

- Basel II incorporates allowances for financial collateral.

EXHIBIT 13.2					
Risk Weight Based on Credit Rating					
Credit Rating	AAA to AA−	A+ to A−	BBB+ to BBB−	BB+ to B−	Below B−	Unrated
Risk Weight	0%	20%	50%	100%	150%	100%

Source: International Convergence of Capital Measurement and Capital Standards, Part 2— The First Pillar Minimum Capital Requirements, Bank for International Settlements, June 2006.

For example, Exhibit 13.2 shows the risk weights based on credit rating for sovereign debt.

Basel II's Internal Ratings-Based Approach

The good news in Basel II is that under its Internal Ratings-Based approach, financial institutions are allowed to use their own internal measures for key drivers of credit risk as primary inputs to the capital calculation, subject to meeting certain conditions and to explicit supervisory approval. The bad news is that the IRB requires a high level of financial rigor and effort by both its business and information technology (IT) groups. The IRB approach allows financial institutions to determine the borrowers' probabilities of default. The Advanced IRB approach (AIRB) allows financial institutions to rely on their own estimates of LGD and EAD on an exposure-by-exposure basis. These risk measures are converted into risk weights and regulatory capital requirements by means of risk weight formulas specified by the Basel Committee.

Exhibit 13.3 captures the high level of financial and accounting rigor required to comply with Basel II's IRB approach to credit risk.

Ratings and Scoring in Credit Risk

Internal approaches to credit risk rely on rating and scoring systems. Ratings are typically applied to organizations and scores are applied to individuals. Ratings use both qualitative and quantitative methods, while scoring relies primarily on quantitative methods.

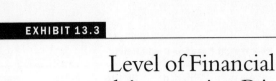

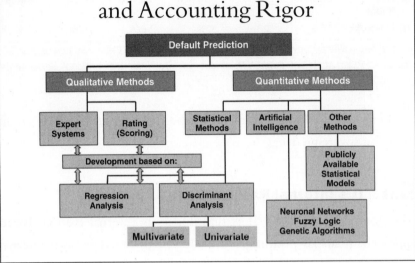

Level of Financial and Accounting Rigor

Rating

Typically, a *rating* is the evaluation or assessment of something, in terms of quality (as with a critic rating a novel), quantity (as with an athlete being rated by his or her statistics), or some combination of both. A rating is a standardized, objective method for quantitative and qualitative evaluation of a borrower by evaluating specific criteria individually and combining them into a final result in order to determine the current and future creditworthiness.

Scoring

Scoring includes a statistical prognosis method of individual borrowers that relies primarily on quantitative analysis of various risk characteristics, including socioeconomic characteristics, such as age or marital status. For example, a mortgage credit score may include payment history on existing and/or previous mortgages, while a consumer credit score may include past-due balances on revolving bank and department-store credit cards. The score may also include public records, such as previous collections, bankruptcies, collections, and foreclosures. Debt ratio is also an important factor in scoring creditworthiness. Lenders calculate debt ratio by dividing the total monthly debts (the housing expenses for the proposed loan plus the borrower's other monthly credit obligations) by the total monthly income. Mortgage lenders and other creditors frequently use credit scores, known as *FICO* scores, to determine the credit risk (FICO stands for the Fair Isaac Company, which originated the system). The higher the credit score, the better the credit risk.

EXECUTIVE INSIGHT

Early Warnings of a Credit Bubble

In 2003, the Bank of International Settlements published a working paper by Linda Alan and Anthony Saunders, "A Survey of Cyclical Effects in Credit Risk Measurement Models," which warned that credit risk models could accentuate "procyclical tendencies of banking" with the potential to impact the global economy. They noted that credit models applied very optimistic forecasts of default risk during boom periods, reinforcing natural tendencies of major and global banks to overextend lending at the very point in the cycle when they should have begun to restrain lending. During contraction periods, the same credit risk models could be overly pessimistic. Even if the central banks create expansionary monetary policies, the banks, relying on these models, will resist lending.

The authors also warned that the Basel Committee's push to utilize such credit risk models as CreditMetrics as the basis for capital adequacy requirements could further "accentuate the procyclical nature of banking unless the credit cycle and its effect on credit risk are appropriately recognized in the model structure."[*]

---

[*]Linda Allen and Anthony Saunders, "A survey of cyclical effects in credit risk measurement models," *BIS Working Papers*, No. 126, (January 2003).

Sovereign Risk

Sovereign or country risk is the threat that a government (a sovereign) will either default on its obligations or will impose regulations that restrict issuers in that country from meeting their obligations. Sovereign debt is financing made with a national government as a contracting party. It is usually accepted as less risky than dealing with local private companies. Sovereign risk management therefore includes assessing the creditworthiness of a national government.

Lending to a national government in its own sovereign currency is often considered to be practically risk-free—or a risk-free interest rate. The accepted argument is that it is risk-free because governments can repay their obligations by raising tax receipts, reducing spending, or by simply printing more money—a common practice during the global financial crisis of 2008. U.S. Treasury bonds denominated in U.S. dollars are usually considered risk-free within the United States, but this disregards the risk to buyers outside the United States of the dollar's depreciation relative to the buyer's home country currency. America's risk-free status implies the stability of the U.S. government and its ability to continue repayments during any financial crisis.

The 2010 sovereign debt crisis in Greece and other European countries highlights that sovereign debt is not always risk-free. Accordingly, market interest rates tend to vary depending on debt levels and overall health of national economies. Politically unstable states are rarely considered risk-free, regardless of their debt levels. Examples include revolutionary Russia in 1917, which refused to accept the responsibility for Imperial Russia's foreign debt.[1]

Subsovereign debt is lending to a local or municipal government. It can be as risky as private lending unless the local or municipal government has adequate authority to tax or reduce spending. In this way, local governments can meet their debt obligations just as national governments can. In some cases, local government debts are guaranteed by national governments to reduce risks.

Using a ratio of debt to gross domestic product (GDP) is one of the most accepted measures of assessing a nation's debt. A commonly used method to calculate the ratio is government debt divided by GDP. Another commonly used ratio is the total debt to GDP, which reflects the nation's entire financial position.

TIPS AND TECHNIQUES

Sovereign Debt Heat Maps

On February 18, 2010, the Royal Bank of Canada (RBC) published a heat map comparing the sovereign risk of several countries based on six indices. Ironically, Ireland is viewed by RBC's heat map as a larger risk than Greece, which was the focus of much of the global financial press in mid-2010.

Developed countries	Percent of Gross Domestic Product						Sovereign Risk Index
	Fiscal Balance	Structural Balance	Gross Public Debt	Net Public Debt	Interest Payments	Government Spending	
Ireland							0.98
Greece							0.90
Portugal							0.59
Britain							0.52
Italy							0.43
France							0.37
Spain							0.33
Japan							0.28
United States							0.21
Belgium							0.15
Austria							0.14
Netherlands							0.08
Germany							-0.06
Canada							-0.19
Finland							-0.39
Denmark							-0.45
New Zealand							-0.49
Australia							-0.52
Sweden							-0.59
Switzerland							-1.06
Norway							-1.32

Extremely higher than average	Significantly higher than average	Somewhat higher than average	Average or below

In calculating the sovereign risk index, RBC included other factors, such as current account, foreign exchange reserves, net external debt, real GDP growth, and inflation, which are not included here.

Source: "Royal Bank of Canada Sovereign Risk Heat Map." www.ibankcoin .com/peanut_gallery/index.php/2010/03/08/12752. March 8, 2010.

Foreign Exchange Risk

Foreign exchange (FX) settlement risk is the risk of loss when a financial institution in a foreign exchange transaction pays the currency it sold, but does not receive the currency it bought. FX settlement failures can arise from operational issues, counterparty default, liquidity constraints, and other factors. Settlement risk exists for any traded product, but given the size of the foreign exchange market, for many banks FX transactions form the greatest source of settlement risk exposure. For large banks, FX transactions can involve credit exposures amounting to tens of billions of dollars each day, and in some cases, exposures to a single counterparty in excess of an institution's capital.

FX settlement risk has both credit risk and liquidity risk dimensions. If a bank cannot make the payment of the currency it sold conditional on its final receipt of the currency it bought, it faces the possibility of losing the full principal value of the transaction. Even temporary delays in settlement can expose a receiving bank to liquidity pressures if unsettled funds are needed to meet obligations to other parties. Such liquidity exposure can be severe if the unsettled amounts are large and alternative sources of funds must be raised on short notice in turbulent or unreceptive markets. Finally, FX settlement risk also has a wider systemic risk dimension.[2]

EXECUTIVE INSIGHT

Bank for International Settlements Has a Big Say in Local and Global Lending

The Bank for International Settlements (BIS), located in Basel, Switzerland, is arguably the world's oldest international organization, founded by the Hague Agreement in 1930. (The Red Cross, also founded in Switzerland, is much older, but consists of several distinct organizations that are legally independent from each other.)

The BIS is the central bank for central banks, and although it has no actual legal authority, it sets the supervisory framework and risk standards for virtually all major banks in the world. The BIS's framework and risk standards trickle down and impact regional and local banks as well.

The bank was originally intended to facilitate money transfers and settlements arising from settling an obligation from the Treaty of Versailles at the end of World War I. Allegations that the BIS had helped Nazi Germany loot assets from occupied countries during World War II led to a movement for its dissolution by the United States. The successful effort to save the BIS was led by the United Kingdom and its delegation leader, John Maynard Keynes.

The influence of the BIS cannot be overestimated. All the leading economies of the world have embraced its Basel II Capital Accords for banks. The reasons are simple: Basel II is essential to establish a nation's banking soundness and transparency, and therefore vital as a means to attract global capital.

Although the accords make some provisions for regional and local banks, the massive weight of the regulations fosters the continued consolidation of banking. It should be noted that most regional and local banks, with their less sophisticated risk frameworks, fared better than the majority of the world's largest banks, especially those in the EU under Basel II.

The BIS web site (http://bis.org) is a valuable resource for anyone interested in best practice risk frameworks and standards for credit, market, operational, and liquidity risk.

Summary

The primary thrust of this chapter is around the credit risk that banks and other financial institutions face, but it should be noted that all institutions that are *not* conducting business on a cash basis are exposed to credit risk.

For most nonfinancial institutions, credit risk as a lender is not a primary concern, but it is a significant issue for a borrower. The availability of credit is essential to all but the most cash-rich organizations. So it is important to understand the fundamentals of credit risk, even if you never intend on making a loan.

A common theme of this book is that all types of risk management failures contributed to the global financial crisis, but credit was by far the biggest factor. What has been commonly described as a real estate bubble of the last decade was actually a credit bubble in which historically sound practices and governance over lending and borrowing were ignored.

Notes

1. Niall Ferguson, *The Cash Nexus: Money and Power in the Modern World, 1700–2000* (New York: Basic Books, 2002).
2. Basel Committee Consultative Paper, "Supervisory Guidance For Managing Settlement Risk in Foreign Exchange Transactions," November 30, 1999.

CHAPTER 14

Corporate Governance and Compensation

After reading this chapter, you will learn how to:

- Improve corporate board performance.
- Reform executive compensation.
- Increase board diversity as a means to improve governance.
- Make the case for a board-level risk committee.

The popular perceptions of corporate governance have changed significantly since the global financial crisis. Prior to the crisis, during a period of expansion and growth, investors and media had little reason to question corporate governance at the level of the board of directors or rising executive compensation packages. The crisis changed perceptions dramatically. Corporate boards were widely blamed for lax oversight, granting overly generous pay packages, and generally failing to perform in a prudential manner. There is a growing realization that corporate governance has at least an indirect impact on enterprise risk management. We make the case that it has a direct and significant impact, and that there are proven approaches to corporate governance that improve risk management.

There are a variety of corporate governance factors that impact enterprise risk management. The following factors have been the subject of much debate and academic research:

- Corporate board diversity
- Chief executive officer/chairman of the board duality
- Executive compensation

Of these, executive compensation has received the greatest level of scrutiny over the past few years, especially after the global financial crisis of 2008, in which the popular media railed against executives receiving multimillion dollar payouts while shareholder values nose-dived. There is research that within the financial services industry, efforts by chief executive officers (CEOs) to substantially increase their compensation resulted in a weakening of board independence, governance, and risk management, contributing to the global financial crisis.

Organizations can take actions to compensate executives while structuring, organizing, and operating corporate boards in a manner to improve their enterprise risk management. Such actions can also improve overall corporate governance while reducing the principal/agent problem—the diverging or conflicting objectives between company owners (principals) and their employees (agents).

It can be argued that corporate boards do not operate in a vacuum, and, like the rest of us, react to changes in their environment. Board members, like millions of investors, were excited about the profit opportunities offered by high growth rates in the value of real estate. Financial service providers created sophisticated instruments tied to the value of real estate that promised and delivered high growth rates with seemingly low risk, until the speculative bubble burst.

The problem with this argument is that corporate boards and c-level executives are supposed to possess more wisdom and maturity than most of their corporate stakeholders—investors, customers, suppliers, creditors, and the community at large. They are expected to demonstrate prudence (exercising sound judgment in practical affairs) and act as fiduciaries to their shareholders. As such, they are tasked to guide their corporations through good and bad times. This includes balancing risks and opportunities while complying with corporate bylaws and regulatory requirements.

The events of the past three years demonstrate the failure of corporate boards to guide their firms through the financial crisis. To the contrary, their actions often have led to the destruction of shareholder value and crippled their firms' survivability. In short, corporate governance at the board level played a significant role in the global financial crisis. The availability of cheap credit, the lure of subprime and other mortgage-backed market opportunities overwhelmed the prudence and fiduciary responsibilities of corporate boards. Board members need to possess the appropriate level of knowledge and expertise to understand the business dealings engaged in by the firm. In situations where they do not, they need the counsel of unbiased subject matter experts.

The crisis clearly demonstrated that boards agreed to investment strategies and complex financial products that were far beyond their levels of comprehension. In many cases boards relied on their firm's internal advisors and executives, who had major compensation incentives to engage in reckless risk taking.

Avoid Chief Executive Officer and Chairman of the Board Duality

Under Western corporate law, there are only three actors in a corporation: directors, employees, and shareholders. Duality permits one individual to assume two of the three roles, violating checks and balances and worsening the agency problem. Preventing duality has proved successful in the United Kingdom (U.K.) with its Combined Code, the European Union (EU), and Australia with its AX10 Principles by creating checks and balances between risk and opportunities, reducing the principal/agent problem, and improving governance.[1]

The pros and cons of duality as opposed to singularity have been argued for many years.[2] CEO/Chairman of the board (CoB) duality can weaken corporate board governance by creating a bias of communications and monopolies of knowledge in which minority opinions are suppressed.[3] With one dynamic and charismatic individual holding the positions of CEO and CoB, financial risk management tends to take a back seat to the pursuit of opportunities. The reason for this is quite simple. Board members are expected to oversee the performance of corporate executives, but are conflicted because the top company executive is also their boss as chairman of the board. This limits the ability of boards from challenging executive management decisions not in the long-term interests of the firm, and tends to make boards more passive and reactionary. A duality environment creates a conflict of interest in which board members, like employees, serve at the pleasure of management, and are challenged in providing independent monitoring.[4]

Duality in the financial services industry has also hurt corporate governance and increased the agency problem. CEOs strive to create more passive boards willing to approve far greater compensation than historically received[5] or justified by increases in employment turnover rates,[6] or potential litigation and prosecution under the Sarbanes-Oxley Act.[7]

This is not to argue that all corporations under a duality environment are at risk. Many successful corporations operate in a duality environment. Steve Jobs as CEO and CoB has guided Apple to the status as one of the most admired and successful organizations in recent history. In the United States, typically over 75 percent of corporations represented on the Dow Jones Industrial 30 Average operate in a duality environment. Approximately 70 percent of larger U.S. firms (mean market value of $7.5 billion), 55 percent of mid-size firms (mean market value of $189.4 million), and 55 percent of smaller firms (mean market value of $9.6 million) operate in a duality environment.[8]

Regardless of their success in a duality environment, there is research to indicate they would operate in a more prudential manner with a singularity environment, in which two individuals are responsible for their organization's well-being. The argument for singularity is that

The Role of Banking Duality in the Global Financial Crisis

As part of the research for an upcoming peer-reviewed journal article, we wanted to investigate the role of CEO/CoB duality among the largest banks, those listed on *Fortune's* Global and U.S. 500. (As of year-end 2009, there were a total of 79 banks on the combined lists.) The two-year (2007 to 2009) changes in stock price, revenue, and profits (the average of which we call a misery index) indicate that banks in a singularity mode fared better than those in a duality mode.

Duality v. Singularity: Banks Listed on Fortune's Global 500 and Fortune's US 500 = 79 Total Banks		Two Year ('07–'09) Change in:			
		Stock Price	Revenue	Profits	Misery Index
CEO/CoB Singularity	Average	-24.2%	23.0%	34.4%	11.1%
	Trim Mean 10%	-28.5%	7.4%	-74.4%	-31.8%
CEO/CoB Duality	Average	-52.8%	6.3%	-406.1%	-150.9%
	Trim Mean 10%	-40.3%	-3.9%	-124.7%	-56.3%

Globally there are 49 banks in a singularity mode and 30 banks in a duality mode. Within the EU duality is rare—4 of 34 banks. In the United States, singularity is rare—4 of 22 banks.

the responsibilities of CEO and CoB can be divergent and possibly in conflict. In this environment, the CEO is responsible for day-to-day operations, striving to meet quarterly financial objectives, and the CoB is responsible for the firm's long-term well-being and meeting its stakeholder responsibilities. These stakeholders include investors, employees, suppliers, buyers, regulators, and local communities. There are a small group of talented executives capable of wearing both hats, but it is a model difficult to scale, and even in the best of environments, corporate governance suffers.

Proponents for an independent structure argue that duality reduces boards' abilities to fulfill their governance functions, may constitute a conflict of interest, and compromises checks and balances.[9] They cite principal-agent theory to argue that performance can only be optimized by separating the decision-making process, with the CEO acting as the decision manager and the CoB as the decision controller.[10] They also argue that duality can result in weakened board governance as characterized by more passive and captive boards made up of gray members (those beholden to the CEO), busy members (those sitting on three or more boards), or older members (typically more than 70 years of age).[11] Such boards appear to be independent, but the great majority of members tend to be beholden to the CEO, at least indirectly.

The classic argument for duality is that having one individual at the corporate helm makes it clear who is in charge and accountable—one throat to choke and one back to pat, as the old saying goes. Duality advocates argue that it creates a clear focus for objectives and operations. They argue that the alternative is chaos within the firm and with the board.[12] They also cite organizational theory to argue that performance can only be optimized when one person exercises complete, unambiguous, and unchallenged authority. They contend that this provides one public face with a clear company mission.[13]

The primary responsibility of corporate boards is to monitor and advise the management of the firm. Lehn, Patro, and Zhao list five functions of boards, with monitoring and advising at the core of each. Monitoring requires directors to carefully evaluate firm management to guard against behavior that could be harmful to the firm.

In spite of the active debate over the two models, earlier empirical studies have failed to provide much evidence that either model results in superior firm performance. Using one year of *Fortune* 200 company performance, Berg and Smith found no differences in many leading financial indices.[14] Chaganti, Mahajan, and Sharma studied bankruptcies of 42 companies and found no significant differences either.[15] Rechner and Dalton took a random sample of 250 of the *Fortune* 500 and did find significant advantages in the individual model over the duality model in return-on-investment (ROI), return-on-equity (ROE), and profitability over a six-year period.[16]

Anecdotal evidence suggests that performance evaluations of U.S. corporations that switched from a combined to a split model are not always a valid indicator. Many corporations make the change during periods of stress in which the CEO/CoB was replaced for poor performance. In the example of Washington Mutual (WaMu), the largest U.S. savings and loan, the company only made the split in June 2008 after CoB/CEO Kerry Killinger had lost his credibility and was blamed by the board for weakening the firm. Killinger was fired three months later and the 119-year-old firm failed in September—the largest bank failure in U.S. history. An evaluation would show a decline in performance after the board removed Killinger as CoB, but it can be argued the split had no causal impact on WaMu's performance. In the case of Bank of America, Kenneth Lewis was stripped of his CoB position but retained his CEO slot in an April board vote after the firm's share price had dropped by more than 70 percent in the past two years.

It is not unusual for U.S. corporate boards to split the ownership of CEO and CoB while forcing out an incumbent CEO, and then to recombine the positions when a new CEO is installed. Brickley, Coles, and Jarrell found that many firms that had separated the CEO and CoB roles were in transition to new CEOs and later rewarded the new CEO with the CoB title. Brickley, Coles, and Jarrell also argue that this is part of the promotion and succession process.[17]

There are some notable exceptions to the combined/duality U.S. model. Of the members of the Dow Jones Industrial 30, five companies operate under a split model: Alcoa, Intel, Microsoft, United Technologies, and Walt Disney. They represent global leaders in materials, technology, and entertainment.

A collateral benefit of splitting the roles between two individuals could be to reduce the large disparity in executive compensation between the United States and the rest of the world, discussed in greater detail in a later section. In an ideal environment, compensation committees would be made up of independent directors reporting to a board of directors led by a CoB who is not the CEO. When a CEO is also the CoB, there are obvious pressures on compensation committees. By splitting the responsibility, board-level compensation committees will be less likely to be dominated by one all-powerful person holding both positions.

Separating the two will permit each to focus on critical company objectives—operations and meeting financial targets on the part of the CEO and oversight and the voice of stakeholders on the part of the CoB. It is needed to stimulate much enhanced board governance in which risks and opportunities are more rationally balanced. With an independent CoB, boards can meet and deliberate free of the influence of the firm's CEO.

EXECUTIVE INSIGHT

Business Continuity Planning Should Include Executive Succession

Business continuity planning has evolved from narrowly focused disaster recovery programs to encompass wide-ranging efforts covering both business and technology. Robust executive succession planning can be viewed as a means of lowering enterprise risk and an extension of business continuity planning. Executive succession planning should translate into corporate boards identifying and grooming talented executives who are capable of assuming leadership positions, including the top jobs, in case the incumbent departs, either voluntarily or involuntarily.

Executive succession is even more critical in duality environments, especially in situations where the firm is identified with a charismatic leader. Unfortunately, duality environments may come with passive boards, unwilling or unable to challenge a powerful individual who is both chairman and chief executive officer, frustrating executive succession efforts.

Create a Board-Level Risk Committee

Risk committees exist at the board level in only a small proportion of financial service firms and are virtually nonexistent in nonfinancial services. More than 15 percent of financial service companies have established separate risk committees at the board level. Outside of financial services, the number drops to less than 4 percent.[18]

A risk committee would give risk management a much better seat at the table of corporate decision making. Risk committees need not be a major financial burden and can be composed of as few as three members, only one of which needs to be a risk expert. A board-level risk committee has the advantage of being more efficient and focused than the board at large. Such a risk committee should be tasked to provide oversight, create a risk profile and risk management function, and assess the effectiveness of risk management systems.

A risk committee operating in a duality environment may find its independence compromised. A firm's CEO is tasked to pursue opportunities. The board is tasked to balance those opportunities against the long-term well-being of the firm. They act as checks and balances against each other. When the CEO also heads the board as CoB, the checks and balances break down.

Audit, nominating, and compensation committees are now mandated in many leading nations' company laws. Just as audit committees are typically mandated to be made up of a majority of independent directors and include financial experts, a risk committee should be independent and include risk experts.

A 2006 survey by the Conference Board indicates wide variations in the quality of risk management from company to company based on feedback from directors who serve on multiple boards, and fewer boards seem to have a well-established risk management process. The survey also found that only 54 percent have clearly defined risk tolerance levels, 47.6 percent of boards rank key risks, and only 42 percent have formal practices and policies in place to address reputational risk.[19]

According to the survey of *Fortune* 100 companies, about two thirds of corporate boards place board risk responsibility in the audit committee, but recommends assigning risk management, not associated with financial reporting, to another a separate committee. This committee would then coordinate its efforts with the audit committee, providing improved operational aspects of enterprise risk management. The survey found that risk management is shared with another committee in 23 percent of companies.

There is no evidence that a greater number of board-level risk committees would have prevented or reduced the severity of the global financial crisis, but independent risk committees would have given boards a stronger and more independent voice—one not as prone to being drawn into the bias of communication, groupthink, and shortsighted thinking that punishes opposition. Firm leadership pursues opportunities and typically has little tolerance for opposing opinions. Therefore, risk committees must operate at a high enough level to be heard, even if their advice is not always heeded.

Increase Board Diversity

Approximately 85 to 90 percent of directors are white males, with an average age of 59, so their backgrounds and perspectives do not well represent their major stakeholders—employees, customers, suppliers, creditors, and stockholders, especially in global firms. Increasing diversity has been proven to improve company performance and governance, while helping to broaden risk management perspectives.[20] Improving the structure of boards to make them less captive and/or disengaged has also been demonstrated to improve governance while lowering executive compensation.[21] In the United States, diversity initiatives include both race and gender. Outside of the United States, diversity initiatives are typically limited to gender.

Many U.S. companies have been moving in the direction of greater diversity for some time, seeing it as much more than improved social responsibility, but also a means to improve shareholder value by expanding the perspective of corporate boards. The CEO of Sun Oil, Robert Campbell, noted more than 10 years ago that minorities or women can bring new perspectives and improved deliberations to boards. Such a perspective is often lacking in all-white, male boards. Adding women and minorities to boards can also inspire today's diverse work force.[22] The arguments for increased diversity can be summarized as:

- Corporate diversity promotes a better understanding of the marketplace, and its corresponding risks. A more diverse marketplace (suppliers, customers, investors) warrants a more diverse board. This will increase the ability to penetrate these markets and avoid risk land mines.[23]

- Diversity increases creativity, innovation, and more effective problem solving, all of which are key to balancing risks with opportunities. Beliefs, attitudes, and cognitive functioning tend to vary, in a systematic way, around such demographic variables as gender, race, and age.[24]

- Diversity enhances the effectiveness of corporate leadership. Although board homogeneity promotes quicker consensus, it results in a narrow perspective. A more diverse board will take a broader view, resulting in improved decision making, including risk management.[25]

There is new research that helps to explain something that many parents of teenagers understand—boys take greater and sometimes more foolish risks than girls do. Researchers at England's Cambridge University discovered that elevated testosterone levels in males lead to greater risk taking—sometimes resulting in greater gains and sometimes, conversely, in greater losses. They recommended that banks and other financial systems as a whole add more women and older men to their boards and risk management practices. This is not to emasculate management, but to bring a better balance of risk taking and sound risk management.[26]

The Conference Board of Canada published a study in May 2002 on the role of women on corporate boards.[27] The study notes a direct correlation between increased female board membership and improved corporate governance. In boards with three or more women, more than 90 percent of boards advocated conflict-of-interest guidelines. This compares to less than 60 percent of boards with only male members. In boards with two or more female members, about three quarters of boards conducted formal board performance evaluations. This compares to less than half of boards with only male members. The study also found that boards with increased female membership tend to provide formal board orientation programs and formally limit board authority.[28]

There is evidence that increased diversity improves company performance as measured by the Tobin Quotient (Q = Market value/Asset value) in *Fortune* 1000 companies. Carter, Simkins, and Simpson conclude in their 2003 study that after making adjustments for industry, size, and other governance factors, they found a statistically significant positive relationship between the presence of two or more women on the board and firm value, as measured by Tobin's Q—1.58 versus 1.03—or by return on assets—5.2 percent versus 2.5 percent. They also found that the proportion of minority and women directors increases with the size of the firm, but decreases with higher numbers of inside board members, and that firms committed to increasing the number of minorities on their boards also have more women on their boards and vice versa. Firms with two or more women directors have more minority directors—8.6 percent versus 2.9 percent. Their results provide critical evidence of a positive relation between the value of a firm and the diversity of its corporate board.[29]

Carter, Simkins, and Simpson also found additional evidence for the positive relationship between corporate board diversity and firm value. They define board diversity as the proportion of African Americans, Asians, Hispanics, and women on the board. Firm value is measured by Tobin's Q. In the first empirical evidence that examines the association between board diversity and improved financial value, they found a significant positive relationship between the ratio of minorities and women on boards and firm value. In their survey they factored in company size, industry, and other corporate governance measures. They also found that increased company size is accompanied by higher proportions of women and minority board members.

Robinson and Dechant and Cox and Blake make strong cases for board and workplace diversity, arguing that it increases short-term and long-term value of an organization.[30] They make the following arguments, all of which impact risk taking, either directly or indirectly. Greater diversity:

- Increases innovation and creativity. This is based on the belief that cognitive functioning and attitudes are not randomly distributed,

but will typically vary systematically with such demographic variables as gender, race, and age.

- Translates into better problem-solving. Greater heterogeneity will
  slow down the decision process with greater discussion and potential conflicts, but with more openness to alternative actions.

- Promotes the effectiveness of corporate leadership. Too much
  executive homogeneity can lead to a narrower perspective,
  whereas more diverse executives can take a broader view.

- Helps to promote stronger global relationships. Today's global
  environment, with its ethnic and cultural diversity, requires corporate leaders to be more sensitive.

- Promotes a stronger understanding of the marketplace, which has
  become more diverse.

In spite of this compelling evidence, female membership on boards
continues to lag even in economies in which half of college graduates
and postgraduates are women and in economies in which women make
up 30 to 40 percent of business executives. In the United States, women
hold about 15 percent of board positions in *Fortune* 500 corporations,
but represent about half of managerial and professional positions.[31]

With the exception of Scandinavia and some of the emerging
Eastern European economies, most European economies lag as well.
Norway (currently at 32 percent of board positions) and Spain (currently less than 5 percent) have imposed quotas to increase female
board membership. Australia, a leader in corporate governance in
most areas according to World Bank metrics, has shown a decline
in female board representation—from 12 percent to 10.7 percent in
the last year.[32]

Although about 30 percent of Europe's senior management positions are held by women, they represent only about 11 percent of
board members. In Germany, with its two-tiered board structure,
the situation is even worse. German women represent 26 percent of

business executives, but less than 8 percent of board members. Of these, about half are elected as trade union and employee representatives. Only one woman was on an executive board of the 100 largest German companies, and only 11 women were on the 200 largest companies' executive boards.[33]

A survey by Heidrick & Struggles International and USC's Marshall School of Business of U.S. corporate board members clearly indicates that female and ethnic representation is not likely to increase by voluntary action. Among directors of publicly held companies, more than half indicated that they did not want to increase board diversity. The results of this survey did not change significantly from one taken 12 years ago.[34]

As long as board membership is looked upon as an executive perk primarily reserved for former and current CEOs, efforts to increase diversity will be frustrated. Incumbent board members have shown an inability to challenge risky decisions that have not been in the best interests of shareholders and other stakeholders. With the many government bailouts enacted in 2008 and 2009, these stakeholders now include the taxpayers in most of the leading economies.

TIPS AND TECHNIQUES

The Primary Argument against Diversity Is Flawed and Self-Serving

As indicated by the Heidrick & Struggles and USC survey, incumbent board members are advocates for the status quo—maintaining a high level of white male–dominated boards. The classic argument against diversity is that a heterogeneous board will slow decision making and increase internal debates.* This argument is self-serving and invalid as evidenced by the overwhelming body of research over the past two decades, some of which we have highlighted.

Reform Executive Compensation

The global financial crisis has elevated the topic of excessive executive compensation even higher. It was widely debated prior to the crisis but is now a favorite topic far beyond business circles. There is evidence that CEOs have weakened corporate governance in their efforts to increase their compensation.[35] An unintended and painful consequence of weakened governance was the reduction of corporate risk management at the critical period when mortgage-based financial products were offered up as a major opportunity for their respective firms.

Countrywide is a poster child for reckless risk taking. Through his options and stock sales, Angelo Mozilo took home $160 million in 2005 and $120 million in 2006 as CEO and CoB. Countrywide's board at the time was all male, met in person only five times per year, operated under a duality environment, had twice as many meetings for its compensation committee as its audit committee, and was paid a minimum of $350,000 per year.[36]

The rise of investor-based capitalism and frustration with the lackluster performance of incumbent corporate management laid the foundation for more charismatic and powerful executives. Executive salaries soared in this market because boards, investors, analysts, and business media all mistakenly believed that such a great leader could cure any and all corporate woes. This had two negative consequences beyond higher executive salaries. First, the new CEO was under inordinate pressure to perform miracles. This led to the company taking on extraordinary risks, which sometimes resulted in major losses up to and including the demise of the organization. Second, it undermined the ability to develop strong subordinate executives who could succeed the CEO and would strive to improve corporate performance.[37]

Executive compensation increases have been dramatic. In 1965 chief executive officers and chief financial officers were paid 20 times more than the average worker. The multiple in 2007 was more than 300 times and compensation averaged $10.5 million for CEOs in the S&P 500. The gap in the United States is much larger than in the rest of the world, with U.S. executives making twice as much as their German, French, and British counterparts and four times as much as their Korean and Japanese counterparts.[38]

One argument for increased compensation is the greater exposure to litigation and criminal prosecution risk today's executives face. Under U.S. Sarbanes-Oxley Act (SOX) Section 302, chief executive officers and chief financial officers are required to sign off on financial statements. Unlike fraudulent acts, there is no requirement to prove intent to deceive if financial statements are found to be erroneous or fraudulent.[39] CEOs and CFOs face civil and criminal penalties, but there have been few civil and criminal charges brought under Section 302. The cases of civil litigation have typically been against smaller organizations in which executives were alleged to have actively participated in fraud.[40] Securities fraud was a criminal offense many years prior to SOX, and these cases would have been prosecuted under existing securities fraud statutes if SOX had not been enacted. Although the risk of civil litigation and criminal prosecution exists under SOX, the question is whether it justifies a risk premium to executive compensation. The research indicates that a large risk premium in compensation is not justified by turnover risk.

The other major risk that executives face is higher levels of unplanned or forced turnovers. An annual survey by Booz and Company shows that although North American executive turnovers have increased from about 10 percent in 1995 to 14 percent in 2009, the increases in the EU have been more dramatic—from about 3 percent to 15 percent in the same time period. Planned turnover is the same in the United States and EU at 7 percent. The survey found that North American and EU turnover declined in 2008 in spite of the major economic downturn.[41] We believe this may be because of reduced opportunities as executives stayed the course through tough economic times. The research concluded by indicating that a large risk premium in compensation is not justified by turnover risk.[42]

The level of executive compensation is the most criticized element of this problem, but it is the nature of the compensation that presents the greatest risks to an organization. Before the 1980s, most executive compensation was primarily fixed and in cash. The culture flipped this ratio so that variable bonuses are now the large majority of executive compensation and are usually share-based.

The share-based nature of variable compensation is an issue because it is often based on increases in the company's share prices through either stock options or restricted stock. This creates major incentives for executives to take extraordinary measures to jack up share prices. This can lead executives to take short-term measures at the expense of the long-term growth of the organization. In the worst situations, a temporary price increase is generated by manipulation and accounting games in order for executives to exercise options—known as *earnings management*.

The best defense against manipulation may be to tie compensation to metrics that are measured and averaged over three or more years, known as long-term incentive programs. Recent Wharton research by Edmans proposes a compensation structure based on long-term escrow accounts set for a period of years, stretching into the executive's retirement. The escrow accounts, known as *dynamic incentive accounts*, would link an executive's compensation to the performance of the firm over a longer time horizon in order to prevent executives from taking short-term actions that may enrich them at the expense of the firm's long-term well-being. The escrow accounts also include a rebalancing mechanism to maintain a constant compensation proportion between cash and stock. This creates sufficient equity in the firm to provide performance incentives, even when share prices fall.[43]

The post–World War II United States prospered to become the largest economy in the world using a compensation model in which the large majority of compensation was fixed, and typically, less than 30 percent was variable. It also prospered in a system in which duality was the exception and not the rule. The argument that higher variable compensation is needed to maximize growth is invalidated by the higher gross domestic product for growth rates in the 30 years after World War II. This is not to suggest that there were no other causal factors, but it does establish that a nonduality and high fixed compensation model was in place for the period of the United States' greatest growth.

The economic theory of agency has been debated for many years. Ross and Macdonald are examples of researchers making efforts to better align the interests of principals and agents.[44] The huge increases in executive compensation in the face of major shareholder losses and the worst economic crisis since the Great Depression argue that the dichotomy between principals and agents has never been greater. The dichotomy has been exacerbated by CEO/CoB duality and the captive or semi-captive nature of their corporate boards.

Summary

Improved corporate governance goes hand in hand with improved risk management. Boards that are characterized as independent, proactive, and diverse have been shown to improve overall governance and risk management without sacrificing profitability or growth. The inertia against reform is understandable, especially from incumbent board members, but is not acceptable, especially in light of the dismal performance of so many public companies.

Notes

1. For an overview of Australia and United Kingdom Corporate Governance related to duality, see Chapters 49 and 65 in Anthony Tarantino, *Governance, Risk, and Compliance Handbook* (Hoboken, NJ: John Wiley & Sons, 2006).

2. For a discussion of the pros and cons of duality, see J. F. Alibrandi, "A CEO's dream board," in E. Mattar and M. Ball (eds.), *Handbook for Corporate Directors* (New York: McGraw-Hill, 1991); C. A. and R. N. Anthony, *The New Corporate Directors* (New York: John Wiley & Sons, 1986); J. Dahya, "One Man Two Hats—What's all the Commotion," (New York: City University of New York, CUNY Baruch College, Zicklin School of Business, August 2005), http://papers.ssrn.com/sol3/papers.cfm?abstract_id=853006; H. S. Geneen, "Why directors can't protect the stockholders," *Fortune,* September 17, 1984; L. Levy, "Reforming Board Reform," *Harvard Business Review,* 59(1): 166–172, 1981; F. W. Steckmest, *Corporate Performance* (New York: McGraw-Hill, 1982); S. C. Vance, *Corporate Leadership: Boards, Directors and Strategy* (New York: McGraw-Hill, 1983); and H. M. Williams, "Corporate Accountability—One Year Later," *Address to the Sixth Annual Securities Regulation Institute,* San Diego, CA, January 8, 1979.

3. H. Innis, *The Bias of Communication* (Toronto: University of Toronto Press, 1951).

4. For the arguments against duality, see: M. Mace, *Directors, Myth, and Reality* (Boston: Harvard Business School Press, 1971); L. Bebchuck and J. Fried, "Pay Without Performance: Overview of the Issues," *Journal of Corporate Law* 30: 647–673, 2005; K. Lehn, S. Patro, and M. Zhao, "Determinants of the Size and Structure of Corporate Boards: 1935–2000," (Working paper, University of Pittsburgh, 2004).

5. J. E. Core, R. W. Holthausen, and D. F. Larcker, "Corporate Governance, Chief Executive Officer Compensation, and Firm Performance," *Journal of Financial Economics* 51 (1999): 371–406.

6. P.-O. Karlsson and G. L. Neilson, "CEO Succession 2008: Stability in the Storm," *strategy+business*, summer preprint, (2009): 3–8. www.strategy-business.com/article/09206?gko=7449c.

7. J. A. Tanega, "Sarbanes Oxley Litigation: On Legal Risk, Potential Liability and Employee Protection," in I. Bantekas, *International and European Finance Crime*: 154–179, 2006.

8. J. S. Lincka, J. M. Nettera, and T. Yang, "The Determinants of Board Structure," *Journal of Financial Economics,* 87 (February 2008).

9. For the argument for an independent board structure, see: K. N. Dayton, "Corporate Governance: The Other Side of the Coin," *Harvard Business Review,* 62 (1), 1984; L. Levy, "Reforming Board Reform," *Harvard Business Review,* 59 (1), 1981; G. Mills, *On the Board*, (Hampshire, UK: Gower Publishing Limited, 1981); R. K. Mueller, "New Directions for Directors," *Strategic Management Journal,* 12(2) (1991): 155–160; S. C. Vance, *Corporate Leadership: Boards, Directors and Strategy* (New York: McGraw-Hill, 1983); H. M. Williams, "Corporate Accountability—One Year Later," *Address to the Sixth Annual Securities Regulation Institute*, San Diego, CA, January 8, 1979.

10. M. Carapeto, M. A. Lasfer, and K. Machera, "Does Duality Destroy Value?" *Cass Business School*, City University, London, January 12:

14–15, 2005, http://papers.ssrn.com/sol3/papers.cfm?abstract_id=
686707.

11. Core, Holthausen, and Larcker, 1999.

12. C. A. Anderson and R. N. Anthony, *The New Corporate Directors*
(New York: John Wiley & Sons, 1986); P. A. Stoeberl, and B. C.
Sherony, "Board Efficiency and Effectiveness," in E. Mattar and
M. Ball (eds.) *Handbook for Corporate Directors,* (New York:
McGraw-Hill,1985), 12.1–12.10.

13. Carapeto, Lasfer, and Machera, 2005.

14. S. V. Berg and S. K. Smith, "CEO and Board Chairman: A Quantitative Study of Dual vs. Unitary Board Leadership," *Directors and
Boards*, 3, 1978.

15. R. S. Chaganti, V. Mahajan, and S. Sharma, "Corporate Board
Size, Composition and Corporate Failures in Retailing Industry,"
Journal of Management Studies, 22, 1985.

16. P. L. Rechner and D. R. Dalton, "CEO Duality and Organizational
Performance: A Longitudinal Analysis," *Strategic Management Journal*, 12, 2, February 1991.

17. J. Brickley, J. Coles, and G. Jarrell, "Leadership structure: Separating the CEO and Chairman of the Board," *Journal of Corporate
Finance*, 3, 1997.

18. K. Brancato, M. Tonello, and E. Hexter, "The Role of the U.S.
Corporate Board of Directors in Enterprise Risk Management,"
The Conference Board, 1390, June 6, 2006.

19. Ibid.

20. D. A. Carter, B. J. Simkins, and G. W. Simpson, "Corporate
Governance, Board Diversity, and Firm Value," *Financial Review*,
February 2003.

21. Core, Holthausen, and Larcker, 1999.

22. J. L. Pierce, "The Federal Reserve as a Political Power," in Thomas
Mayer, *The Political Economy of American Monetary Policy* (Cambridge, UK: Cambridge University Press, 1993).

23. Carter, Simkins, and Simpson, 2003.

24. Brancato, Tonello, and Hexter, 2006.

25. G. Robinson and K. Dechant, "Building a Business Case for Diversity," *Academy of Management Executive,* 11, 1997.

26. R. Schmid, "Male Hormone Linked to Irrational Risk Taking," *San Francisco Chronicle,* April 15, 2008.

27. David A. H. Brown, Debra L. Brown, and Vanessa Anastasopoulos, "Not Just the Right Thing But the 'Bright' Thing," *The Conference Board of Canada,* May 2002, www.europeanpwn.net/files/women_on_boards_canada.pdf.

28. R. E. Rosen, "Risk Management and Corporate Governance: The Case of Enron," *Connecticut Law Review,* 35, 2003.

29. Carter, Simkins, and Simpson, 2003.

30. G. Robinson and K. Dechant, "Building a Business Case for Diversity," *Academy of Management Executive,* 1997; T. H. Cox and S. Blake, "Managing Cultural Diversity: Implications for Organizational Competitiveness," *Academy of Management Executive,* 1991.

31. Catalyst, "Statistical Overview of Women in the Workplace," 1–2, 2007, www.catalyst.org/file/172/qt_statistical_overview_of_women_in_the_workplace.pdf.

32. See Chapter 65, "United Kingdom's Combined Code," in A. G. Tarantino, *Governance, Risk, and Compliance Handbook* (Hoboken, NJ: John Wiley & Sons, 2008).

33. European Union Commission, published in DIW, Berlin, 2006.

34. Heidrick & Struggles International Inc., "Majority of Corporate Directors Do Not Want to Increase Minority Representation On Boards," December 15, 2008, http://biz.yahoo.com/pz/081215/156340.html.

35. Core, Holthausen, and Larcker, 1999.

36. J. R. Finlay, "Countrywide's Subprime Corporate Governance Echoes Enron," *Finlay on Governance,* October 3, 2007.

37. R. Khurana, *Searching for a Corporate Savior: The Irrational Quest for Charismatic CEOs* (Princeton, NJ: Princeton University Press, 2002).

38. See A. R. Hunt, "Letter From Washington: As U.S. Rich-Poor Gap Grows, So Does Public Outcry," *Bloomberg News*, February 18, 2008; H. Landy, "Behind the Big Paydays," *Washington Post*, November 15, 2008.

39. Tarantino, 2006.

40. J. A. Tanega, "Sarbanes Oxley Litigation: On Legal Risk, Potential Liability and Employee Protection," in I. Bantekas, *International and European Finance Crime* (New York: Routledge-Cavendish, 2006).

41. Karlsson and Neilson, 2009.

42. Ibid.

43. A. Edmans, X. Gabaix, T. Sadzik, and Y. Sannikov, "Dynamic Incentive Accounts," May 5, 2009, http://ssrn.com/abstract= 1361797.

44. See S. A. Ross "The Economic Theory of Agency: The Principal's Problem," *The American Economic Review*, 63(2), Papers and Proceedings of the Eighty-fifth Annual Meeting of the American Economic Association, May 1973; G. M. Macdonald, "New Directions in the Economic Theory of Agency," *The Canadian Journal of Economics/ Revue Canadienne d'Economique*, 17(3), August 1984.

CHAPTER 15

Faith-Based Risk Management—Shariah

After reading this chapter, you will learn how to:

- Compare the pros and cons of faith-based risk management.
- Consider the value of a Shariah approach.
- Evaluate Shariah-based investments.

The notion of faith-based risk management is more than 3,000 years old. References to morally responsible investing and risk management can be found in the scriptures of Judaism, Hinduism, Christianity, and Islam. Of the major religions, Islam has taken the most comprehensive and disciplined approach to applying religious principles to risk management and investments: a system of religious scholars that evaluate business practices and investments as to their compliance to Shariah principles.

Prior to the global financial crisis, Islamic-based investments with their Shariah rules were considered too conservative for many investors. Shariah renounces interest, translating into limits to how much debt a company can have or how much profit it can derive from interest-based investments. This restriction prevents holding stocks in financial services companies. It also prohibits selling assets you do not own, selling someone's debt, and engaging in high-risk investments. Shariah's restrictions became a blessing during the crisis by preventing investments in the most risky financial products—the ones that suffered the greatest losses, such as complex derivatives, short-selling, and the $30 trillion market in credit default swaps.

Shariah-based finance, investments, and risk management are growing globally, not just in the Muslim countries of the Middle East. More than 70 Islamic banks and investment funds are now in operation with $80 billion under management. Therefore, it is important in conducting business in or with the Middle East and in countries with a Muslim majority, such as Indonesia and Pakistan, to be aware of the main principles applicable to Islamic finance and risk management.

There is another compelling reason to understand Shariah-based risk management: its faith-based conservatism tends to avoid the most risky and volatile investments and has fared well in the global financial crisis. Shariah is also compelling because of its stewardship approach to corporate governance that stresses an ethical tone-at-the-top.

EXECUTIVE INSIGHT

Western versus Islamic Governance

The major distinctions between Western and Islamic approaches to governance can be found in the concepts of Shariah, *shura*, and religious supervision and audit.

- *Shariah* is an Arabic word meaning the way to the source of life and is now being embraced as a legal code of behavior. Shariah includes a ban on usury in favor of a shared risks and rewards system.

- Islamic law also calls for a *shuratic* decision-making process to encourage consultation and participation in an open and frank discussion with the goal of making the most appropriate decisions. The shuratic process is comprehensive and flexible, providing opportunities for participants to create and develop necessary laws to satisfy specific needs.

- Religious supervision and audit are required in Islam, because all resources are seen as given by God and therefore accountable to God. Man is only a trustee of God-given resources, and the audit of corporate boards and executives is a means to inform shareholders and other stakeholders that the organization is acting in an acceptable manner.

Shariah Basics

There has not been a uniform application of Shariah, nor is there a uniform codified text of Shariah. Countries in the Middle East, Africa, and the Far East with predominantly Muslim populations have, to varying degrees, adopted laws based on Shariah. In spite of similarities, they relied on varying interpretations of Shariah according to the predominant Islamic sect in that specific country.

At the core of Islamic finance and risk management is the fact that usury (*riba*) for some interest payment is forbidden (*haram*). Money in Islam is not allowed to be used to make more money. However, profits (*arbah*) from business are allowed (*halal*). The Qur'an quite clearly specifies that while profit and usury may seem similar, profit is allowed, but usury is prohibited, as explained in the following section.

The challenge therefore for Islamic finance is to structure transactions in such a way that interest is not involved, while profits and fees are utilized to achieve the required returns. In conjunction with this, there will always be subtle differences in the underlying risks that are part of the product or deal.

Trade

Shariah rules typically allow trade. Therefore, trade and investment are allowed in things considered lawful. Trade and investments are neither allowed nor permitted in things considered sinful, such as gambling; related activities, such as using drugs, alcohol, or products and goods that are prohibited; and other activities deemed immoral, such as prostitution or pornography.

Usury

Usury is usually defined as charging a fee for the use of money borrowed and is also generally interpreted to mean charging excessive and compounded interest for money lent. During the dawning of civilization in Babylon, a system of credits was developed, based on the major commodities known at the time, that prohibited excessive charges. Historically usury was universally condemned as an immoral act. Holy books of all religions have supported this attitude, particularly since the concept generally symbolizes greed and exploitation of the needs of the borrower. In fact, even in modern Europe usury was, until the mid-nineteenth century, considered illegal in some countries, such as the United Kingdom.

Usury is clearly prohibited in Shariah, as numerous verses of the Qur'an exemplify that prohibition, particularly the verse that states that "those who devour usury will not stand except as stands those whom the devil has touched with madness; they say that trade (sale) is like usury but God has permitted trade and forbidden usury."[1]

Interest

Interest is generally defined as charging a fee for the use of money. Although many Islamic jurists and scholars have argued that all forms of interest charged constitute usury, others have argued that only excessive compounded interest charged at exorbitant rates is usury and that agreed-on simple uncompounded interest does not constitute usury.

TIPS AND TECHNIQUES

Why the Islamic World Is Important

There are 24 nations with a Muslim population of 10 million or more—the largest being Indonesia (196 million), India, and China (each with 133 million). Of these 24, 19 nations have both a majority Muslim population and more than 10 million Muslims. They represent:

- Fully 75 percent of the 1.3 billion Muslims in the world.
- Some 7.6 percent of global gross national product as measured by purchasing power parity.
- Three African, nine Middle Eastern and North African, and three South and Southeast Asian nations.
- Three of the world's largest oil-producing nations—Saudi Arabia, Iran, and Iraq.
- Two countries at war—Iraq and Afghanistan.
- One country with nuclear weapons—Pakistan.
- One NATO member—Turkey.

Islamic Finance

Islamic finance is becoming an important offering for the world's 1.3 Muslims and for those attracted to its conservative, risk-adverse, and moral foundations.

Banking

The banking system established in most of the countries in the Middle East is based on globally applied Western banking policies and procedures. The general banking sector in the Arab Middle East is reported to have about 470 Arab banks managing assets that are worth more than US$1 trillion, $632 billion of which is deposit-based. It is further reported that in spite of the fairly steady growth of the banking and investments sector in the Middle East, banks and investment funds in the area are reported to be looking for expansion beyond the Middle East, with the Far East, Asia, and Europe providing potential investment opportunities.[2]

In spite of its expansion, Islamic finance still represents a small portion of the global banking system, and general skepticism still remains in some financial quarters concerning the application of Islamic finance concepts and principles. But in the past few years there has been a notable overall change in the attitude in financial centers toward this expanding banking and investment system, coupled with keen interest in learning how it operates. This interest is enhanced not only by the possible flow of available funds mentioned earlier but also by the global increase of the number of Muslims living in the western hemisphere.

Western-style banking is generally based on charging or paying interest on deposits, borrowing, and for providing facilities. In contrast, the predominant overriding principle of Islamic finance is that it should be interest free. Shariah is based on the concept that the banks and their clients are partners in investments or trades that are performed by the Islamic bank using deposited funds.

Islamic banks, like conventional banks, are profit oriented. They are also supposed to be compassionate as well as be aware of and uphold the overall welfare of the community where they operate. One of the practical applications of this principle is that banks should comply with a verse in the Qur'an that states that a person in need, such as a debtor who owes the bank money, should be given leeway until he can improve his situation.

Another important general basic principle of Islamic finance is that funds should be invested in matters that are allowed and lawful and not in anything that is forbidden, in accordance with Shariah principles, as explained earlier.

Therefore, Islamic investment, similar to trade, should conform to Shariah rules, and should not be used in matters that are prohibited or considered immoral in accordance with Shariah. It is also important to note that although trading in goods and products is allowed, the selling of debts and the generation of money from the use of money is prohibited in Shariah. Other prohibited matters that were mentioned earlier include any that involve gambling, drugs, alcohol, products and goods that are not allowed, or prostitution and pornography.

Banks operating on Islamic principles are required to establish and appoint advisory boards, committees, or consultants that are considered Shariah experts to advise the bank. They review investment policies and assist the management in making decisions concerning specific business prospects to avoid any controversial businesses and ensure that the operations and activities of the bank comply with Shariah principles.

Investment Products

Even though Islamic banks and finance usually have an overall traditional community welfare aspect to their operations, they have, similar to conventional Western banks, the ultimate objective of creating profits for their shareholders and depositors through specific Shariah-compatible investment devices or products. However, the overriding principle of Islamic finance is that it should be interest-free and its investment instruments should conform to and be in accordance with Shariah. The main Islamic finance products/devices are listed next.

Deposits

Deposits are usually defined as a sum of money paid by a customer or depositor for a specific period to a bank, to be repaid to the customer on agreed terms. In both conventional and Islamic finance, deposits usually form the main source of investment revenue. However, the difference between the two methods of banking is that while in conventional banking the repayment of the deposit is guaranteed by the banks, in Islamic banking the bank is considered the keeper and trustee of funds to be invested on the basis of partnership between the depositor and the keeper; consequently, the bank does not guarantee the repayment of deposits.

Investment Finance

Investment finance (*mudarabah*) is one of the oldest forms of Islamic investment and finance, whereby the capital owner/financier/Islamic bank agrees to provide specific investment funds to an entrepreneur (*mudarib*) to be invested as he deems fit using his skills and expertise. Although the bank will not participate in the management of the businesses financed, it will usually supervise it to ensure that funds are invested in accordance with the agreed terms. Traditionally, this form of finance involves providing finance for the purchase and sale of goods and products for a share of the return. In providing this type of investment finance, the Islamic bank will be considered as capital owner/financier to the entrepreneur, and at the same time as an entrepreneur that manages deposited funds of the depositors. This is usually described as two-tier investment (*mudahrabah*).

An important condition of this type of investment is that while both parties share in profits as agreed, only the capital owner or provider will bear the losses incurred unless such loss is caused by the misconduct or negligence of the mudarib. The investment finance will continue until the funds are repaid. In this investment, the bank will consider itself compensated for the time value of its money in the form of a floating rate that is calculated on the basis of profits made.

Partnership

Partnerships or joint ventures (*musharakah*) are another established form of Islamic finance, whereby a partnership is concluded between the financier, who will mainly provide the finance, and another party or parties to perform a specific business venture that will include the management arrangements of the venture and its supervision. Profits made and losses incurred will usually be divided and shared on an agreed ratio based on the equity participation. Providing qualified management personnel by Islamic banks for the venture could pose a difficulty for the banks, which, bearing this difficulty in mind, would be more generally inclined to invest funds in stocks and shares of public or private companies rather than enter into business partnership ventures.

Resale Contracts

The Islamic investment concept is essentially considered a resale contract for the purchase of generally durable goods (and possibly real estate) identified by the buyer or businessperson to be financed and purchased by the bank in its own name. It is then resold to the buyer on an agreed immediate or deferred payment arrangement. This will include a profit margin agreed on by the parties. The purchase and sale price, other costs, and the profit margin must be clearly stated at the time of the sale agreement. This type of finance is considered to comply with Shariah because it is a resale of an asset by the bank that takes title of the asset to resell it.

The mechanism for calculating the agreed-upon resale price could in fact be on the basis of time value of money, similar to calculating interest on a loan, but the asset will remain the property of the bank until full repayment of the agreed-upon sale price. However, the bank should not charge interest on late payments. These types of *murabahah* transactions might be considered similar to hire-purchase or rent-to-own arrangements for assets in some jurisdictions.

Lease to Own

Rent usually indicates the transfer of the right of use of an asset or property by the owner to another party for an agreed-upon term and price.

In essence it is fairly similar to the lease or rent-to-own arrangements referred to earlier, and is more generally used for real estate purchases in which the intended buyer will identify the property to be purchased and agree on a price with the vendor. The financier/bank will purchase the property in its name and lease it to the buyer for a specified periodic rental amount for a specified period. At the end of that period and the payment of the installments the title will be transferred to the buyer as agreed.

This concept is similar to a conventional mortgage, but with the difference that funds are not borrowed for interest to purchase a property. The bank will share with the ultimate buyer the purchase of the property at the agreed-upon price. The buyer will pay rent on the bank's share in the property and can also purchase the property earlier.

Fabrication Finance

Istisna'a can be translated as "fabrication" or "industrialization." This indicates that this type of product is essentially a contractual agreement; cash payments are advanced to finance the fabrication of goods and commodities for delivery at a later date, to be sold to repay the advanced payments. Istisna'a is also used for financing construction of houses, buildings, plants, industrial projects, and construction assets. The contracting parties will agree on the specifications of the house or building to be constructed, either on land owned by a customer or to be purchased, as well as the construction costs and repayment terms thereof.

Bonds

Sukuk, which can be translated as "documents" or even "checks," is an expanding innovation in Islamic finance and designates a financial debt product that is similar to conventional banking bonds. However, in following the Shariah requirement to be interest-free, the issuance of tradable fixed-interest-bearing bonds is not permissible. Therefore, the issuance of sukuk should be on the basis of investment products that are allowed and acceptable in Shariah, and the funds raised should be used to generate revenue from Shariah-compliant assets and products. A good analogy for the type of business for sukuk to be invested in might be ethical or green investments. Numerous innovations are being introduced into the growing sukuk market, such as contracts described as *bai al-arboon*, translated as down payment sales, which are similar to options. Malaysia has been quite active in the sukuk market and has recently announced the issue of $750 million worth of tradable Islamic bonds by the Malaysian Government Investment Company (National Khazna).

Islamic Equity Funds

Trading in stocks, shares, and similar equities is allowed in Shariah, and it is usually done through Islamic equity funds that will, like sukuk, invest in Shariah-compatible equities. The Islamic investment equity funds market is again one of the growing sectors within the Islamic financial system. It has been reported that there are currently about 100 Islamic equity funds worldwide that manage total assets of approximately US$1 billion and the market is growing by 12 to 15 percent per annum. In spite of skepticism about the performance of some of these funds (some of which had to close down), it is still expected that the continued interest in Islamic finance will lead to more similar Islamic equity funds being launched, probably by some major Western banks and financial institutions.

Sales Contracts

Although Shariah recognizes different types of sales, depending on the transactions concluded, it prohibits others. In addition to murabahah and other contracts mentioned earlier, which involve sales contracts as well, Islamic banks can finance certain types of sales contracts for customers. These could be contracts for the sale of goods at an agreed-upon lump-sum price to be paid at a later date or in installments (*bay' mu'ajjal*). The bank buys the goods on behalf of the customer and then sells them to him with an agreed markup to be paid later. This type of sale is similar to conventional deferred payment sales without the need to specify the bank's profits. Another type of controversial sale contract is to make an advance payment for the purchase of goods to be delivered at a later date (*bay' salam*). This is similar to forward buying. However, it should be for defined goods to be delivered at a specific date and should not include gold or silver, which are usually equated with money, so that trade is not acceptable in Shariah.

Another type of unacceptable sale is called *bay' al gharar*, which is usually described and translated as a sale that includes an unknown or deceptive element. In Shariah, contracts that could involve deception of a contracting party or uncertainty about essential elements of a contract are prohibited. Gharar contracts are typical of contracts where sales of an unknown or unspecified matter are not allowed. Gambling is a typical form of prohibited gharar.

Joint Liability in Lieu of Insurance

Although insurance has become an essential factor in modern conventional business to reduce risks, it is neither recognized nor allowed in Shariah, mainly because it involves an element of uncertainty and ambiguity, described earlier as gharar. However, the concept of *takaful*, signifying joint responsibility or cooperation, has been accepted since the advent of Islam. This concept is similar to mutual insurance, whereby members share losses of assets or properties with other members.

Summary

In the San Francisco Bay Area, residents who bought homes through an Islamically compliant lender in San Jose, the Ameen Housing Cooperative, do not have to worry about whether their lender will work with them if they lose their jobs. Islamic lenders are required to work in good faith with distressed borrowers to figure out ways to make payments manageable—and co-op leaders say they will.[3]

The Amana and Iman are examples of well-established and respected Shariah-based investment funds, and have either matched or outperformed the performance of the S&P 500 over the past five years. The two Amana Income and Growth funds, the largest Islamic mutual funds in United States with $1.2 billion in combined assets, outperformed the S&P 500 in 2009 by 13 percent and 7 percent, respectively.[4]

This is not to suggest that Islamic finance is a better model than Western finance. It is a system of morally responsible investing supported on an institutional level, avoiding many of the highest-risk investment options. Conversely, it may not enjoy the high returns of Western finance during good times.

The notion of faith-based investment comes with most of the major religions and philosophies in the world today and dates back to their earliest texts—the Old and New Testament, the Qur'an, the Analects of Confucius, and the Hindu Vedanta, to name a few. Although Islamic finance is only about 30 years old, Muslims have always been encouraged to follow Shariah's ethical rules in their banking practices and investment decisions.[5] Islam's Shariah-based investments typically prefer a conservative approach, avoiding organizations with heavy debt loads and volatility in earnings and shunning short-term financial instruments.

Prior to the global financial crisis, Islamic faith-based investments were typically seen as fairly safe but too conservative to compete with Western investments that enjoyed double-digit growth rates prior to the crash. During the crash, Islamic-based investments fared better than their Western counterparts. As markets imploded, triggering the largest crisis since the Great Depression, Islamic-based investments enjoyed a degree of immunity from the worst of the declines. The prohibition from charging interest kept Islamic banks from investing in financial services companies. Islamic investments also forbid selling assets that you do not own, or selling someone's debt—therefore there was no short selling, derivatives trading, or participation in the $30 trillion market in credit default swaps. Some Islamic funds limit the amount of debt of companies they invest in. This policy caused them to withdraw from Enron prior to its downfall.[6]

Islamic finance, in spite of its growth and expansion, still represents a small portion of the global banking system, and general skepticism still remains in financial quarters concerning the application of Islamic banking concepts and principles. Islamic finance concepts are fairly simple and straightforward, but the application mechanism could be problematic when making arrangements in which a bank will essentially become its customer's partner.

In certain areas, the practices of some Islamic banks have been opposed because, it is argued, the banks do in fact charge and deal in interest and apply conventional banking methods—but provide the necessary legal cover by giving the product or transaction a Shariah description, while the application mechanism is the same as conventional banking products, or alternatively by giving interest other names or descriptions, such administrative costs or charges.

There are faith-based investment funds outside of Islam. They include the Catholic-based Ave Maria Mutual Funds[7] and the Christian-based GuideStone Funds.[8] The primary difference is that Islamic-based investments and business practices are more widely accepted and rigidly enforced by Muslims than their Christian counterparts. In terms of investments and risk management, Muslims can rightfully claim that they practice what they preach.

Notes

1. Qur'an 2:275.
2. "Islamic Banking," Blogsome, accessed August 23, 2010, http://islamicbanking.blogsome.com/category/islamic-banking-news/Qatar.

3. Ibid.

4. See the Iman and Amana web sites: www.investaaa.com and www .amanafunds.com.

5. Susan Tramell, "Can centuries-old religious law incorporate modern investment theory? A new generation is exploring the possibilities," *CFA Magazine,* April/May 2005. http://anglorand.co.za/ files/cfamag/200503Islamic.pdf.

6. Matthai Kuruvila, "Muslim Investors Profit by Adhering to Faith," *San Francisco Chronicle,* February 9, 2009, www.sfgate.com/cgi-bin/ article.cgi?f=/c/a/2009/02/09/MN2D15J4HD.DTL&type=pri.

7. See the Ave Maria web site: www.avemariafund.com/home.htm.

8. See the GuideStone web site: www.guidestonefunds.org.

CHAPTER 16

Reputational Risk

After reading this chapter, you will learn how to:

- Improve reputation management at the board level.
- Evaluate reputation monitoring technologies and service.
- Consider the impact of operational failures on reputation and brand.
- Accept personal reputation as your most valuable asset.

Reputational risk is growing as an enterprise-, brand-, and career-ending threat. The risks are compounded by nonstop media coverage and bloggers that can make or break reputations in days or even hours. In a 2003 survey of financial services institutions, more respondents cited reputational risk than any other risk class as the greatest potential threat to their firm's market value.[1] A 2005 survey showed that most firms listed reputational risk as their largest threat—over regulatory, credit, market, human capital, or operational risk. More than 80 percent of global firms say their brand is their most important asset.[2] In spite of its accepted importance, there is little industry or sector consensus as to who should own or how to manage reputational risk.

Organizational reputation can be defined as the overall estimation that stakeholders (investors, employees, suppliers, customers, regulators, and communities) have of an organization. In simple terms, is the company thought of in positive or negative terms; is it trusted or not?[3] Unlike other types of risk, reputations are built on belief and emotion. They are a subjective value judgment about an organization by its stakeholders.

Existing media clipping services only look at external data while internal sources are often the first indicators of growing threats to an organization. The reason for this is simple: Operational-level employees usually share their concerns among their peers in a variety of informal ways—blogs, e-mail, instant messages, and so on. It is typical for scandals to be accompanied by revelations of internal communications raising concerns. Often this is not in the form of formal communication to superiors. The discussion in Chapter 7 of the retaliation whistleblowers face suggests that upward communication of enterprise threats is not an attractive option to most internal sources.

Capital, financial, operational, social, and intangible risks are the lead indicators of corporate reputation risk. But they are not the only sources of this risk. For example, Judy Larkin, in her book *Strategic Reputation Risk Management*, suggests that what is driving much of the adverse sentiment expressed about companies is a changing society as reflected in:

- The rising expectations of stakeholders about the social responsibility of business.
- A decline in trust of companies and their leaders.
- A more simplifying and sensational media.
- The emergence of a victim culture.
- The rise in antibusiness and antitechnology activism.[4]

In short, the community's beliefs and expectations about business are changing, and boards and senior managers are struggling to understand how these changes will impact the perceptions of their corporate behavior.

Thus, the misalignment of corporate and social expectations is another lead indicator of corporate reputation risk. It sends an open invitation to the activist groups and critics to become more vocal. It also encourages politicians and lawmakers to intervene, as they have done with the Sarbanes-Oxley Act in the United States. The agenda and timetable for debate and change is now being set outside the corporate boardroom. Many social commentators welcome this move. Many economists and business executives oppose it.

Reputational Risk Management by Corporate Boards

How can corporate boards do a better job of managing reputational risk in order to protect their corporate and personal reputations, and stem the move towards more regulation?

Here are some suggestions:

- Be well briefed about how the company can create a better corporate reputation.

- Work with the chief executive officer (CEO) to develop a strategy to enhance the perceptions of the company held by key stakeholder groups and a story to communicate this to stakeholders, social critics, and business commentators.

- Put corporate reputation on the formal board agenda and in the key performance indicators of the CEO.

- Regularly audit the drivers of corporate reputations and monitor the effectiveness of the corporate reputation strategy by measuring the expectations and perceptions of employees, target customers, opinion makers, (institutional) investors, and other key stakeholders on a regular basis—at least once a year if the company's reputation is good and more often if it is not.

Manipulating Corporate Images

Can investors and other stakeholders' perceptions of organizations be influenced by image or reputation manipulation? There is a growing acceptance that the old adage is true—perception is reality, and that perceptions of organizations of all types can be manipulated to some extent.

The ways in which stakeholders expect an organization to perform and operate can be a vital asset. The reputation an organization enjoys can generate profits and growth, lead to innovation, open new markets, help to avoid ethical and legal land mines, and translate into a large gap between a public company's book value and its market capitalization. A strong positive reputation is a major advantage that market leaders enjoy, as evidenced by their higher price-to-earnings ratios.[*]

But there are limitations to spin. Ultimately, an organization's spin must be grounded in reality, and its reputation is built over years. Negative perceptions based on poor financial performance, reliability, or ethics cannot be resolved by a clever public relations firm. Underlying problems must be resolved. At the end of the day, the largest driver of an organization's reputation and its stock performance is its financial performance.[†]

---

[*]"What Price Reputation," *BusinessWeek*, July 9, 2007.
[†]Phil Rosenzweig, *The Halo Effect* (New York: Simon & Shuster, 2007).

Reputation Monitoring Technology and Services

What began in the mid-nineteenth century as newspaper cutting and clipping services has evolved into media monitoring services, providing documentation and analysis of all types of media and Internet blog content of interest to their clients. These services use advanced data mining and text mining to search and retrieve a great variety of both positive and negative reactions to the actions of individuals and organizations. Such services can be helpful in monitoring reputation in the marketplace. More advanced solutions permit users to define taxonomy technologies to create attributes as to what constitutes negative and positive comments about an organization, its board members, and executives.

Spending on public image research by large public corporations is growing and now can cost as much as $2 million per year. To better gauge how companies are perceived by their stakeholders, they are engaging firms that utilize powerful search engines to track a wide variety of databases. For example, one monitoring service charges about $100,000 to evaluate a database of more than 10,000 media sources from more than 150 countries and 10 million blogs to inform their clients whether the press is positive or negative on critical issues.[5]

Reputation monitoring services can be valuable, but sometimes reputations are ruined by a single catastrophic event; for example, Arthur Andersen LLP's single-count indictment over its role as Enron's auditor (discussed in the Executive Insight box below). In such cases, media monitoring will only confirm what the organization should have already known—that it was in serious trouble. But there are many situations where media monitoring services can function as a wakeup call for executives who surround themselves with like-minded staff caught in a groupthink that all is well. A few examples, but far from an exhaustive list, of the players in the field include Cision,[6] Mediamiser,[7] Media Monitors,[8] IBM's Cobra,[9] and Dow Jones Factiva.[10]

According to Dr. Ying Chen, a leading authority in information analytics, reputation monitoring and information analytics solutions are typically based on two technologies: data mining and text mining.[11]

Data Mining

Data mining is focused on structured data stored in relational database management systems (RDBMS), with the goal of discovering hidden patterns in data and relationships by mining large relationships in databases. Typically the process includes three technology suites:

1. Extract, transform, and load (ETL) solutions for data processing, cleansing, and data warehouse building.

2. Data-mining analytics algorithms that identify hidden patterns and relationships.

3. Visualization and reporting front-end technologies that allow end-users to quickly review analytics results and compose analytical reports.

Text Mining

Text mining is focused on mining unstructured text—an area of growing interest with the explosive growth of e-mail, instant messaging, blogs, social networking, and other forms of unstructured text. Text mining faces much greater technology challenges due to the unstructured nature of text. Although the three basic technology suites used in text mining are the same as in data mining, they require major innovations when dealing with unstructured data.

EXECUTIVE INSIGHTS

The Demise of Arthur Andersen LLP

Arthur Andersen founded what would become one of the world's most prestigious and admired accounting firms in 1913. Andersen, who ran the firm until his death in 1947, was a champion of high ethical and professional accounting standards. He maintained that an accountant's responsibility was to investors, and not to management of their clients, refusing to compromise the firm's ethical standards even if meant losing clients.

Standards in the accounting industry declined in the 1980s as accountancy firms sought much greater revenue and profitability by providing consulting services to their audit clients. In spite of the obvious conflict of interest, regulators failed to curtail the expansion of audit firms into consulting. By 2000, the firm had tripled its revenues, but struggled to balance its faithfulness to accounting standards with the desire to maximize profits.

The firm was alleged to have engaged in fraudulent auditing and accounting practices at a variety of firms, Enron being the most infamous. Andersen's work for Enron led to the firm's demise. In June 2002, Andersen was convicted of obstructing justice by its shredding Enron audit documents. Ironically, the conviction was later overturned by the U.S. Supreme Court, but it was far too late to save the firm.

Once it was indicted, its clients quickly abandoned the tarnished firm. As with our earlier example of Toyota, Arthur Andersen LLP forgot what made it great. Regardless of the obvious lapses by regulators to prevent an obvious conflict of interest, Andersen and other audit firms should have policed themselves to retain their creditability and basic professional standards. It did not take an accounting genius to realize that Enron's business model was fatally flawed and that hiding massive debts via off-balance-sheet tricks (special purpose entities) would backfire.

The lesson here is simple: An organization has to establish a high ethical tone-at-the-top and codify it with governance policies, procedures, and practices that are reinforced and audited. The governance should not be lowered to regulatory requirements or industry practices that are obviously shortsighted and unsound—a race to the bottom. Andersen would be alive and well today if they had only followed the guidance of its founder, who famously walked away from clients rather than compromise his ethics.

The Relationship between Operational and Reputational Risk

There is a direct and powerful relationship between operational and reputational risk. Research by Cummins, Lewis, and Wei assesses the impact of operational loss announcements on the market value of financial institutions by examining the relationship between Tobin's Q and operational losses. Their analysis covers all publicly reported banking and insurance operational risk events affecting publicly traded U.S. institutions from 1978 to 2003 that caused operational losses of at least $10 million—totaling more than 400 bank events and more than 80 insurance company events. Their research indicates "a strong, statistically significant negative stock price reaction to announcements of operational loss events. On average, the market value response is larger for insurers than for banks." Significantly, they conclude that "the market value loss significantly exceeds the amount of the operational loss reported, implying that such losses convey adverse implications about future cash flows." The losses suffered are proportionately larger for financial institutions with higher Tobin's Q ratios, which suggest that events around operational losses are more costly in market value terms for firms with strong growth prospects.[12]

Perry and de Fontnouvelle examined 115 operational losses within financial firms between 1974 and 2004. They propose a method of measuring reputational risk by evaluating an organization's share price reaction to major operational loss announcements. Loss percentages are calculated as dollar losses divided by the organization's market capitalization, and a market model is used to determine abnormal returns for each organization. "The abnormal return for a firm is defined as the difference between the firm's actual return and the expected return based on a one-factor market model." They conclude that any decline in an organization's market value that exceeds the announced loss amount can be considered reputational loss.[13]

Perry and de Fontnouvelle also suggest that market declines can be much greater than the actual operational loss. In particular, they found that market declines were six times the actual internal fraud losses for organizations with strong shareholder rights. Markets can quickly and significantly react to operational losses, even when operational losses are small relative to firm size.[14]

EXECUTIVE INSIGHT

Personal Reputation—Your Most Valuable Asset

My business students enjoy hearing old war stories that they can utilize as lessons learned to guide their careers. One of their favorites is the story of a young purchasing manager who was dealing with large Japanese trading companies. In those days it was typical for trading companies to call their customers for quarterly steel mill commitments. These were informal phone discussions, which would be followed up with formal purchase contracts over the coming weeks. The young purchasing manager had the advantage of a good mentor who had taught him that his word must be his bond, that it is essential to be true to one's verbal commitments.

It was not unusual that there were periods of rapid market contractions and expansions when the young manager wished he could withdraw his verbal commitments, but this was not possible because the trading companies had already converted the verbal commitments into purchase orders to the largest steel mills in Japan and other countries. If the buyer had reneged, the trading companies would be stuck with thousands of tons of steel.

One quarter, when there was a major decline in business activity, the young manager had ordered more steel than he would be able to use during the quarter. A much more experienced purchasing manager worked for a peer organization, but not a competitor. He, too, had ordered too much steel, but decided to renege to his Japanese trading companies by refusing to place the appropriate follow on purchase orders.

As with most industry sectors, there are no secrets; everyone knows everyone, and bad news spreads quickly. The breach of ethics and protocol quickly became a favorite topic over industry lunches and happy hour drinks. The trading companies never forgave the experienced manager. Although he was able to save his company a temporary increase in inventory, the trading companies increased his prices for all future orders and always found ways to punish him for his misdeeds over the years to come—his personal reputation was ruined, and none of his suppliers would ever trust him again.

The following quarter witnessed a large increase in demand. The young purchasing manager approached the trading companies to increase his original commitments long after the deadline. To his surprise, his request was granted. He came to learn from his contacts that this was possible because they had placed his new orders ahead of the orders from the experienced purchasing manager, which had been placed on time. The trading companies called the experienced manager and informed him that steel mills were running at full capacity and they would have to move out his shipment dates by several weeks.

The lesson in this story is basic. During a typical career, it is likely that you will have to leave your job for a variety of reasons. In most cases, you can get another job, but you cannot get another reputation.

There is also a lesson in organizational reputation. The experienced manager's company experienced operational losses— paying a premium price and extended lead times for its bad business practices. Tone-at-top must cascade down to directors, managers, and supervisors.

Summary

The final two chapters of this book cover the most ubiquitous and most elusive areas of risk management—reputation, liquidity, and solvency. None of them enjoy a widely accepted method of measurement, risk management framework, or standard.

Although there are examples of organizational failures caused by one of the three areas alone, often they are interconnected and tied to failures in operational risk. Arthur Andersen's bad audit practices were an operational failure. Once its operational failure was exposed through the Enron scandal, its reputation was shattered. Clients cancelled contracts en masse, destroying its liquidity and leading to its de facto insolvency (de facto in that Arthur Andersen LLP is technically still an enterprise with 200 employees, down from 80,000 globally, and is addressing more than 100 lawsuits).

Media monitoring and information analytics are useful tools in assessing an organization's reputation and helping to share image and brand, but they can do little to prevent reputational disasters caused by catastrophic operational risk failures, such as those that occurred with Arthur Andersen, Toyota, and British Petroleum.

Notes

1. Basel Committee, "Sound Practices for the Management and Supervision of Operational Risk," 2003, Bank for International Settlements.
2. The Economist Intelligence Unit, *Reputation: Risks of Risks*, December 2005.
3. Grahame Dowling, "Reputation Risk: It Is the Board's Ultimate Responsibility," *Journal of Business Strategy*, 27, 2 (2006).
4. Judy Larkin, "Strategic reputation risk management," (New York: Palgrave Macmillan, 2003).
5. "Google Yourself—And Enjoy It," *BusinessWeek*, February 9, 2008, www.newsweek.com/2008/02/09/google-yourself-and-enjoy-it.html.
6. See Cision web site: http://uk.cision.com/about-cision.
7. See Mediamiser web site: http://info.mediamiser.com/demo?gclid=CK6m7rmDwaICFRA2gwod_llz5Q.

8. See Media Monitors web site: www.mediamonitorsgroup.com.

9. See IBM's Cobra web site: http://domino.watson.ibm.com/odis/odis.nsf/pages/solution.18.html.

10. See Dow Jones's Factiva web site: http://factiva.com.

11. See Ying Chen, "Analytics: Secrets to Deriving Business Value and Insights out of Information," in Anthony Tarantino and Deborah Cernauskas, *Risk Management in Finance* (Hoboken, NJ: John Wiley & Sons, 2009).

12. T. J. David Cummins, Christopher M. Lewis, and Ran Wei, "The Market Value Impact of Operational Loss Events for US Banks and Insurers," *Journal of Banking & Finance*, 30(10) (October 2006): 2605–2634.

13. Jason Perry and Patrick De Fontnouvelle, "Measuring Reputational Risk: The Market Reaction to Operational Loss Announcements," *Social Sciences Research Network*, October 30, 2005, http://papers.ssrn.com/sol3/papers.cfm?abstract_id=861364.

14. Ibid.

CHAPTER 17

Liquidity and Solvency: Enterprise-Ending Risks

with Deborah Cernauskas, PhD

After reading this chapter, you will learn how to:

- Understand the causes of liquidity risk.
- Apply sound practices in liquidity risk.
- Respond to increased regulatory oversight.
- Relate solvency to liquidity.

Liquidity is the ability of an organization to fund increases in assets and meet obligations as they come due without incurring unacceptable losses. This seems to be a fairly straightforward definition, but the difficulties in defining liquidity are clearly depicted by Crockett (2008), "Liquidity is easier to recognize than to define," reflecting the fact that, in recent history of financial systems, economic agents have used a large variety of financial instruments and techniques to plan and regulate their cash needs.[1]

There are three types of liquidity risk:

1. **Funding liquidity risk** is the risk that an organization will not be able to meet efficiently both expected and unexpected current and future cash-flow and collateral needs without affecting either daily operations or the financial condition of the firm. This is the risk under the focus of the Bank of International Settlements/BCBS, the G-30 regulators, and ratings agencies.

2. **Market liquidity risk** is the risk that an organization cannot easily offset or eliminate a position at the market price because of inadequate market depth or market disruption.

3. **Contingency liquidity risk** is the risk caused by organizational issues, such as a lack of internal controls and oversight, reputation risk, and legal risks.

The risk for financial institutions comes with being forced to borrow or sell assets in a short period of time under stressed conditions. It is the risk that a sudden surge in liability withdrawals may require a financial institution to liquidate assets in a short period of time and at low prices, such as when liability holders demand immediate cash for their financial claims, resulting in low prices. Serious liquidity problems can result in a "run" in which all of an organization's liability claimholders demand to withdraw their funds. This can lead to solvency problems.

Liquidity risk is sometimes called consequential risk because liquidity problems generally occur after a firm experiences a severe loss from credit, market, or operational risk. Because of its tendency to compound other risks, it is difficult or impossible to isolate liquidity risk. In all but the most simple of circumstances, comprehensive metrics of liquidity risk do not exist. Certain techniques of asset-liability management can be applied to assessing liquidity risk. A simple test for liquidity risk is to look at future net cash flows on a day-by-day basis. Any day that has a sizeable negative net cash flow is of concern. Such analysis can be supplemented with stress testing.

The fundamental role of banks is to transform short-term deposits into long-term loans, making them inherently vulnerable to liquidity risk. When limited to an individual bank it is known as enterprise risk; when it is part of a contagion, it becomes systemic risk, impacting entire national and global economies. Virtually every financial commitment impacts a bank's liquidity. The role of risk management is to ensure a bank's ability to meet cash-flow obligations, which can be challenging given the uncertain nature of external events. External events have become much more complex with globalized financial markets and the reliance on short-term interbank lending.

According to Gualandri, Landi, and Venturelli (2009), a bank's liquidity risk is associated with its ability to fulfill its obligations to depositors and borrowers by transforming their deposits into legal money, such as receiving cash by drawing down credit lines, and the bank's function of maintaining a balance between the ingoing and outgoing cash flows derived from managing payments made using the banking money. "Means of payment are created and cash flows managed under the direction and control of the Central Banks, which guarantee the availability of the monetary base needed to sustain the ordered creation of banking money. The Central Banks also play a key role in the creation and strengthening of the infrastructures needed to settle payments within the financial system."[2]

Financial innovation, along with its securitization process, has weakened the ability of financial institutions to manage liquidity risk during periods of financial stress. Financial innovation has also made financial institutions more reliant on the stability of financial markets—thus making market and credit risk more correlated.[3]

Causes of Liquidity Risk

Liquidity risk arises from situations in which a party interested in trading an asset cannot do so because nobody in the market wants to trade that asset. It becomes particularly important to parties that are about to hold or currently hold an asset because it impacts their ability to trade.

Manifestations of liquidity risk are quite different from a market price drop to zero. When a price drops to zero, the market has determined that an asset is worthless. However, there are other situations where one trading partner cannot find a counterparty interested in trading an asset. This became a major issue under mark-to-market accounting rules, with the potential of a complete write-down of an asset if no buyer could be found. Uncertain liquidity is also an issue in lower-volume and emerging markets. An organization might lose liquidity if its credit rating falls, it experiences sudden unexpected cash outflows, or an event causes counterparties to avoid trading with or lending to the institution. An organization is also exposed to liquidity risk if markets on which it depends are subject to loss of liquidity.

Liquidity risk tends to compound other risks. If a trading organization has a position in an illiquid asset, its limited ability to liquidate that position quickly can compound its market risk. For example, when an organization has offsetting cash flows with two different counterparties and one of them defaults, the firm will have to raise cash from other sources to make its payment. If it cannot do so, it will also default, creating credit risk.

Basel's 17 Principles of Sound Liquidity Risk Management

In June 2008, the Basel Committee published recommendations to improve liquidity risk in the face of the growing credit crisis in financial markets,[4] known as Liquidity Guidance Assumptions. The basic recommendations include:

- The importance of establishing a liquidity risk tolerance.
- The maintenance of an adequate level of liquidity, including a cushion of liquid assets.

- The necessity of allocating liquidity costs, benefits, and risks to all significant business activities.
- The identification and measurement of the full range of liquidity risks, including contingent liquidity risks.
- The design and use of severe stress test scenarios.
- The need for a robust and operational contingency funding plan.
- The management of intraday liquidity risk and collateral.
- Public disclosure in promoting market discipline.

The Basel guidance is arranged around 17 principles.

Management and Supervision of Liquidity Risk

Principle 1: Banks need to establish robust liquidity risk management frameworks, ensuring that they maintain sufficient liquidity, including a cushion of high-quality, unencumbered, liquid assets, in order to withstand a range of stress events, such as those involved with the loss or impairment of both unsecured and secured funding sources.

Governance of Liquidity Risk Management

Principle 2: Banks need to clearly articulate the liquidity risk tolerance appropriate for their business strategy and roles in financial systems.

Principle 3: Banks should develop strategies, policies, and practices to manage liquidity risk in accordance with the risk tolerance and to ensure that they maintain sufficient liquidity.

Principle 4: Banks should incorporate liquidity risks, benefits, and costs in their performance measurements, product pricing, and new product approval processes.

Measurement and Management of Liquidity Risk

Principle 5: Banks need sound processes for identifying, controlling, monitoring, and measuring liquidity risk.

Principle 6: Banks need to actively manage their funding needs and liquidity risk exposures across and within business lines, legal entities, and currencies, which takes into account operational, legal, and regulatory limitations to liquidity transferability.

Principle 7: Banks need an established strategy providing effective funding diversification in the tenor and sources of funding.

Principle 8: Banks need to manage intraday liquidity risks and positions to meet settlement and payment obligations on a timely basis for normal and stressed conditions that contribute to smooth functioning of settlement and payment systems.

Principle 9: Banks need to actively manage their collateral positions and differentiate between unencumbered and encumbered assets.

Principle 10: Banks need to conduct regularly scheduled stress tests for a variety of market-wide and institution-specific stress scenarios to ensure that current exposures remain in accordance with their established liquidity risk tolerance and as a means to identify sources of potential liquidity strain.

Principle 11: Banks need to develop formal contingency funding plans (CFPs) clearly establishing strategies that address liquidity shortfalls in emergency situations.

Principle 12: Banks need to maintain a cushion of high-quality, unencumbered, liquid assets as insurance against a range of liquidity stress scenarios, including the impairment or loss of unsecured and typically available secured funding sources.

Principle 13: Banks need to disclose information on a regular basis, enabling market participants to make informed judgments about the soundness of their liquidity risk management frameworks and liquidity positions.

The Role of Banking Regulators (Supervisors)

Principle 14: Banks need to regularly perform comprehensive assessments of their overall liquidity risk management frameworks and liquidity positions to determine whether they deliver an adequate level of resilience to liquidity stress, given their role in the financial system.

Principle 15: Bank regulators need to supplement regular assessments of a bank's liquidity positions and liquidity risk management frameworks by monitoring market information and prudential and internal reports.

Principle 16: Bank regulators need to intervene when required to take timely and effective remedial action by banks to address deficiencies in their liquidity positions or liquidity risk management processes.

Principle 17: Bank regulators need to communicate with other national banking regulators on a timely and regular basis in order to facilitate effective cooperation around the supervision and oversight of liquidity risk management.

Increased Regulations over Liquidity Risk

Liquidity risk has not been directly considered in the Basel capital accords, because of the notion that a strong capital base would restrict the impact of liquidity shocks. The global financial crisis exposed major weaknesses in liquidity risk management by major financial institutions and in the Basel framework. Prior to the crisis, cheap and plentiful credit funded buoyant asset markets. The collapse of the real estate market sparked the evaporation of liquidity, forcing the central banks to intervene in a massive way to prevent the collapse of financial markets. Many of the leading banks had failed to follow basic principles of liquidity risk management when liquidity was plentiful.

Many of the exposed banks did not have an adequate framework to satisfactorily account for the liquidity risks posed by their individual products and business lines. Many banks and other financial firms had not considered the amount of liquidity they might need to satisfy contingent obligations under adverse conditions, which were deemed to be highly unlikely. Many of these banks failed to conduct stress tests that considered a major market contraction, even though history indicates such contractions are inevitable.

The Basel committee of the Bank for International Settlements (BIS) has admitted that its Basel II framework lacks the means to adequately regulate liquidity risk. Management of liquidity risk now is a key element of new regulation. It will be included as an additional regulatory component with specific liquidity reserves, with levels established by stress testing and models. These models will be separate from those used in market, credit, and operational risk.

TIPS AND TECHNIQUES

What to Look for in New Liquidity Regulations

Although specific regulatory requirements are still evolving, they can be expected to include:

- The need to allocate liquidity risks, costs, and benefits to all major financial activities.
- Maintaining adequate liquidity levels, including a cushion of liquid assets.
- Establishing liquidity risk tolerances that are periodically reviewed and calibrated.
- Measuring the full range of liquidity risks—funding, market, and contingency.
- Creating and deploying severe liquidity stress test scenarios.
- Establishing a dynamic and agile contingency funding plan.
- Managing intraday liquidity risk and collateral.
- Both public and regulatory disclosure in order to promote market discipline.

At a national level, regardless of the Basel guidance, many leading economies are enacting liquidity risk management requirements under the force of law. Key elements include:

- **Board and senior management oversight.** Boards and executives should possess a working knowledge of the inherent risk from business activities, review and approve appropriate policies to limit key risks, periodically evaluate and approve risk exposure limits, ensure that business lines are adequately staffed with employees having sufficient expertise, provide adequate supervision of daily business activities, respond appropriately to risks arising from changes in competitive environment and/or market innovations, and ensure that the proper infrastructure and internal controls are in place prior to embarking on new activities or products.

- **Policies, procedures, and risk limits.** Risk managers should provide for proper identification, measurement, monitoring, and control of key risks; delineate accountability and authority; and address new activities prior to implementation. For example, policy components may include delegation of clear lines of authority, quantifiable liquidity risk limits, specifications for measuring and reporting liquidity risks, and guidance for completion and review of contingency funding plans.

- **Risk measurement, monitoring, and management information systems.** Adequate measurement and monitoring require reporting mechanisms that sufficiently address all material risk areas, contain appropriate and reasonable inputs, communicate consistency with established limits, goals, and expected performance, and provide accurate, timely, and sufficiently detailed information to identify adverse trends and current risk exposures.

- **Scenario analysis and contingency funding plan.** Contingency funding planning, like other areas of risk management, will include both quantitative and qualitative components. Quantitative components will analyze adverse scenarios (i.e., those significant enough to cause problems) with reasonable estimates. Qualitative components will include descriptions of stress scenarios, steps to declare a crisis and trigger events, contact information for critical team members, identification of responsible parties to initiate external communication, and relevant reporting requirements.

The Close Relationship between Solvency and Liquidity

Liquidity and solvency are very much related. Short-term funding issues are typically treated as liquidity risk, whereas long-term issues are treated as solvency risk—an organization without liquidity eventually becomes insolvent and fails. Solvency can be defined as the ability of an organization to hold adequate assets to cover its liabilities. Solvency is often confused with liquidity, but it is not the same thing. Liquidity is defined as an organization's ability to meet financial obligations as they come due, without incurring unacceptable losses. Unlike liquidity, solvency is often measured as a ratio of the total current assets divided by the total current liabilities:

$$\text{Solvency Ratio} = \frac{\text{After-Tax Net Profit} + \text{Depreciation}}{\text{Long-Term Liabilities} + \text{Short-Term Liabilities}}$$

Solvency ratios vary by industry, but the higher the solvency ratio the better. Conversely, the lower a company's solvency ratio, the greater the probability that the company will default on its debt obligations. As a general rule of thumb, a solvency ratio of greater than 20 percent is considered financially healthy. An organization that is insolvent, whether public or private, for-profit or not-for-profit, is bankrupt. Solvency ratios are related to debt management, also known as the gearing ratios. Solvency ratios can point out weaknesses in a corporation that could lead that business into a bankruptcy proceeding.

EXECUTIVE INSIGHT

The Roles of Liquidity and Solvency in Surviving Bankruptcy

The close relationship between solvency and liquidity has been researched for many years. Research by Bryan, Tiras, and Wheatley (1999) differentiates long-term stress as solvency risk and short-term stress as liquidity risk.[*] The combination of high- or low-solvency risk with high- or low-liquidity risk changes the chances of emerging from bankruptcy.[†] Bryan, Tiras, and Wheatley predict that firms that exhibit low solvency risk and high liquidity risk are most likely to emerge from bankruptcy. Firms that exhibit high solvency risk and high liquidity risk are predicted to be least likely to emerge from bankruptcy.

[*]Samuel Tiras, Daniel Bryan, and Clark Wheatley, "The Interaction of Solvency with Liquidity and its Association with Bankruptcy Emergence," October 1999, http://papers.ssrn.com/sol3/papers.cfm?abstract_id=189410.
[†]See K. Chen, and K. Wei, "Creditors' decisions to waive violations of accounting based debt covenants," *The Accounting Review* 68 (1993): 218–233.

Summary

Liquidity and solvency go hand in hand. Although liquidity risk management may cover short-term funding issues, it is a mistake to think of it on a tactical level. A viable liquidity and solvency risk management framework must take a strategic view that accepts the potential, no matter how remote, of sudden and severe downturns in markets and responds with contingency funding plans. For financial institutions this must include scenario analysis and stress testing, along with both quantitative and qualitative techniques and procedures.

Notes

1. Andrew Crocket, "Market Liquidity and Financial Stability," *Financial Stability Review,* February 2008, www.banquecentrale.eu/gb/publications/telnomot/rsf/2008/rsf_0208.pdf#page=23.

2. Elisabetta Gualandri, Andrea Landi, and Valeria Venturelli, "Financial Crisis and New Dimensions of Liquidity Risk: Rethinking Prudential Regulation and Supervision," *Journal of Money, Investment and Banking*, 8(2009).

3. T. Adrian, and H. S. Shin, "Liquidity and Financial Cycles," 6th BIS Annual Conference, Financial System and Macroeconomic Resilience, June 18–19, Brunnen, Switzerland, 2007.

4. See Basel Committee on Banking Supervision, "Principles for Sound Liquidity Risk Management and Supervision," September 2008, www.bis.org/publ/bcbs144.pdf?noframes=1.

Links to Risk and Compliance Organizations, Standards, and Frameworks

Risk and Compliance Organizations

Accounting Standards Board of Japan (ASBJ)	www.asb.or.jp/asb/top_e.do;jsessionid= 7AE9A1A626BEA423CBB8A743BC435773
Association of Insurance and Risk Managers	www.airmic.com
Association of Local Authority Risk Managers	www.alarm-uk.org
Bank for International Settlements	www.bis.org
BITS Financial Services Roundtable	www.bitsinfo.org
British Standards Institute	www.bsi-global.com/en/Standards-and-Publications
Business Continuity Institute	www.thebci.org
Committee of Sponsoring Organizations (COSO)	www.coso.org

Disaster Recovery Institute International	www.drii.org
Financial Services Agency, Japan	www.fsa.go.jp/en/index.html
Information Systems Audit & Control Association	www.isaca.org
Institute of Risk Management	www.theirm.org
International Association of Insurance Supervisors	www.iaisweb.org
International Auditing & Assurance Standards Board	www.ifac.org/IAASB/About.php
International Risk Governance Council	www.irgc.org
International Society of Six Sigma Professionals	www.isssp.com
International Standards Organization (ISO)	www.iso.org/iso/home.htm
IT Governance Institute	www.itgi.org
Ministry of Finance, People's Republic of China	www.mof.gov.cn/mof
Ministry of Finance, China Securities Regulatory Commission	www.csrc.gov.cn/n575458/n4001948
Open Compliance & Ethics Group (OCEG)	www.oceg.org
Public Company Accounting Oversight Board	http://pcaob.org
Securities and Exchange Board, India	www.sebi.gov.in
Securities and Exchange Commission (SEC)	www.sec.gov
Standards Australia	www.standards.org.au
Standards New Zealand	www.standards.co.nz
U.K. Office of Government Commerce (OGC)	www.ogc.gov.uk/guidance_itil.asp
U.S. National Institute of Standards and Tech Computer Security Resource Center	http://csrc.nist.gov

Risk-Related Standards and Frameworks

AS/NZS 4360:2004 Set, Australia and New Zealand	www.saiglobal.com/shop/Script/Details.asp?DocN=AS564557616854
Basel II Capital Accords for Banking	www.bis.org/publ/bcbsca.htm
Basic Standard for Enterprise Internal Controls, China	www.casc.gov.cn/gnxw/200807/t20080715_751587.htm
BCI Good Practices	www.thebci.org/gpgdownloadpage.htm
BITS Shared Assessment Program SIG and AUP	www.bitsinfo.org/FISAP/index.php
BS 25999-1	www.bsi-global.com/en/Shop/Publication-Detail/?pid=000000000030157563
BS 25999-2	www.bsi-global.com/en/Shop/Publication-Detail/?pid=000000000030169700
Clause 49 of the Listing Agreement, India	www.sebi.gov.in/Index.jsp?contentDisp=Search
COBIT	www.isaca.org/Template.cfm?Section=COBIT6&Template=/TaggedPage/TaggedPageDisplay.cfm&TPLID=55&ContentID=7981
Combined Code, United Kingdom	www.frc.org.uk/corporate/combinedcode.cfm
COSO ERM Integrated Framework	www.coso.org/ERM-Integrated Framework.htm
DRII/BCI Generally Accepted Practices	www.drj.com/GAP
Eighth EU Directive (2006/43/EC), Euro SOX	http://eur-lex.europa.eu/LexUriServ/LexUriServ.do?uri=OJ:L:2006:157:0087:0107:EN:PDF
FED Notice of Proposed Rule Making (NPR) - Basel II	www.federalreserve.gov/generalinfo/Basel2/DraftNPR/npr
Financial Instruments and Exchange Law, Japan	www.fsa.go.jp/common/law/fie01.pdf
Fourth EU Directive (Fourth Council Directive 78/660/EEC), Euro SOX	http://eur-lex.europa.eu/smartapi/cgi/sga_doc?smartapi!celexplus!prod!DocNumber&lg=en&type_doc=Directive&an_doc=78&nu_doc=660

Guidelines for Assurance Engagement in Relation to Assessing Effectiveness of Enterprise Internal Controls, China	www.cicpa.org.cn/Professional_ standards/comments/200807/ t20080701_13474.htm
Implementation Guidelines for Enterprise Internal Controls, China	www.casc.gov.cn/gnxw/200807/ t20080715_751591.htm
International Standards of Auditing (ISAs)	www.ifac.org/IAASB/Pronouncements .php#Standards
IRGC Framework Introduction	www.irgc.org/IMG/pdf/An_introduction_ to_the_IRGC_Risk_Governance_ Framework.pdf
ISO 31000 Risk Framework	www.iso.org/iso/catalogue_detail .htm?csnumber=43170
ISO 31010 Risk Management Techniques	www.iso.org/iso/catalogue_detail .htm?csnumber=51073
ISO 27000 Series	www.iso.org/iso/iso_catalogue/ catalogue_tc/catalogue_detail.htm? csnumber=42103
ISO Publication 73	www.iso.org/iso/catalogue_detail? csnumber=34998
ITIL	www.itil-officialsite.com/Publications/ Core.asp
Japan SOX	www.fsa.go.jp/en/refer/legislation/ index.html
Loi sur La Sécurité Financière (LSF), France	www.casewise.com/ModelsAnd Frameworks/NationalAccounting Standards/LSF
Motorola University for Six Sigma	www.motorola.com/motorolauniversity .jsp
New Corporate Law, 2006, Japan	www.acga-asia.org/public/files/Japan %20WP_%20May2008.pdf
NIST (especially 800-30, 34, 58, 53, 84)	http://csrc.nist.gov/publications/ PubsTC.html
OCEG Governance Risk and Compliance Foundation	www.oceg.org/View/Foundation
PCAOB Audit Standards 1–6, United States	http://pcaob.org/Standards/index.aspx

Performing Assurance Engagements in Evaluating Effectiveness of Enterprise Internal Controls, China	www.casc.gov.cn/gnxw/200807/ t20080715_751591.htm
Risk Management Standard from AIRMIC web site	www.airmic.com/en/Library/Risk_ Management_Standards/
Risk Management Standard from ALARM web site	http://www.alarm-uk.org/PDF/ rmstandard.pdf
Risk Management Standard from IRM web site	http://www.theirm.org/publications/ PUstandard.html
Sarbanes-Oxley Act Section 401, United States	http://www.sec.gov/news/studies/ soxoffbalancerpt.pdf
Sarbanes-Oxley Act Section 404, United States	http://www.sec.gov/news/studies/ 2009/sox-404_study.pdf
Seventh EU Directive: Consolidated Accounts of Companies with Limited Liability (83/349/EEC), Euro-SOX	http://eur-lex.europa.eu/smartapi/cgi/ sga_doc?smartapi!celexplus!prod! DocNumber&lg=en&type_doc=Directive &an_doc=83&nu_doc=349
Solvency II (EU European Insurance Std.)	www.iaisweb.org/index.cfm?pageID=37
Val IT	www.isaca.org/Template.cfm?Section= Val_IT4&Template=/ ContentManagement

Index